CAMBRIDGE LIBRARY COLLECTION

Books of enduring scholarly value

Spiritualism and Esoteric Knowledge

Magic, superstition, the occult sciences and esoteric knowledge appear regularly in the history of ideas alongside more established academic disciplines such as philosophy, natural history and theology. Particularly fascinating are periods of rapid scientific advances such as the Renaissance or the nineteenth century which also see a burgeoning of interest in the paranormal among the educated elite. This series provides primary texts and secondary sources for social historians and cultural anthropologists working in these areas, and all who wish for a wider understanding of the diverse intellectual and spiritual movements that formed a backdrop to the academic and political achievements of their day. It ranges from works on Babylonian and Jewish magic in the ancient world, through studies of sixteenth-century topics such as Cornelius Agrippa and the rapid spread of Rosicrucianism, to nineteenth-century publications by Sir Walter Scott and Sir Arthur Conan Doyle. Subjects include astrology, mesmerism, spiritualism, theosophy, clairvoyance, and ghost-seeing, as described both by their adherents and by sceptics.

Experiences in Spiritualism with Mr D.D. Home

First published in 1869, this book describes the spiritualist activity of Scottish-born Daniel Dunglas Home (1833–86), who emerged as a medium in the United States in the wake of the Fox sisters' alleged 'spirit rappings' in the mid-nineteenth century. Written by the Irish journalist and politician Windham Thomas Wyndham-Quin, Lord Adare (1841–1926), who befriended Home in 1867, the book records Adare's observations of seventy-eight spiritualist sittings over two years, and reports verbatim the conversations between Home and the spirits with whom he was allegedly in contact. Adare also describes Home's supernatural interactions away from the formal setting of a séance. The accounts were originally written as private reports to Adare's father, the landowner and archeologist Edwin Wyndham-Quin, third Earl of Dunraven. Dunraven was deeply interested in spiritualist activity and wrote the introduction to this work, which also includes a classification of all spiritualist phenomena.

T0381615

Cambridge University Press has long been a pioneer in the reissuing of out-of-print titles from its own backlist, producing digital reprints of books that are still sought after by scholars and students but could not be reprinted economically using traditional technology. The Cambridge Library Collection extends this activity to a wider range of books which are still of importance to researchers and professionals, either for the source material they contain, or as landmarks in the history of their academic discipline.

Drawing from the world-renowned collections in the Cambridge University Library and other partner libraries, and guided by the advice of experts in each subject area, Cambridge University Press is using state-of-the-art scanning machines in its own Printing House to capture the content of each book selected for inclusion. The files are processed to give a consistently clear, crisp image, and the books finished to the high quality standard for which the Press is recognised around the world. The latest print-on-demand technology ensures that the books will remain available indefinitely, and that orders for single or multiple copies can quickly be supplied.

The Cambridge Library Collection brings back to life books of enduring scholarly value (including out-of-copyright works originally issued by other publishers) across a wide range of disciplines in the humanities and social sciences and in science and technology.

Experiences in
Spiritualism
with
Mr D.D. Home

VISCOUNT ADARE
INTRODUCTION BY
THE EARL OF DUNRAVEN

CAMBRIDGE
UNIVERSITY PRESS

CAMBRIDGE UNIVERSITY PRESS

Cambridge, New York, Melbourne, Madrid, Cape Town,
Singapore, São Paolo, Delhi, Mexico City

Published in the United States of America by Cambridge University Press, New York

www.cambridge.org
Information on this title: www.cambridge.org/9781108052979

© in this compilation Cambridge University Press 2012

This edition first published 1869
This digitally printed version 2012

ISBN 978-1-108-05297-9 Paperback

EXPERIENCES

IN

SPIRITUALISM

WITH

MR. D. D. HOME.

BY

VISCOUNT ADARE,

WITH

INTRODUCTORY REMARKS

BY THE

EARL OF DUNRAVEN.

LONDON :

PRINTED BY THOMAS SCOTT, WARWICK COURT,

HOLBORN.

INTRODUCTORY REMARKS.

THE subject of Spiritualism was first brought under my notice about fifteen years ago, by reading two or three accounts of the occurrences which were taking place in America. To some extent I was prepared for the fair consideration of very strange and startling phenomena, from having previously examined fully into the subject of mesmerism. The result of this enquiry, carried on for several months, under most favourable circumstances, was a thorough conviction of the reality of the phenomena of mesmerism, from the simple sleep up to clairvoyance. At that time, scientific men in general, and the medical profession in particular, were loud in condemnation of what they considered sheer imposture; and one of the most eminent of the profession, the late Dr. Elliotson, lost a considerable portion of his very extensive practice by his bold and uncompromising assertion of the truth of mesmerism and its great importance as a curative agent. Since then a great change has taken place in the opinion of the public on this subject. Judging by the literature of the day, as well as by the remarks current in society, the general phenomena of mesmerism, are widely accepted as true; and even those who believe in the higher phenomena, including clairvoyance, are no longer necessarily considered to be the victims of imposture.

When table turning became one of the amusements of the day, I witnessed and tried various experiments which clearly demonstrated the inadequacy of Professor Faraday's explanation of the manifestions by involuntary muscular action. I was also present at a *séance*, where Mrs. Hayden was the medium, and an attentive examination of what took place sufficed to satisfy me that the subject was worthy of careful examination, to be made whenever an opportunity should occur for a full investigation into a class of phenomena, opening a new field of research of a very strange and startling description. This opportunity has been afforded by Lord Adare's acquaintance with Mr. Home, which commenced in 1867. I soon perceived from his letters, that the manifestations were so remarkable that they deserved to be duly chronicled and preserved. At my request he has carefully noted, as fully as could conveniently be done, the occurrences of each day, and has permitted me to print the whole series for private circulation. Publication is out of the question, as much that is interesting and a valuable portion of the record, relates to private domestic affairs, and to near relatives or intimate friends.

Even after the unavoidable suppression of some curious and instructive details, it was not without much reluctance that we made up our minds to give even a very limited circulation to this series of *séances ;* but, after full consideration we have deemed it best to print—as nearly as we possibly could venture to do—the entire record ; notwithstanding the pain, to ourselves and others, which necessarily accompanies the mention of communications professing to come from those whose memories call up the deepest and tenderest feelings of our nature. It is obvious that the chief value of such a record must depend upon the trustworthiness of the narrator. Fidelity of description is very rare, even where honesty of purpose is undoubted. I believe that in the present case scrupulous accuracy, a retentive memory, and an unexcitable temperament are combined in an unusual degree, forming just such a combination of qualities as is indispensable for one who undertakes to record phenomena of this exceptional and startling character. In several of the latter *séances*, portions of them have been written by both Lord Adare and myself, and then carefully compared ; some were looked over by more than one of the persons present: thus everything has been done to ensure the greatest accuracy. In addition, each of those mentioned. as present at the *séances* (except a few who are not within reach) has received a copy of the printed account, and replies have been received from all, affirming the accuracy of the reports. A list of these names will be given further on, and thus the following pages, it is hoped, will be found to contain the fullest and best authenticated account of the phenomena of Spiritualism which has as yet appeared in this country.

It must be borne in mind that an actual record of facts, and not the adoption or refutation of any particular theory, is the main object in view. Spiritualism, will, therefore, in the ensuing remarks, be regarded chiefly in its scientific or phenomenal aspect, and I have purposely avoided expressing any decided opinion on questions so complicated, and about which at present such conflicting opinions prevail, as upon the character of the phenomena, the source from which they proceed, and the tendency of the teaching to be derived from them.

The whole subject of Spiritualism is one which must soon command the attention of thoughtful men in this country, as it has very fully done in America, and to some extent in France and other countries of Europe. In America, the belief in Spiritualism may be considered as a *fait accompli*. Its adherents are said to be reckoned by millions ; varying from three to eleven, according to different accounts ; but, even should the lowest calculation be beyond the exact truth, as is probably the case, there can be no doubt that a considerable portion of the people of the United States, including many men eminent in science, literature, politics, &c., (among whom was to be reckoned the late President Lincoln) believe that a means of communication is now open between the inhabitants of this world and intelligent beings belonging to a different state of existence ; thus affording a new and astounding evidence for the reality of another life, and of a spirit-world. It is remarkable that this new source of evidence should be discovered at a time when materialism, and the denial of a future state are on the increase, apparently in all parts of the world, and are said to prevail to an alarming extent in America, the country, be it remarked, where first these manifestations occurred on a large or striking scale. The timidity or apathy of men of science in England on this subject is to be deplored. A remarkable example of the former was seen in the case of the late Sir David Brewster. He was present at two *séances* of Mr. Home's, where he stated, as is affirmed on the written testimony of persons present, his impression that the phenomena were most striking and startling, and he does not appear then to have expressed any doubt of their genuineness, but he afterwards did so in an offensive manner. The whole discussion may be read in Mr. Home's book entitled, " Incidents in my Life." I mention this circumstance, because, I was so struck with what Sir David Brewster—with whom I was well acquainted—had himself told me, that it materially influenced me in determining to examine thoroughly into the reality of the phenomena. I met him one day on the steps of the Athenæum; we got upon the subject of table-turning, &c.; he spoke most earnestly, stating that the impression left on his mind from what he had seen, was, that the manifestations were to him quite inexplicable by fraud, or by any physical laws with which we were acquainted, and that they ought to be fully and carefully examined into. At present I know of only three eminent men of science in England, who have gone fully into the subject; and in their case the enquiry has resulted in a conviction of the genuineness of the phenomena. I allude to Mr. De Morgan the mathematician, Mr. Varley the electrician, and Mr. Wallace the naturalist, all, as is well known, men of high distinction in widely differing departments of science.

In investigating this subject, the greatest patience is required. As in the somewhat analogous case of clairvoyance, the recurrence of similar phenomena is most uncertain, owing partly to the varying physical conditions of the medium, partly to the physical state of one or more of those present, or even to the state of the atmosphere; partial or even total failures must, therefore, occasionally be expected. I remember at a *séance* held to witness the clairvoyant phenomena of Alexis, how the effect of the presence of one lady sufficed nearly to obliterate his power; she, fortunately for us, left the room in disgust at what she designated as humbug, as Alexis's power returned almost immediately after her departure, and we had a most interesting and beautiful *séance*. A very analogous example in the case of Spiritualism will be found at p 110 of the following *séances*. Great caution must, therefore, be observed, and great allowances made, wherever a *bonâ fide* desire to arrive at truth is the real object of the enquirer.

Taking a general view of the subject, there are five hypotheses, three of them widely accepted, for explaining the so-called spiritualistic phenomena. The first, adopted by the world at large, maintains that they are the result of tricks or clever contrivance; in other words, that the mediums are impostors, and the whole exhibition humbug. According to the second, which is advocated by some scientific and medical men, the persons assisting at a *séance* become, then and there, the victims of a sort of mania or delusion, and imagine phenomena to occur, which have no real objective existence. The third maintains that the manifestations are referable to cerebral action, conscious or unconscious. This theory is evidently incapable of embracing the whole of the phenomena, and is not very widely advocated. The fourth, adopted almost unanimously by Spiritualists, is that the manifestations are caused by the agency of the spirits of departed human beings; and, generally speaking, by those who profess to be present. According to the fifth, which is held chiefly by believers in dogmatic Christianity, and also by many of the Low Church and Calvinistic school, the phenomena are supposed to be due to the agency of evil spirits or devils, personifying departed human beings, who have obtained this new power apparently for the purpose of undermining that conception of Christianity which has hitherto been almost universally received.

No amount of written or oral testimony seems to be sufficient to carry conviction on this mysterious subject to the minds of the vast majority of persons; yet a candid enquirer, reading a record such as that contained in the following pages, embracing so great a variety of phenomena, witnessed under varying circumstances and conditions, and attested by so many persons, can hardly avoid, without putting aside the narrator's testimony as utterly untrustworthy, admitting the possibility that some of the occurrences here recounted are the work of an agency beyond that of the persons present. The examples are so numerous that it would be difficult to make a selection for illustration; but the reader's attention may be called to those

instances where Mr. Home had never before entered the room
in which the *séance* was held; as for example, at No. 5,
Buckingham Gate, mentioned in p. 8; or where, as in *Séance
No.* 1, and indeed many of the others, he had no possible
opportunity of making any preparatory arrangements. It is
perhaps as well here to mention, that we have not, on a single
occasion, during the whole series of *séances*, seen any indication
of contrivance on the part of the medium for producing or
facilitating the manifestations which have taken place. The
larger has been our experience, and the more varied the
phenomena, the more firmly have we been convinced that a large
portion of them are but explicable on the hypothesis that they
are caused by intelligent beings, other than the persons in the
room; the remainder being probably due to the action of
physical laws as yet unknown.

The phenomena may be divided into two classes:—Physical
manifestations; and communications or messages. The former
are divisible again into those which are solely or partly due to
physical forces acting by a law—not yet ascertained—and
those which imply a power exercised by an invisible and
intelligent agent. To the first division of the physical manifestations, certain movements and vibrations of the table, or
other articles of furniture may be referred; and perhaps the
cold currents of air so often felt at the commencement of
séances. As an example of the second may be mentioned the
case of the table rising above our heads, described in page 131;
but a more decided illustration is afforded at page 137, where
a table was raised (no one touching it) and placed most carefully
upon another table; also may be cited those occasions on which
the accordion was played, when not held or touched by mortal
hands. One very curious example of vibration of the table will
be found at the end of *Séance No.* 51, p. 100, where the
manifestation can only be referred to an intelligent agent, or to
fraud on the part of some one present. I was so struck by the
synchronism of the vibration with each stroke of the clock, as
indicating an intelligence at work somewhere, that I examined
closely but failed to detect any indication that it was caused by
any one of those sitting at the table.

The communications may be divided into six classes; those which come through the alphabet; through the planchette; writing by the influenced hand; direct spirit-writing; audible spirit-voices; and, lastly, by the medium in a trance. The first and last methods are those employed in the following *séances*. Those delivered by the medium in a trance are obviously unsuited to convince persons of the existence of spirits; generally they afford no actual proof of the utterances being other than the thoughts of the medium; there are, however, exceptional cases, as where a communication is made to some person present, detailing circumstances unknown to the others, and of which the medium is almost certainly ignorant. Generally, but not always, these examples may be referable to the powers of mind-reading, similar to that manifested by clairvoyants. A genuine message, spelled out by the alphabet, is best suited to produce conviction that a communication is really from a spirit, especially where the raps, indicative of the letters which compose the words, are made at a distance from the medium, or are of such a nature as to have rendered it impossible for him to have caused them. The most striking cases are those where the mode of marking the letters is unknown to the medium or to any one present, except the person addressed. Examples will be found at pp. 111, 112, and 121, where the letters were indicated by my being touched on the knee. Not only are the two modes of communication of very different value as to their power of producing conviction in the reality of the phenomena, but likewise as to the reliability of the messages sent; and this must be carefully borne in mind when judging of the tendency of, or teaching derived from the communications. When Mr. Home speaks in a trance, there is no certainty whether his utterances are those of a spirit alone, or how far they may be mixed up with his own ideas or principles. Sometimes the communications are striking, at other times vague, sometimes trivial. Messages through the alphabet, on the other hand, carry at least a strong probability that they convey the thoughts of a spirit; although even they too in some cases exhibit indications of being affected by the medium, and are therefore not quite reliable.

The foregoing remarks will suffice to shew that in my opinion the first of the five hypotheses is utterly untenable. The second is disposed of by such cases as are detailed in pp. 137, 141. In the first example, the table lifted up and placed upon that at which we were sitting remained in the same position after the *séance* was broken up. In the second, the traces of the snuff which had been poured out on the shelf under the window were visible after supper. The third hypothesis requires no particular comment, being held by a very limited number among those who believe in the reality of the phenomena. Only two, therefore, need occupy the reader's attention, namely, that by which the manifestations are supposed to be caused by deceased human beings, or that which affirms them to be entirely due to the agency of lying spirits or devils. It is worthy of notice how the majority of the communications can be pressed into the service of either hypothesis.

The probability of the latter of the two theories being the correct one, extravagant and repulsive as this must appear to so many in the present day, results from the difficulty of reconciling the announcements of Spiritualism with the belief in certain doctrines hitherto uniformly maintained by all portions of Christendom. The necessity of a sacrificial atonement through Christ to obtain our salvation; the separation of mankind at death into two classes, the saved and the lost; the former destined to live for ever in union with God and in happiness, the latter in perpetual separation from Him, in punishment and misery; and the existence of a personal devil, and of fallen angels, whose unceasing efforts are directed to procure the loss of men's souls, are beliefs or doctrines which have been universally held by all churches. Now, the first and most important of these doctrines, one which has been regarded almost as the basis of Christianity, is seldom if ever alluded to in the following *séances*, while the two others are absolutely denied by Spiritualists in all countries. Thus, too, the miracles of the Old and New Testament are referred to natural laws, as exemplied, p. 74, in the passage of the Israelites through the Red Sea; and in p. 83, where the phenomena which occurred on the day of Pentecost are imitated. More might be cited having the same tendency, as for example the views put forward in p. 56; but, as has been already stated, the principal object here is to place on record a series of actual occurrences and communications, and then to indicate very slightly such points as are most worthy of the attention of an enquirer into their bearing upon the prevailing opinions of the day, on questions of social and religious importance. It should, however, be borne in mind that the majority of the statements here alluded to were made by the medium in a trance, and cannot be regarded as so probably the sayings of spirits, as if they were derived from messages through the alphabet. I must also observe that I have read many communications received through writing and drawing mediums which are distinctly Christian in their teaching, they are full of reference to our Lórd and to his office as the Mediator of mankind; but all, as far as my knowledge extends, have a latitudinarian character about them. Most fearful pictures are drawn of the consequences of sin, and of the way retribution must be made for evil done in this world. Many Spiritualists affirm that communications coming from these sources are of a higher kind than those conveyed through the ordinary physical means, such as raps, table tiltings, &c.

In other important particulars there is an apparent contrast between Christianity and the tendency of Spiritualism. In the New Testament, submission to authority and child-like obedience are inculcated as qualities peculiarly appertaining to the Christian believer, whereas the teaching of the spirits, as here recorded, seems rather to bring everything to the test of our reason. The spirit of Christianity has generally been antagonistic to the spirit of the world, and frequently to what may be called the spirit of the age. Latitudinarianism; opposition to ecclesiastical rule and authority; and dislike of forms as well as dogmas, are characteristic of the present day; and these principles are in accordance with the general teaching of Spiritualism, which is decidedly latitudinarian, and in harmony with the spirit of anti-sacerdotalism as opposed to that of dogmatic Christianity.

The reader of the following pages will not fail to perceive that a high and pure morality is taught in them; that the love of God, the value of prayer, and the importance of cultivating a truthful spirit are strongly inculcated; the terrible effects of sin, and the necessity of leading a good life in this, in order to occupy a high place in the next world, are forcibly pointed out. But what must perplex an orthodox Christian reader of these *séances* is the startling fact, that all reference to our Lord's office and work, as the sole passport to heaven, is practically omitted, and that He, whom all Catholics and most Protestants recognize as the sun of their religion, and the centre of their worship, seems to form so small a part of the thoughts or teaching of the spirits that here speak to us from beyond the grave.

That every variety of religious opinion, and all forms of Christianity are taught by spirits, is fully shown in an excellent book on Spiritualism, designated by rather an ill-chosen title, "Planchette; or, the Despair of Science." This, however, is quite in accordance with the general belief of Spiritualists, namely, that spirits hold various views because they retain in the next world their complete individuality, and to a certain extent their ignorance; they do not therefore know for certain that one system is better than another. They teach immortality; a living Providence; the possibility of communicating with us; that God has condemned no one to an eternity of punishment; and they usually imply that a good life in itself, rather than as springing from our union with Christ's merits, is the passport to a happy position in the next world. If what Spiritualists affirm be true, that the spirits are really those of departed human beings, and not demons, no harm can be done by narrowly scanning the tendency of some of their announcements in an opposite direction; and on the contrary, if they are demons or devils, the importance cannot be overrated of warning those who are interested in the subject, lest they find themselves implicated in the adoption of a system, which must on that hypothesis be looked upon as a very formidable conspiracy against the Christian religion, as hitherto believed in all countries.

It must, however, be evident to a thoughtful peruser of these pages, (and still more should he extend his reading to larger works on Spiritualism; such, for example, as the "Life of the Seeress of Prevorst,") that the evil-spirit or devil hypothesis is surrounded by such formidable difficulties, that hasty judgments and rash conclusions cannot be too strongly deprecated. Not to go so far back as the opposition made to Galileo and others, when their discoveries appeared to militate against the letter of Scripture; how many of us remember the sensation caused, and the alarms expressed by pious and learned persons, when the discoveries in geology demonstrated the impossibility of the world being created in six days, a few thousand years ago, but that it has existed and been peopled with animals for millions of years. Again, the universality of the Flood, so clearly declared in the words of Scripture, is found to be incompatible with the results of careful observation of the actual state of the surface of the earth. Among the beliefs exploded by geological research, may be mentioned the doctrine that pain and death, not only in man but in animals, are the result of Adam's sin. The fact being that the remains of animals, fitted to prey upon and kill each other, are found in strata formed millions of years ago, and in many cases the smaller creatures which were devoured are found within the stomachs of those by whom they were killed and eaten. Later still, the short amount of time during which man has existed on the globe, as deduced from even the longest Scripture chronology, is irreconcilable with recent researches in geology, in archæology, and in philology; the accuracy of which is every year more and more confirmed by additional observations, clearly indicating that man has inhabited this world for a period, not to be reckoned by thousands but by tens of thousands of years. This subject might be pursued much further, and additional illustrations given, tending to inculcate the necessity of modifying preconceived opinions on questions of great importance. To mention only one—that of miracles;—certain phenomena which have been universally considered as miraculous, or, to use the current expression, supernatural, are identical with those which are manifested by clairvoyants. How far this may extend cannot at present be known, but sufficient is established to render it advisable to pause before denouncing those who deny that certain phenomena are miraculous; some of which are, and others may be, referable to physical laws that have only recently been included within the domain of natural science, and which are as yet only partially understood. I would also point to the wonderful healing powers of certain mediums, as affording a subject of most serious consideration and reflection, but which need not be entered upon here as not bearing upon the following *séances*.

Arguing by analogy, it need not surprise us to find, as must be the case should the announcements of Spiritualism be true, that the conceptions hitherto held by Christians of all denominations, of the state of existence in the next world, may require considerable modification. We are informed that the spirit-world is very analogous in some respects to this; that it is one of continued progression ; that we are not suddenly brought to the full knowledge of religious truth; that the belief we hold here we shall in all probability, at least for a time, retain there, in proportion as we are more bigoted in this life, and consequently more difficult to teach in the next. We are told, p. 38, "*There is a contest*" going on, "*same as on earth*;" but, "*purity when freed from the mortal is strongest, as truth overcomes error.*" At different epochs of the world, the same subject is regarded from very different points of view. For example, the idea of the punishment of hell being a material fire was for many ages almost universal; it certainly is not so at present, even among the most orthodox believers in the doctrine of eternal punishment.

A difficulty of another kind, one not easily got over, stands in the way of the adoption of the evil-spirit theory, namely the fact that conversions have been made by the agency of Spiritualism, from Atheism and from simple Deism to Christianity. To take one instance ; Dr. Elliotson was a strong materialist, and unbeliever ; he was converted, through Mr. Home's manifestations, to Christianity. In accordance with this fact we have a message from a spirit purporting to be his, (vide *séance No.* 10) "*I now know that my Redeemer liveth,*" &c. Again others, among whom are four or five of my own acquaintance, have been led by the same means from Unitarianism to a belief in the divinity of Christ. Still more striking are the cases where persons have been brought into the Church of Rome, several examples of which have occurred in America, and a few in England. The case of Dr. and Mrs. Nichols (Americans) affords a most remarkable instance in point; and it would be strange could any of these individuals be brought to believe that their advance from a lower to a higher religious creed was due to the agency of the devil; nor can the express testimony be overlooked of some pure-minded, earnest persons, as to the elevating effect of the belief in Spiritualism upon their hearts and souls. Take for example the interesting and striking account of the closing years and death of a very beautiful character, the late Mrs. Home, as described by Mrs. Howitt and Mrs. S. C. Hall,* where the happiness and the blessings which Spiritualism has produced, not only in her case, but in their own, are portrayed in a tone strikingly earnest and yet quite free from anything like excitement or exaggeration. To ascribe such peace and joy in believing, such love of our Lord, and resignation to His will as led the Bishop of Perigueux—who administered the last sacraments to Mrs. Home—to remark, " Though he had been present at many a deathbed for heaven, he had never seen one equal to hers;"—and she a professed Spiritualist, and the wife of one of the most noted mediums in the world!—To ascribe, I repeat, such results to the agency of the father of lies and the arch enemy of mankind, must appear as impossible to many, as it must be revolting to the two gifted writers whom I have quoted, and who bear such strong testimony to the blessed influence which Spiritualism has exercised upon their own lives and faith. Attention should also be called to the *séances* at Homburg, especially *Nos.* 19, 21, 22, where the action of the spirits was decidedly exercised in various ways to promote bodily health and comfort, and also to inculcate and reiterate the advantage of good practices, such as examination of conscience at night; still more striking was the evident anxiety on their part to prevent and counteract grievous sin, as must be quite clear to those who read these accounts with attention. Remarks upon this subject might be considerably amplified; but enough has been pointed out to indicate some of the difficulties which surround the adoption of the evil-spirit hypothesis. Indeed the only answer

---

* *Vide* Mr. Home's " Incidents in my Life," chap. xii.

which can be given, by those who maintain this view, is that Satan is allowed an unlimited power, of which he makes copious use, of transforming himself into an angel of light.

Setting aside the religious question, and admitting even that the spirits are those of departed human beings, the difficulty of identification renders the whole subject in its present stage rather unsatisfactory. This opinion, I know, is to a considerable extent shared in by persons who have been for several years believers in Spiritualism. Among those who took part in the following *séances*, some seem to find little or no difficulty in believing that the spirits in communication with them are the relatives or friends they professed to be. I confess in this confidence I cannot share. To take an extreme case, the idea that the former possessor of Adare Manor should be present at a *séance*, and yet only manifest that presence by shaking his son's chair (*No.* 57, p. 116), seems as improbable as absurd.*

Whatever view be taken of the source of the phenomena, the subject is one deserving serious treatment, and careful investigation. The tone of levity which prevails in some amateur *séances*, and the fashion now prevalent among young ladies of playing with planchettes, cannot be too strongly deprecated. A power, which practically may be looked upon and treated of as new, has almost suddenly been developed among men; a power which may be fraught in many cases with serious consequences. Are we in a position at present to pronounce from what sources this power proceeds? The veil which separates this world from the next is partially raised; can we say why this partial unfolding of the future is permitted; into what extent it may be developed, or what is the main purpose for which this unexpected source of knowledge, or deception as the case may be, is revealed? A partial but decisive answer may be given to some of these questions. A proof, derived from a physical and material source is opened to men of an existence beyond the grave. The tendency of the present age being materialistic and sceptical,

---

* Since these *séances* have taken place, communications have been made to Lord Adare (*vide* p. 164) which, if genuine, would account for and explain why none were given at the time from the source mentioned; the probability, however of identity is scarcely strengthened, in my mind, by the terror of these later communications.

the evidence of the senses is required as a ground for belief, to a degree far surpassing what has hitherto been the case; that evidence is now afforded for the most important of beliefs, namely, that of a future existence. The true answer to those who require the *cui bono* of Spiritualism would appear, therefore, to be, that through its instrumentality an incontrovertible proof is afforded to all who will fairly, fully, and patiently investigate a world of spirits. This teaching stands out clear and unmistakable above any conflicting theories as to the kind of spirits who are the source of the communications.

That Spiritualism is not unaccompanied by danger is allowed, even by its most earnest believers. This chiefly springs from the great power of deception which may be exercised by spirits, while the power of identification remains so unsatisfactory as it is at present. For example, messages are sent, or communications in the trance state given, purporting to come from deceased members of a family, commenting on family affairs; it is obvious that this may be a source of serious mischief. If, as is allowed by all Spiritualists, bad and lying spirits can and do communicate, what is to secure one from being deceived by them in a particular case? A friend of mine believed that a spirit present at a *séance* was a gentleman who had been lately poisoned; he asked if B—— was concerned in the matter and was answered in the affirmative. This he appeared to believe, and thus B——, who lives in his parish, to some extent lies under the imputation of being concerned in a murder; and this on the declaration of a spirit whose identity seemed to me to rest on no solid ground.

One of the most remarkable features in these *séances* is the frequency of Mr. Home's trances. This peculiar phase of his power has become much developed of late; while others, such as his being raised in the air, have comparatively diminished. To those who are familiar with mesmeric trances, the genuineness of Mr. Home's is easily admitted. To me they are among the most interesting portions of the manifestations which occur through his mediumship. The change which takes place in him is very striking; he becomes, as it were, a being of a higher type. There is a union of sweetness, tenderness, and earnestness

b

in his voice and manner which is very attractive. At first sight
much might appear to be skilful acting; but after having so
frequently witnessed these trance states, I am fully convinced
of their truthfulness. Sometimes his utterances are most
impressive; the language beautiful, conveying his thoughts in
the most appropriate words. That he is possessed by a power
or spirit, not his own, and superior to himself, a very little
experience will suffice to render manifest. I can most fully
endorse the statement in Lord Adare's preface—of the very
imperfect conception of the impressiveness of some of these
séances as conveyed by our meagre reports. They are, as it
were, mere skeletons, as for example, *No.* 55; no one could
imagine the beauty and interest of that *séance*, from the very
inadequate account given there of what occurred. To be
appreciated or realized they must be witnessed, and that
under favourable circumstances. Those who have been present
will, I am sure, agree with me that some of them are very
touching and beautiful. A pure, lofty, and religious tone more
or less pervades them. The solemnity which is always manifested at the name of God is remarkable. After reading Mr.
Chevalier's pamphlet I was anxious to apply the test of using
the invocation of the Trinity. I never mentioned this to
Mr. Home; but it was unexpectedly suggested by him when
entranced during the *séance*, *No.* 59, and with a totally opposite
result, as the reader will see.* The effect produced upon
Mr. Home by Pressencé's "Life of Christ" was very striking.
I have never seen such reverence paid to the Bible in real life;
it reminded one of the devotion exhibited by a Catholic to the
Blessed Sacrament.

Another very remarkable feature and well worthy of attention, is the account given by the spirits of the mode by which
they are able to make manifestations, as is detailed in pp. 54, 126,
and other places; also the extreme difficulty experienced in
making them, and the slight causes which interrupt the power.
In fact, when one considers the number of favourable conditions

---

* Mr. Chevalier states that when he asked the spirit who it was, using the
names of the Father, Son, and Holy Ghost; the word " *Devil*" was spelled out.

necessary in order that manifestations should succeed, the wonder is that they do not oftener fail. Nothing can be plainer than that the power of spirits over matter is one of degree, varying each night, and indeed almost every minute. This is the answer to those who are constantly remarking " If they can do this, why cannot they do that? If a spirit can raise an object an inch, why not a yard? If Mr. Home could float in the air last week, why can he not to-day? " and so forth. The causes of failure are well exemplified in the last *séance* at Garinish, *No.* 63, when apparently, numbers were present, and evidently they had intended giving us a series of manifestations as a wind up to the *séances* in Ireland; but this design was partly frustrated by the state of the weather and Mr. Home's health, as well as our own rather unfavorable condition.

A very common misconception on the general subject ought to be here pointed out. The idea seems very prevalent that Mr. Home invokes or evokes spirits. This notion is totally destitute of foundation. Neither Mr. Home, nor any medium, as far as I know ever professes to call up spirits. Several persons sit round a table, and Mr. Home, while deprecating levity, desires to promote cheerful and social conversation on general matters, without any premeditated design or wish expressed that particular things should happen or particular spirits be present. Some Spiritualists begin every sitting with prayer, and generally with a chapter in the Bible. I was at one lately, where, as soon as the presence of spirits was announced by raps, they were asked, should we begin by reading a chapter; " *Yes*," was the reply; and they were then asked, what chapter it should be, and they rapped out, "*Acts*, xi. *chapter, verses*, 5 *to* 18." One more appropriate could not readily be selected.

Before concluding these introductory remarks, I would remind the reader, that the primary object of this little work is to place on record a series of observed facts upon a very mysterious and startling subject. It is only by such means, pursued under varying circumstances, as to time, place, and mediums, multiplied by different observers, that a conclusive answer can be hoped for to the question, *Will the result of Spiritualism be good or evil?* is the tendency of the movement as a whole to the glory of God, and the happiness of mankind in the next world, or, is it a great system of deception, carried on by the powers of darkness, and fraught with danger to our souls? Setting aside the great majority of the world, who refuse all enquiry into a subject which they consider to be imposture, or ridiculous nonsense, unworthy of serious thought, many shrink from it as the work solely of evil spirits; others, from a fear of the danger derived from the difficulty of identification, and the consequent deception which may be practised; and others again from an instinctive dread of communing with the departed, and from an intense pain caused by the idea that the state of those whom they have loved should be so widely different from, and apparently so much lower than what they have fondly believed in, through the traditionary teaching under which they have been brought up. Nor can we omit in fairness the opinion of many of the opponents of Spiritualism who maintain, that the examples of its being productive of good effects are exceptional, and that the system must be judged by its general results, which, as developed in America, are, they say, drifting away from anything like orthodox Christianity. This statement I am not in a position to be able to pronounce upon one way or the other.

Without attempting to conceal my own state of doubt as to the source from which the phenomena of Spiritualism proceed, and my decided impression of the danger which in some respects seems possibly to accompany its pursuit or adoption, I have been most desirous not to bias unduly those who are anxious to investigate a very interesting and most curious subject of enquiry; especially as Lord Adare takes a more favourable view than I can at present conscientiously hold, of the points about which such opposite opinions are entertained by men of earnest and truth-loving character. Why then, it may be asked, take any part in enquiring into a subject, the tendency of which seems so difficult to determine? The answer is simple:—Chiefly, to examine for my own satisfaction; next, to enable others, who may consider a similar spirit of enquiry advisable or interesting, to have the benefit of the experience derived from the following *séances;* and also, to shew to those who are already struck by, or much occupied in, the pursuit of this mysterious subject, the dangers by which it is surrounded, through the possible tendencies of its teachings, or the deceptions practicable by bad or mischievous spirits. I maintain that we are entitled to investigate all the physical phenomena which may come before us, provided we do so earnestly and with a desire to arrive at truth. Acting upon this principle, I enquired into the remarkable phenomena of mesmerism and clairvoyance, when the propriety of so doing was doubted by some for whom I entertained the highest respect. Upon the same principle I now avail myself of the opportunity which Lord Adare's acquaintance with Mr. Home has afforded, of investigating the still more interesting and startling phenomena of Spiritualism; content that time will clear up that which is at present so perplexing, and enable honest enquirers to decide whether the subject is one which they can with propriety continue to pursue, or one which they feel themselves bound, as sincere followers of Christ, and for the safety of their souls, to abandon.

DUNRAVEN.

NAMES OF PERSONS PRESENT AT THE SEANCES

[All the persons present at the following *séances*, with the exception of three or four to whom access cannot be obtained, have received a copy of the account of the *séances* which they witnessed, with a request that if the report coincided with their own recollection of what took place, they would kindly allow their names to be appended, as testifying to its accuracy. Every answer has been in the affirmative as to the correctness of the accounts; but a very few have, for prudential reasons, preferred that their names should not appear. By accuracy is meant, that nothing has been inserted that did not occur, or has been exaggerated. A great deal has necessarily been omitted.]

Mr. H. JENCKEN, Barrister-at-Law, Temple.
Mrs. HENNINGS, 9, Thicket Road, Norwood.
Mrs. SCOTT RUSSELL, Norwood.
Miss GALLWEY, 7, Lower Belgrave Street.
Mr. S. C. HALL, 15, Ashley Place.
Mrs. S. C. HALL,   „   „
Mr. H. T. HUMPHREY, 1, Clifford's Inn.
Mr. HAMILTON, Sundrum, Ayr.
Mrs. HAMILTON,   „   „
Miss HAMILTON,   „   „
Mrs. COX, Stockton House.
Miss BROOKS,   „   „
Mr. ION PERDICARIS, 2, Heathcote Villas, Twickenham.
Mrs. MAINWARING, Ashley House, Victoria Street.
Countess DE MEDINA DE POMAR, Grafton Hotel, Albemarle Street.
Mrs. HONEYWOOD, 52, Warwick Square.
Dr. GULLY, Malvern.
Mr. JONES, Enmore Park, South Norwood.
Mrs. MACKDOUGALL GREGORY, 21, Green Street, Grosvenor Square.
Lady FAIRFAX, 45, St. George's Road.
Major DRAYSON, 6, York Crescent, Woolwich.
Mr. HART, 30, Duke Street, St. James's.
Mr. SARL, 45, Cornhill.
Mr. J. COLLINS, Royal Military Academy, Woolwich.
Miss SMITH, Adare Manor, Ireland.
Miss BERTOLACCI, Vine Cottage, Fulham Road.
Miss E. BERTOLACCI,   „   „
Hon. F. LAWLESS, Maritimo, Black Rock, Ireland.

Capt. CHAS. WYNNE, Lissadell, Sligo.
Mrs. C. WYNNE,   ,,   ,,
Mr. B. DE C. NIXON, 1, Queen's Gate Gardens.
Mrs. B. DE C. NIXON,   ,,   ,,
Mr. JAMES GORE BOOTH, R.E., Aldershot.
Sir ROBT. GORE BOOTH, Bart., 7, Buckingham Gate.
Miss GORE BOOTH,   ,,   ,,
A. SMITH BARRY, M.P., 26, Chesham Place.
The Hon. The MASTER OF LINDSAY, 9, Grosvenor Square.
Major BLACKBURN, 35, Beaufort Gardens.
Mrs. BLACKBURN,   ,,   ,,
Mrs. WYNNE, Corris, Bagnalstown, Ireland.
Miss WYNNE,   ,,   ,,
Mr. J. BERGHEIM, 34, Hill Street, Knightsbridge.
Mr. H. A. RUDALL, 17, Langham Street.
Mr. F. FULLER, 12, St. James's Place.
Miss DOUGLAS, 81, South Audley Street.
DOWAGER DUCHESS OF ST. ALBAN'S, 4, Princes Gate.
Mr. CHAS. BLACKBURN, Park Field, Didsbury, Manchester.
Capt. GERARD SMITH, Scots Fusilier Guards, 13, Upper Belgrave Street.
Mr. STANLEY J. MACKENZIE, 32, Bernard Street.
Mrs. STOPFORD, 7, Grosvenor Gardens.

CLASSIFICATION OF PHENOMENA.

PREFACE.

BEING personally acquainted with Mr. Home, and having resided for some little time with him in London during the autumns of 1867 and 1868, and having travelled in his company in Germany in the summer of 1868, I have had considerable opportunity of witnessing the phenomena of *Spiritualism*, not only at regular *séances*, but also at times when we were quite alone, and without any premeditation on our part.

My father, being interested in the subject, requested me to write him a short account of anything remarkable that occurred. I did so, and of the letters so written the following narrative is composed. At the time I wrote them I had not the slightest notion that my letters were destined to be printed; had I thought so, I would have endeavoured to express myself with greater clearness. Frequently remarkable incidents followed each other in such rapid succession, that without transgressing the bounds of ordinary correspondence, I had scarcely time or space to give my father a full account of what took place. In preparing the letters for the press, I have found the statements in many instances much curtailed and embodied in language not so carefully chosen as it should have

been had I known that they were to be submitted
even to private circulation. I have however thought
it better not to interfere with the originals, and the
following pages are printed nearly word for word
from the letters that I wrote to my father immediately
after each occurrence took place. There are four
things I wish to mention :—

1st.—It has been my object throughout to divest
my accounts of all the sensational element; and
partly for the sake of brevity, partly from a fear of
exaggerating in any particular, in writing to my
father I simply recorded the bare facts I witnessed.
I know that in so doing, I have not treated the
subject fairly. Take any interesting and exciting
incident, a shipwreck—or a fearful railway catas-
trophe—put down the bare facts on paper, that a
goods train ran into an excursion train, so many
people were killed, and so many legs and arms broken,
and the story seems very prosaic. Hear it recounted
by an eye-witness and participator in the danger, and
you will carry away a very different impression. For
this reason, the reader may consider the following
accounts rather stupid and uninteresting, and sometimes they may appear even trivial. I can assure
the reader that to those engaged in the investigation,
they did not appear so, and were they clothed in
language sufficiently powerful to produce upon the
mind of the reader the same impression that was
produced at the time upon those who witnessed the
phenomena, they would appear not trifling, but full
of interest, and worthy of the deepest attention.

2nd.—To put down on paper accurately, even the substance of what Mr. Home says when speaking in a trance, is extremely difficult. Unless a writer be acquainted with some method of short-hand writing, it is impossible to keep pace with a speaker delivering a long discourse with ordinary rapidity of utterance. This difficulty is further increased by the fact, that in many cases the addresses were delivered in a partially darkened room. I am well aware that in some cases I have represented Mr. Home as talking with little connection between the sentences, and sometimes the meaning is obscure, and the ideas badly expressed; this is the result of the impossibility of transmitting his utterances accurately to paper without the assistance of a short-hand writer. In all cases of trance-speaking witnessed by me, Mr. Home has expressed himself with perfect clearness, his language has been remarkably well chosen and to the point, frequently interspersed with truly poetic ideas and symbols. In some cases when my notes were very imperfect, I have contented myself with merely saying that Mr. Home spoke on such and such a subject. On other occasions I have endeavoured to write down, as well as I could, the substance of what he said. In one case, I have requested Mr. Jencken to write out some sentences delivered by Mr. Home in a trance, as I was quite unable to make out the meaning of the notes that Mr. Jencken succeeded in taking at the time.

3rd.—Even in the original letters to my father, I was obliged to omit a few circumstances of great interest; in some cases on account of their having reference to persons who did not wish those circumstances mentioned; in others, because the communication, although referring to myself, was of such a private nature that I preferred making no mention of it. In looking over the letters previous to sending them to press, I have found it absolutely necessary to suppress certain other facts and communications. Owing to this, the reader will find some passages incomplete; in two cases I had an explanation given to me of a long train of puzzling circumstances; the reasons for certain occurrences that took place were told me, the object to be gained, and the result. I was as it were let behind the scenes, to see the "reason why" for a number of strange events that I could not previously account for. I am unable to mention either of these cases because other people are much involved in them. Some of the events however are mentioned, and must appear meaningless to the reader, as they did to me until I was furnished with the explanation of them.

4th.—It may perhaps appear strange to some that I did not, at the commencement of my investigations, take greater pains to determine that the manifestations were not the result of trickery, collusion or mechanical contrivance. From what I had heard from reliable sources, I had come to the conclusion that the phenomena were the result of some power or intelligence, other than that of the medium, or any of the persons present. I had therefore little difficulty on this point, and the scrutiny that

I did make was more to satisfy Mr. Home, and to be able to tell others that I had done so, than to convince myself. My father had early opportunities of testing for himself, and soon arrived at the same conclusion. I therefore in writing to him have generally omitted all mention of the various tests I had seen used, in order to save myself useless labour. It is, however, as well now to mention, that I have witnessed many persons make, at their first *séance*, every effort to account for the phenomena by trickery and mechanical contrivance, and failing that, to reduce them to the effects of some unknown force. I have invariably found them (provided of course that the *séance* was successful) very soon obliged to admit that these phenomena cannot be accounted for, except on the supposition that they are caused by an unseen but active and reasoning intelligence. I have printed names in full whenever I have obtained leave to do so, knowing how little value is generally attached to statements unsupported by the testimony of more than one person. It will be noticed that spirits rarely give their names. In some instances, however, they do so, and occasionally they fix upon some sign by which their presence is to be recognized. It would be out of place in a narrative of this kind were I in each case to enter into a discussion as to the probability of the identity being correct. I have merely recorded that which I heard and saw. The persons mentioned in the following pages are not, therefore, to be identified with any particular belief about Spiritualism; but are only witnesses, if necessary, to the correctness of the facts I have stated. I myself make no attempt here to offer any explanation of the following phenomena, or to build up any theory upon them, I only say that they occurred as I have stated them. Many books have been published on the subject by able and thinking men in England and America and on the Continent, which can be referred to by those who are anxious for information. The object of placing my letters in this their present form is simply to preserve a series of well-authenticated cases of the occurrence of very wonderful phenomena. Interesting as they are now, they are likely to become of still greater value in the future, either as recording a very marvellous and transitory condition of things, or as marking the first faint indications of a great and permanent change.

ADARE.

No. 1 Séance.

Malvern, November 1867.

YESTERDAY, Mr. Earl, a total disbeliever in Spiritualism, Home and I, went to spend the evening with Mrs. Thayer, an American lady, a friend of Dr. Gully's. We were shown into the back parlour, a small room, the furniture consisting of a heavy round mahogany table, without any cover, with one leg in the centre, and of a piano and several ordinary chairs. The room was lighted by a fire, a large lamp standing on the piano, and two wax candles on the table.

After Mrs. Thayer came in we sat and talked for a few minutes by the fireside, until at Home's suggestion we sat round the table, which was in the middle of the room. Home was on my left, Mrs. Thayer opposite me, and Earl on my right. The room was perfectly light. After talking on ordinary subjects for perhaps ten minutes, raps were heard by us all in various parts of the room, on the table and on the floor and walls. Home requested the raps to be made in various places and it was done. He asked that they would rap under my feet, and I not only heard the noise, but distinctly felt the jar while the raps were taking place. I repeatedly looked under the table, as did also Mr. Earl, to satisfy ourselves that, however they were done, it was not by any movement on Home's part. It was quite impossible that Home could have made them, for while they were distinctly audible, I looked under the table and could have detected even the slightest movement of his legs or feet ; Mr. Earl watched his hands and arms. Similar raps were occasionally heard during the whole *séance*. At the commencement of the *séance* we all felt cold currents of air passing over our hands. The table began to vibrate with the greatest rapidity, and then was moved about and tilted up in various directions. Mrs. Thayer had previously to this placed a pencil and writing paper on the table. The table was repeatedly tilted up at an angle I should say greater than 45°. The surface was smooth polished mahogany, yet the candles, paper, and pencil, did not move. Home asked that the candles might slip (as they naturally would) and they did slide down the table until near

A

the edge, when at his request, they remained stationary. While the table was tilted up very high, Home said to Earl, "Take a candle and look under the table." He took one of the candles on the table, and in lifting it said, good gracious, how heavy it is! I afterwards tried the same thing, and found that when the table was tilted up there was a difficulty in removing the candle from the surface that made it appear very heavy. The table was moved up against my chest, and as I pushed back my chair, it followed me up until the back of my chair was against the window, and I could go no further; the table was then pushed close up against me. I now felt cold currents of air passing across my face and hands, and a chair that was standing against the wall, at a distance of perhaps five yards, came suddenly and quickly out from the wall, and placed itself beside me at the table. The effect was startling. There was a lady's cloak on it, which was pulled off under the table. Mrs. Thayer said, "She could see a shadowy form standing between Home and me." I saw nothing, but I was touched lightly on the head, and distinctly as with a sharp tap of the finger on the knee. I do not think it possible that anybody at the table could have touched me. I could see all their hands, and had it been done by a foot I must have perceived the difference of touch, and have seen the motion. Some time previously to this Mrs. Thayer had sent out the servant to ask a friend for an accordion, and it had been placed upon the table. The alphabet was called for (by five raps) and the following words were spelled out (I am not sure that I remember the exact words but they were to this effect):—"*I could not come the other night because of H——. Yours ever, Fred.*" Mrs. Thayer understood the meaning of this message it having reference to a previous *séance*, the first one, I believe, at which she had been present. After a few minutes the alphabet was again called for, and the following words were spelled out :—"*My boy, I am near you.*" I naturally referred this to my mother.

After this, the accordion was moved about on the table. Home took it, holding it by the lower part, with the keys hanging down over the edge of the table. It is manifestly impossible for a person so holding an accordion either to touch the keys, to inflate the bellows, or to expel the air from it. Almost immediately the keys were touched in an uncertain manner, and then the accordion began to play. It played something resembling a voluntary on the organ: the melody was perfect, and the expression beautiful. I am sure that if I had heard it so played anywhere, under any circumstances, it would have occurred to me how like the music was to what I had often heard my mother play, when running over a few chords on the piano. While the accordion was being played, I looked at it two or three times under the table. Home was on each occasion holding it as I have stated, and the instrument was pulled out horizontally from his hand. I could see the bellows drawn in and out, and the keys move. At one time it was pulled violently under the chair at my side towards me. Home asked me to name some air. I wished to think of one that might help me to identify whoever was playing the accordion, but I could not. Earl asked for "The Last Rose of Summer." It was beautifully played: first, the air quite simply, then with chords and variations. After this Mrs. Thayer took the accordion, and Mr. Earl also, but it did not play again. During what I have narrated, the table was occasionally moved, and raps were now and then heard in different parts of the room. All manifestations ceased when the accordion stopped playing. My hands during the whole time were as cold as ice; when the manifestations ceased they became suddenly warm. I said, "Dear me, my hands have become quite warm!" Home said, "Oh, then I am afraid there will be nothing more." We waited perhaps five minutes; and, finding there were no more manifestations, we got up and moved the table over to the fire. Home began reading to us some poetry. The last thing he read was descriptive of the passing away of a poor old widow; and, after a passage speaking of the love of Christ for her, strong raps of approval—that is, three raps in succession—were heard on the floor behind him. We then said Good night to Mrs. Thayer, and went back to Tudor House. I turned into the dining room and sat down by the fire alone. A few minutes after, Home came in and sat down by me, and we talked about ordinary subjects. We heard a sound that I thought was the door creaking. He said it was not that, and asked that the sound should be repeated, and it was. He then asked that it should rap where I usually sat at dinner; and it did so right at the end of the table. We were both sitting with our backs to the table. Then came a noise as if furniture was moving. I turned but saw nothing move. Home looked and said a chair had moved up to the table. I looked again at the other side of the table, and saw that a chair was standing against it; all the others were against the wall. I did not see it move. We then heard a sort of whistling sound flying up and down the room; then a sound as of something rushing up and down, and then, laughter, unmistakable but not pleasant sounding laughter. After this one of the servants came in, and nothing more occurred. When in the dining room, Home asked whether the spirit that was there in the room was one that loved me. It answered "Yes." By answered, I mean that three raps were given, which means "Yes." He asked if the spirit would like me to have another *séance* with him in London. "Yes," was answered.

_____

No. 2 Séance.

About a fortnight after this I had occasion to go to London. I went down to see Home at Mr. Jencken's, at Norwood. We had a *séance* in the evening. There were present, Home, Mr. Jencken, Mrs. Hennings, and myself. Nothing very remarkable occurred; at least, I do not remember anything. The usual manifestations took place, such as the table moving, and raps were heard; the table, a light card table, was lifted off the ground completely. During the first part of the *séance* the manifestations seemed all directed to Home, afterwards the table was in the same way as at the first *séance* moved up against me. The accordion was played in Home's hand. The last thing that occurred was that my chair began to vibrate rapidly in the most violent way; it gave me a curious tingling sensation up my arms to the elbow, and up my legs as though I was receiving an electric shock. Knowing that this vibration almost invariably preceded any movement, or lifting of the table, I thought that I was going to be raised into the air, and most unwillingly I became very nervous and frightened. If I had not done so I think some phenomenon would have occurred; but as soon as I became alarmed, the vibration of my chair ceased. That was the last thing that occurred that evening.

_____

No. 3 Séance.

This day week I again went down to Mr. Jencken's to see Home. After tea we had a *séance*. There were present: Mr. Jencken, Mrs. Jencken (his mother), Mrs. Hennings, Mrs. Scott Russell, Miss D—— R——, another lady whose name I forget, Home and myself. We sat round the card table, all except Mrs. Jencken, who sat in her arm chair in another part of the room. We had a very beautiful *séance*. Miss D—— R—— had never been present at one before, and was most of the time engaged in looking under the table, and investigating what took place. Very few raps were heard. The manifestations began by the usual vibration of the table, the floor, and our chairs; and by the cold currents of air passing round the table over our hands. The table moved, and we followed it until it was in a corner close to the wall. Home had his back to the wall. On his left, at a little distance, was a small square table, with a vase of flowers on it; and on his right was a small round table, on which stood a large vase containing a fern.

The chief part of the manifestations consisted in the movement of these tables. They were brought close to Home, and then were sometimes raised in the air and inclined towards him; sometimes simply tilted on one leg, so that the flowers touched his face. The flowers were in like manner also, as it were, presented to Mrs. Hennings and Mrs. Scott Russell. Before moving the small round table up to us, it was necessary to clear a space for it, as the table at which we were sitting was close to the window. Our table moved a little back, and we then saw the window curtains drawn on one side out of the way. This table was repeatedly raised in the air to the height of 4 or 5 inches, Miss D—— R—— placing her hands between it and the floor; and it was also frequently inclined at such an angle, that the vase must inevitably have fallen off under ordinary circumstances. The flowers on the square table and the fern on the round table were frequently agitated and moved, but were not broken off or plucked. On placing the ear against the small table, it was found to be full of minute raps, like a current of small electric sparks.

The phenomena connected with the movement of these two tables occupied some time, during which we talked about various matters and subjects. Miss D—— R—— and Mr. Jencken were talking about Spiritualism, and he got rather excited, and was saying something to the effect that he lost his patience when people said it was all trickery and conjuring, and that instead of that it was a great and real blessing and dispensation vouchsafed to us by God for our comfort. Approving raps occurred at this, and he said "Is it not to shew us without doubt that it is so," or some words of that sort. Assent was signified to that remark so emphatically that it made me laugh. It seemed so energetic—first, "Yes" was rapped on the floor and walls, then the small tables tilted themselves three times, and then the table we were sitting round tilted itself up towards each corner in turn three times, and lastly, being raised right off the ground, was moved up and down three times in the air, and then came down with an emphatic bang that shook the floor. During this *séance*, it was remarkable how the spirits joined as it were in our conversation, two or three times signifying approval in the most emphatic way. I noticed a remarkable circumstance in connection with the small round table. When it was inclined at a considerable angle I saw the vase move, but instead of slipping down the slope, it moved up against it.

As I before mentioned, the small table with the fern was raised in the air, and presented as if in greeting to Mrs. Hennings, Home, and Mrs. Scott Russell. After this had been done several times the alphabet was called for, and the following message given (the exact words I cannot answer for): "*We would do more to shew our love; these* (referring to the flowers) *are emblems of God's love.*" The letters were indicated sometimes by the small table tilting, sometimes by raps on the large table. Soon afterwards the alphabet was again called for, and the following message given :—"*Sit alone in a corner with Adare.*" Accordingly Home and I left the table, and sat in another corner of the room at the small round table, having previously removed the vase ; immediately the table was raised up and tilted against my chest. The table had one leg terminating in three claws, one of them just touched my toe, and the letters were indicated by the claw tapping my toe. The following message was thus given :— "*My own boy, I go with you, fear nothing, God will give a mother power to protect her own boy. I will yet speak to you when alone.*" The table was then raised off the ground, presented to me close to my face, two or three times, and replaced on the floor. Home was not touching the table; but during all this time was sitting beside me in an arm chair, and I distinctly felt—and so did he—some one standing between us. We then went back to the large table and Home took the accordion in his hand. He asked some questions, which were answered in the affirmative by three single notes on the accordion. Home in asking these questions became very much affected—I do not know why—and his voice was quite broken; he asked whether the spirit holding the accordion was the same that brought the chair to me at Malvern ?* Whether it had not stood between me and him when we were sitting in the corner? The accordion then played something like a voluntary on the organ. The peculiarity being that the last few notes were drawn out so fine as to be scarcely audible—the last note dying away so gradually that I could not tell when it ceased. I do not think it possible for any human hand to produce a note in that way. Sometime before this we had all heard a whistling over Home's head, similar to that which I had heard in the dining room at Tudor House. It is a curious sound, something between a bird chirping and the whistling produced by birds' wings rapidly moving. After it ceased we all heard sounds as of a voice, but not articulate. Home then asked if a spirit was endeavouring to make the voice heard, and was answered "*Yes,*" and he asked if it would be repeated, and was answered "*Perhaps.*" It was not repeated until we left the table. During the time the sounds were heard Home was talking, which I was glad of, as I wished to feel sure the sounds were not the result of ventriloquism on

---

* There is no answer recorded to Home's questions, but I believe the answer to have been in the affirmative.

his part. I believe I may also safely say that we were all engaged in conversation at the time, so that the sounds could not have been produced by any accomplice among us. I did not, however, observe any of the others so closely as I did Home.

After the accordion had played I took it in my hand, but immediately after I had done so the alphabet was called for and the words were spelled out, " *We can do no more now.*" All the manifestations then ceased. We waited a few minutes, and Home asked if the spirits were gone. No answer was returned, so we left the table. I have particularly noticed three things.

1st. That the commencement of each *séance* appears the same, namely, currents of cold air passing over the hands of those at the table as if some sort of chain was being formed. Any abrupt breaking of which by some one suddenly leaving the table will stop the phenomena.

2nd. That if the attention be too much concentrated it prevents the phenomena. They take place best when those at the table are keeping up a general conversation. If anything occurs, such as a table moving, and everybody stops talking and looks at it, it is almost sure to stop. In the last *séance*, I noticed that when anything of that sort was being done, if every one turned to look at it and stopped talking, the table or some other piece of furniture moved as it were to attract attention. I forgot to mention that Home at the last *séance* was thrown into a trance. He remained entranced two or three minutes, but said nothing. We foolishly all stopped talking to look at him, and I think that broke the trance, as he awoke, passed his hand across his forehead, and remarked how quiet we all were.

At the commencement of a trance Home generally tells the spectators to go on talking; not to fix their attention on him too much at first. I think that as negative a condition of mind as can possibly be maintained is almost a necessity to ensure strong manifestations. This is not however the case, I believe, with all mediums. The presence of dogs in the room, or much tobacco smoke, will entirely prevent manifestations with Home as medium. The effect of these things is, no doubt, upon the medium, not upon the spiritual influence.

3rd. That the name of God is always treated with peculiar reverence. In spelling out a sentence, if you guess an ordinary word, they say "Yes;" and go on to the next. But though you may guess it, they spell out each letter in the name of God, and instead of indicating the letters quickly, as usual, it is done in a slow manner that impresses the mind with an idea of great reverence.

Mr. Home came to my house, only Miss Gallwey and Adare
being present. We sat round a small table in my study.
We talked upon indifferent subjects, which Mr. Home says is
preferable to silence, or to thinking or wishing too much on
the one subject. Soon slight raps were heard, followed by
slight vibrations of the table. We all agreed that the noise in
the street was very disagreeable, so we adjourned to the dining
room, which Mr. Home had never been in. I took in the table,
and, placing it near the fire place, we sat round it. Raps soon
came again, and slight vibrations. Some one remarked that
the table was rather creaky, when Mr. Home observed, " I have
taken a dislike to this table; let us sit at another. Here, this
dining table will do." " What," I said, " surely that huge
table will not move !" " Oh, I daresay it will," he replied.
The table was very large, above seven feet long and five feet
wide, and very heavy, requiring considerable force to move it at
all. Under it is a Turkey carpet ; there were also quantities
of Adare's things upon it. Mr. Home and I sat opposite each
other at the sides, and Adare and Miss Gallwey at the ends. Raps
were heard at different parts of the table, and near the fire
place, and on the round table we had brought in. Presently the
table vibrated very strongly—this was a most strange phenomenon, the vibration was so uniform and powerful. The table
then moved at *right angles* to Mr. Home. I may remark that there
was a green cloth on the table, and when pressure was used,
the hand would simply slip on the polished mahogany. The table
moved towards Adare about a foot; and it soon moved towards
Miss Gallwey, that is, in exactly the opposite direction. She
said, " May I stop it?" " I don't think you can," Home replied.
" Yes I can," she said, as she pressed her hands forcibly against
the edge ; then suddenly withdrawing them from the table,
it made one move, or rather spring forward, of nearly one foot
in length, thus shewing the great strength of the pressure which
must have been exerted by some mysterious power. We heard
sounds from the little table, and I saw it moving by itself. It
had advanced more than a foot towards Mr. Home ; and it came
still nearer afterwards. He sat rather back from the table, with
his hands laid lightly on it.

I expressed a hope that the power would become stronger.
These messages were given :—" *We would fain do more if
we could ; did love give strength, we should be strong indeed.*"
And then " *God bless you all !*" The indications for " God "
differed from the others, being three strong vibrations of the

table. After this we heard or felt nothing more. As to collusion or contrivances, none such could have taken place; the change of room, and our close observation, rendered this impossible. The idea of our hands being able to move such a table is simply absurd. The table, too, moved at right angles to where Home was sitting. The vibration was very singular; the candles shook, and other things trembled visibly. Once the candles very decidedly diminished in brightness for a short time.

No. 5 Séance—November 23rd—Recorded by my Father.

A *séance* was held at Norwood. Present: Mr. Home, Mrs. Hennings, Mr. Jencken and his mother, Mrs. Scott Russell, Adare, and myself. We sat at an ordinary card table in the middle of the room, with two candles on the chimney piece, and a bright fire. After about ten minutes, raps were heard: the table vibrated a little, and soon moved in the direction of Mr. Home, and towards the piano. We followed, and were soon close to the broad end of the piano. Raps were heard on and about the table, and on a small table a few feet distant. Our table gradually tilted up, at an angle of about 30 degrees or more. This was done more than once. The narrow end of the piano moved from the wall two or three times, and altogether about one foot, and pressed Mrs. Scott Russell between itself and the table. The floor vibrated strongly; this was very striking. The five raps were heard for the alphabet, and the following sentence was spelled out:—"*You are over anxious, and not sufficiently prayerful.*" Different movements of the table occurred, and then the following sentence was given:— " *On (? in) seeking for physical facts you lose sight of God.*" It was very remarkable that the indications for the word " God " were made, not by common raps, but by the table giving sudden movements, whilst it was either partially or wholly off the ground. At the end it was clearly so ; and it made the sign of the cross by moving forward and backward, and from side to side. Before this the little table moved of itself, and I went close to it, and I saw it move again slightly. It vibrated slightly when Mr. Home did not touch it, but more strongly when he did. We then got the accordion, and Mr. Home held it just under the table. After a little while it moved about and at last played, but apparently at first with effort, a sort of plaintive melody, very pretty, but nothing I had ever heard. I looked under the table more than once while Mr. Home's hand held it, and I saw it playing. At one time it was held up without his aid, for he put both his hands on the table, and I was then watching it. It stretched from Mr. Home towards Mrs. Russell, who took it, and it played, but faintly. Home took it back. Alphabet then called for, and the following message came :—"*It was A. who touched the keys.*" After this the accordion stretched nearly horizontally towards me, and I took it,—and held it a long time, but it did not play, though it was moved about strangely, and distinct raps were made on it. Before this Mr. Home said he distinctly saw a spirit between Mrs. Scott Russell and me, and before he spoke, she said she was touched in the side.—I was conscious of nothing. The cold currents were very sensible to-night. After this the manifestations became feeble, and while remarking this, the alphabet was called for, and the following given :—"*Daniel is not in a good state.*" We waited longer, but nothing occurred. Mr. Home on one occasion said, "There are curious influences to-night;" and he then said his feet were moved about in a strange way, and he was touched more than once. Just before the *séance* began, Mr. Home was called suddenly away to see a man on business, and this rather disturbed him. When the floor was vibrating strongly some one said it could be felt in the next house; and it was proposed that one of us should go in there, and note the time. Raps of approval were given twice; but, somehow, Mr. Home said nothing, and no one went. I forgot to mention that when the sheet of paper was on the table, Mr. Home touching one corner, the other end was lifted up more than an inch, just at the time when Adare felt the cold currents very strongly, as might happen if a bellows were blown near it. The paper was also rather curled up.

No. 6 Séance.

We had a *séance* the other night at Mr. Jencken's, at Norwood. Home went gradually into a trance; his eyes were quite shut; he got up, moved one or two chairs, walked up and down the room, then sat down again and began to speak. Mr. Jencken had been telling us how one of the servants, Mally, was ill, and had been seeing phosphorescent balls of light in her room at night. Home being in a trance, said, " It was Hans made the lights in Mally's rooms; if you all go presently into the next room, he will show them to you. Mally's mother will pass away within, (I forget the exact time mentioned), Mally must not be told this. After a pause, he turned to me and said, " Do not let Daniel leave your house on Saturday, as he wishes to do, because your friend is coming; we want to let you hear music in your room, and we wish Daniel to stay." He then said, " Adare's mother and Caroline are here." After a pause he said again to me, " Daniel will be able to see you from time to time when you are away." After sitting a little time in his chair, in an attitude of prayer, he got up and walked round the table to me, and stood behind me with his hand raised as in prayer, and then proceeded to make passes over me ; I felt nothing. He held his hand out, made a hollow of it as if to hold a fluid, and went throught the action of pouring out something upon my head ; he then walked behind me, and apparently prayed for some time, then placing his hands upon my shoulders, he drew me back towards him and pressed his head firmly against my back ; I felt a strong current of heat flow out of his hands into my shoulders, and out of his head into my back. It was very hot indeed. He then went back to his place and sat down, then raising his hands, as if praying, he spoke as follows :—(Mr. Jencken took notes as well as he could of what was said, but as Home spoke rapidly without any stop, it was impossible to put down more than the heads of his address.)

" Father of light, we, thy children, do approach thee in all humble reverence and confidence. We do beseech thee, Father of love, to grant us patience, charity, love, that we may love others who are less fortunate than ourselves. We pray that thou mayest remove the veil that shrouds the eternal life from our sight, and that knowledge not of earth be given us. Grant that we may be purified in heart and body : that we may lay aside our grosser earthly body and existence, and assume the robe of our eternal being. Grant that hope be given us, hope! that is the star that guides us ; guides us who know so little of the great world of spirits beyond the grave. (*after a pause*) We, children of God, linger near you, the spirits, guardian angels, hover around you, and guard and aid you in your hour of trial and suffering. To us the spirit-land of higher spheres is like a beautiful planet, luminous, shining forth as our goal—and spheres higher and higher still, brighten as we advance in the vista of everlasting progress. We cannot tell you all we know, for it is the desire of more and more knowledge that impels you onward and upward. As men see a star and desire to know about it, and know that others are beyond it, and invent instruments, and spend their lives in scientific research and in seeking after truth, so it is with you; it would not be good for you to know all, for there would be no object for improvement and research. We know all your sufferings and shortcomings, and what you have to contend with, for have we not too been mortals, have we not wearied on the roadside, and had our times of agony and doubt ; but God, at the evening of our day, brought us home, and called in the weary travellers. God called us into his fold and brought us home, that we may be nearer to thee, O God. Our Father in creating beautiful things on earth, created them for ever and ever, for all eternity, though they may fade to our sight; so beauty, poetry, sunlight, and all that is harmonious are garnered up for ever. Even sound having left the influence of this earth, goes on for ever down the everlasting corridors of space. Thus summer is again and again refined into autumn, toned and softened down, softening down the wintry sky of the future, so too, purer impulses, nobler aspirations, leave their impress for ever upon the waves of eternity—like a wave of sound, the impulse moves on for ever. All of you have to grope your way in the dark paths of life, but we hover near you, carry your minds upwards from earth, whisper to your heart that it may learn to aspire to God. Hope and love are component parts of the Godhead. Truth is God; waves may rise mountains high, but the great beacon truth shines forth over all the waves to guide us, lighting us on our way. From the eternal source goes forth the eternal light to which we aspire. From this great source emanates the small particle of light called our soul, dwelling in this body we live in—The great God who is light itself, for ever light us through all eternity."

Home now spoke in a language none of us ever heard, then said "Oh, how very wonderful, how extraordinary!" and turning to me, he said " A spirit has been approved to go with you, sent by a higher spirit, one who has charge of your past, your present and your future, your high guardian spirit. He knows the country and has been a chieftain in it. On earth he wore a large cross of iron round his neck, it is brilliant and shines; he was a good soul on earth, but was in a bad soil, tended by bad gardeners; too bad was the soil to develope his soul. He speaks two languages, he is not far from you. He lived near—Oh, I cannot get the name of the place; no matter, he has been where you are going, and is charged to take care of you. He will save your life on two occasions, you will know his name." Here Home spoke two strange words. I said to Mr. Jencken, " Have you written that down, for I have already forgotten it." Home smiled and said, " You cannot write it down, and you cannot remember it, but you will recognize it when the time comes." " Guardian spirits are given to those who go to foreign countries, to guide and aid them, whereby they benefit themselves; charity brings good to those that use it, more charity is gained by charity. Nothing prevents you going, he has breathed on you once, he will again, and once again, when you return, then never more; he will accompany you if nothing occurs to prevent your going; he is very strong." Home now got up, walked round to me, kneeled beside me as in prayer, and again drew me back by the shoulders, and pressed his head against my back, and I felt the same current flow from his forehead as before. Home stood up and said, " He is very strong and tall," and standing there beside me, Home grew, I should say, at least, six inches. Mr. Jencken, who is a taller man than Home, stood beside him, so there could be no mistake about it. Home's natural height is, I believe, 5 feet 10 inches. I should say he grew to 6 feet 4 inches or 6 feet 6 inches. I placed my hands on his feet, and felt that they were fairly level on the ground. He had slippers on, and he said, "Daniel will shew you how it is," and he unbuttoned his coat. He was elongated from his waist upwards, there was a space of, I suppose, 4 inches between his waistcoat and the waistband of his trowsers. He appeared to grow also in breadth and size all over, but there was no way of testing that. He diminished down to his natural size, and said, " Daniel will grow tall again;" he did so, and said, " Daniel's feet are on the ground," he walked about, and stamped his feet. He returned to his natural size, and sitting down, he said, " Daniel is coming back now, sit down, and do not tell Daniel at once what he has said." In a few seconds he awoke. After sitting a few minutes, he said, " What can it mean, I hear a voice saying ' Go into the next room, go into the next room?' " We all went into the drawing room; it was quite dark. Home sat at the piano, and played a few notes. Mrs. Hennings sat near him; Mrs. Jencken a little way off; Mr. Jencken and I stood near the piano. Soon we observed the light that we had been told we should see. A small luminous ball flitting about, sometimes very brilliant; the chords of the piano were swept, but the keys were not touched. The piano was lifted off the ground about 2 inches. I had my hand underneath, and it was again lifted about 2 inches, and then without any effort, I should say 8 inches higher. It was not tilted, but lifted bodily. We now heard loud raps, the alphabet was called, and " *Good night* " spelled out. Nothing more occurred.

No. 7 Séance.

We had a *séance* at No. 5, Buckingham Gate, the other night. Soon after sitting down the table began to shew evidence of some powerful influence about it. Mr. Jencken had unfortunately to go away by the ten o'clock train. After he left, we went into the dining room, and sat at the small round table. We had paper and a pencil on the table, and when the table was tilted the paper slipped off, which it does not generally do. I had been mentioning to Brinsley the fact that things on the table generally remain stationary, though it be raised to a great angle; and we were all remarking how curious it was that it would not do so now. The next phenomena that occurred were

entirely in connection with making the paper stay upon the
table. Home said in all his experience he had never seen the
same sort of thing. His hand and arm were taken possession
of, that is to say, they became perfectly rigid, and were moved
quite independently of his will; his fist was so firmly closed
that his fingers could not be opened; and the muscles of his
wrist and arm felt like iron. He got up, and altered the
position of one of the candles on the large table a few inches,
and removed all our hands from the table; he then commenced to mesmerise the paper, pointing at it with the first
and middle finger—the others being clenched—making rapid
passes over it, and making circles round it on the table with
great rapidity. The table was gradually tilted up till its edge
touched the floor. Being a table with one central support
it was nearly, but not quite, perpendicular—the paper remained
without slipping for some little time. We requested that it might
be moved. His hand was agitated above it, and the edges of
the paper were blown up, apparently by the current caused by
his hand. The paper slipped to the ground; he took it and
rubbed it round and round on the table, and then tried to leave
it on the centre of the table. It would not, however, remain
quite fixed, slipping a little. Getting rather tired of this, Home
asked if we might not put the table in its place and all sit round
it again. We were told "Yes;" and did so. The following
sentences were then spelled out: " *We did it to gratify you;*"
" *We have power to make the table heavy.*" We tried, asking
it to become heavy and light, and it did as we required. A
number of messages were then given, all having reference to
Miss D—— R——. None of us knew the people they purported
to come from, or anything about the circumstances they had
reference to. She had some difficulty in believing that an uncle
of hers was present as represented, and as a test of identity the
following was spelt by some one else: " *He always signed his
name —— ——,*" mentioning a peculiar way in which he signed.
All the rest of the *séance* consisted in messages and answers
to Miss D—— R——, amounting to a conversation, and having
some reference to matters that we did not understand. We
were wished Good night at the end. The table was sometimes
very violent in its movements.

No. 8 Séance.—November, 1867.

My dear Father,—I went down yesterday to Norwood, and
dined with Mr. Jencken. I was very much disappointed to find
that Home had settled to go up to London after dinner, to hear a

lecture by Miss Emma Hardinge. I should much have preferred spending the evening quietly there. We all tried to persuade him to stop, but in vain. However, after dinner he recited us some poetry, and to our great satisfaction he went on until he missed the train. We then talked for some time, and had some music. Mrs. Jencken played us some very pretty little musical airs. While Mrs. Jencken, Home, and Miss D—— R—— were at the piano there came raps upon it. Mr. Jencken and I were sitting some way off at the table. Shortly after, Home suggested that we should sit round the table. The room was lighted by a bright fire and two candles. Almost immediately after sitting down, we heard raps; and the usual currents of cold air were felt, also the vibration of the table and floor. We had very little of rapping or movement of the table during the *séance*. The table was, however, two or three times raised off the floor, and sustained in the air for a considerable time. We were talking about a gentleman (a friend of the others); abusing him a little for being conceited and unpleasant in different ways. Home said, "Oh, don't let us talk about our neighbours now." However, they went on talking about him, not in what one would usually call an ill-natured way; but still, cutting him up a little. The table was moving slightly all the time, and at last the alphabet was called for. The four following sentences were spelled out, with short intervals between them: "*There is one God, He is the Father of all.*" "*God is tolerant—he bears with our shortcomings.*" "*Love and charity—God gives the one and expects the other.*" "*We are all but mortals.*" After such a beautiful rebuke as that, I need not say that we did not talk any more about the shortcomings of our neighbours.

I should say that Mr. Jencken had, soon after the phenomena commenced, put out the candles. The fire-light was, however, in a small room, quite sufficient to show everything clearly. The name of God was, in every case, marked in a manner different to that in which the letters in the other words were indicated; sometimes by the table being raised and waved about. Once, when the table was in the air during the whole sentence, by slow strong vibrations, instead of raps. Home now said he was touched for the accordion, and took it, holding it in the usual way. Almost immediately, without any apparent effort, it began to play powerful, clear, and beautifully harmonious chords.

It played for some considerable time when the alphabet was called for and this was spelled:—"*You are quite correct, it was Augusta.*" I said, I did not see exactly to what the sentence applied. The alphabet was called again, and the words "*The other night*" spelled, making the sentence complete, and referring to what you and I had been speaking of in the train about the message on Saturday night, "*It was A—— touched the keys.*" After this the accordion was again played for some little time most beautifully, the notes being drawn out so fine, that it was only by bending the head and listening attentively, that the harmony could be heard dying away and then swelling again. The accordion was drawn out from under the table, Home still holding it lifted over his head, and brought round to Miss D——R——; it was lifted up and presented towards her, the same was done to me, and it was rested on my left shoulder, and while there, close to my ear, it breathed out the softest sounds. There was a noise as of some one breathing behind me, which the others also heard, but, I think, that must have been caused by the instrument. The accordion was in like manner presented to Mr. and Mrs. Jencken, and then went under the table again. A very remarkable thing now occurred, the accordion was seized by some influence that evidently could not play it, and which disturbed that previously acting. It abruptly left off playing, then began again quite differently, playing three or four notes with a powerful loud touch, and then it broke down altogether. Home, before the change said, "Ah, there is some strange influence at work now." After the discordant notes, the accordion was raised above the table, Home still holding it, he said his arm felt quite paralyzed, and that he was obliged to follow it; it drew him from his chair, and went near to D—— and remained there some time oscillating backwards and forwards, and waving itself about, the accordion then led him back to his chair, after which it went under the table and recommenced playing as before the interruption. Soon the alphabet was called, and the following spelt:—"*We do all we can to shew you that we do not forget*"—and then the accordion finished the sentence by playing "Auld lang Syne," first quietly, then with full loud chords. Home said, suddenly, "Oh, this is a very powerful spirit." He stood up, or rather he was raised up, and his hand was violently agitated in the air; he then sat down, and his hand was extended towards the flowers on the small table, the fingers pointing towards them. His hand remained there a few seconds, and was then brought round, and with a motion like sprinkling, cast the perfume of the flowers towards each of us in turn; the perfume was so strong that there could be no mistake about it. This was done twice. His hand was then raised a little above my head, the fingers pointing towards me, and went through motions something like mesmeric passes, or as I thought as though blessing me. His hand was then placed upon mine, and stroked my fingers gently, first one then the other; it then was carried to his own face, and passed across it two or three times. His hand was now swung violently to and fro, then remained quiet, and presently it was extended to the flowers again. I could distinctly see it with the fingers pointing towards the flowers, about six inches above them; I am sure it never touched them. His hand became quite luminous, and was brought slowly round and across the table, until it remained with the fingers still extended, over my hand. I raised my hand towards it, and a leaf of sweet-scented geranium fell apparently from under his hand into mine, the leaf was not held in his fingers, neither could I see it until it fell. (Home said, when his hand was extended over the flowers, that it felt to him, as though it was resting on a solid or semi-solid substance.) At the same moment, the alphabet was called for and this spelled, " *Take it with you, my boy.*" This sentence followed immediately, " *We have done what we promised, look under the handkerchief.*" Mrs. Jencken had, on the evening they had had such beautiful manifestations, a short time ago, asked that a flower might also be given to her. They had announced that it would be done, and now under her handkerchief there was a piece of geranium; her handkerchief had been on the table all the time, and no one had touched it.

This sentence was now spelled, " *Next for dear D——.*" Home's hand was extended again to the flowers; it certainly was not nearer them than 6 inches; it became luminous, and a flower was given to D—— in the same way it had been given to me. The alphabet was again called, and this spelled, " *This is for you,*" and at the same moment, a flower dropped at Mr. Jencken's hand; none of us heard it broken off, or saw it, but it fell on the table just in front of his hand. " *Our joy*" was now spelled, and the accordion played, and then " *Our thanks to God*" and it played again. The alphabet was called, and " *Weep not*" spelled. Dear old Mrs. Jencken was quietly crying, not as she said for sorrow, when the words " Weep not" were spelled, her handkerchief was gently taken from her under the table, and afterwards replaced upon it. After this, " Good night" was spelled, and nothing more occurred.

No. 9 *Séance—July* 26*th,* 1868.

Present: Mrs. Jencken, Mrs. Hennings, Mr. Jencken, Home, and myself. Physical manifestations very slight, Home passing almost immediately into a trance, in which he delivered the following address, purporting to come from the spirit of Dr. Jencken; to prove identity several tests were given.

B

Dr. Jencken, during the last few years of his life, had been quite blind, and was in the habit, when dictating, of going through the form of writing with great rapidity on his knee with his finger; he also had a peculiar habit of clasping his hands together, and speaking with his head bent very low down. Home imitated him in both respects to the very life, and also mentioned some circumstances that had occurred many years before at Mayence.

The first words Home spoke were in a very low voice, telling us to go on talking. He then got up, threw away a silk cushion he had been sitting on, and said, "Remember, Dan must not sit on a silk cushion while this very hot weather lasts." He remained silent for a few minutes, and then commenced speaking with a clear voice, and in a very impressive manner. Part of the discourse was in verse, but owing to the partially darkened state of the room and the rapidity of his utterance, it was quite impossible to write it down. The following notes taken by Mr. Jencken are for these reasons very imperfect.

"There are laws which govern the approach of spiritual beings to earth, and their organic life, and there are epochs of darkness when the spiritual spheres are far removed from the earth; when the approach of spirits is all but impossible. These epochs have been called by those on earth the *dark ages;* they mark the absence of spiritual intercourse. There are also times of near approach, not unlike your winter and summer seasons. This alternate action is a great law; great principles rule all things. There was such an epoch of easy approach at the time of the Ancient Egyptians. They knew this and understood the laws better than you do. Before that time spirits had not taken sufficient pains to encourage the invention of means for the perpetuating of knowledge. There was no printing, nor mechanical contrivance, in those days. Since then, during the period that their approach to earth was more difficult, they have turned their attention more to those matters, so that now knowledge can never be so lost again. You are now entering upon a period of very near approach. It is coming like the tide in a river—irresistible, overriding the current, overcoming all; it is coming grandly and Godly. What has already been seen is but the smallest wavelet of the tide that is coming upon the earth. Some of you here present will see it; others among you will have joined us, and will be helping on the great work we have in hand. The echoes of it are coming; they sound like the notes of the organ rolling up the aisles of those grand old cathedrals that men have built—notes signifying the heart-felt prayer of an earnest soul ascending to the throne of God; never lost but echoing on for ever. Spiritual truth must come ; truth is a lighthouse, a beacon, a speck, a point, leading onward to realms of love. We have no power, we can do so little, that we often wonder that we are able to do anything for you. Language is too imperfect, we cannot convey to you our meaning; you cannot understand us; our state is so different from your material state, that is it with great difficulty that we can work upon it to make our presence known; not that it is painful to us—no, no, it is a labour of love. But still it is an actual labour to us. The earth is still so imperfect—so undeveloped—that we have much difficulty in dealing with material objects. Why, even such a little thing as the silk cushion that Dan was sitting on, prevented us from making physical manifestations to-night ; yet we did succeed in giving you each a token of our presence, though it was very slight. Henry, the floor vibrated under your chair. Adare, your chair was touched. Amelia and Mary, you both felt the current of cold air pass over your hands." You all felt something.

" The earth is as yet very immature, but progressing. A period of very near approach is at hand; after that there will be one, probably two epochs of darkness. We are entirely de-pendent upon atmospherical conditions. Now, to-night, the atmosphere is so surcharged with electricity, that it appears to us quite thick, like sand. It is so unlike our own, that it is almost impossible for us to get near you. We feel like men wading through a quicksand—slipping back as fast as we advance. At other times, when your earthly atmosphere is in a natural state, it is more like our own, and we have no difficulty in being near you. You wonder if we wish you to be better than you are. You are all good. The germs of good are in all. We can see further than you can; and know all your trials, all your doubts and difficulties. Were we not once mortals as you are? We see the troubles and the thorns that beset your path. Stretch forth your hands—thrust them through the brambles—draw them not back or the blood will flow—stretch them out and let them remain, there shall they find rest. We know not of time ; to us yesterday, to-day, to-morrow are all one. Had we hours, days, years, even ages, like you, we should say time passes slowly, or time passes fast. We never tire ; we are eternity. Happiness is not idleness. Labour is joy, the labour of love. Even on earth it is not the spirit that wearies of a labour of love ; it is the poor weak body that tires, that faints, that falls to sleep. We have work to do, to elevate ourselves, and to draw you onward and upward. We constantly watch over you, and sympathize with all your cares. We never weary ; we do not judge you ; we were as you are.

God alone is the Judge. You ask why we always speak of love; it is love that brings us to you. God is Love. Spirit messages are always breathing love for God. God is Love.

Henry, your father is pleased that you are engaged upon his works, he too has his work to do. He was aided in writing, and knows now that higher spirits aided him. Do you remember at Mayence, how he was affected? (Here Home imitated his peculiar mode of writing upon his knee, and manner of speaking). An inferior spirit had got influence over him. I see him now, he had great self-esteem, and was very opinionated, and only wanted his own ideas to become prominent; this is very dangerous, and must be guarded against. Truth, truth—worship truth: particle by particle build up the temple of truth; be consistent, for God is Truth. Here we have no narrowing creed, no four church walls, with a cushioned pew for the rich, and a plain board for the poor man, to limit the worship of truth. The great four walls of eternity; the blue ether, set with sparkling stars, gems made by the hand of God, ever lustrous diamonds of the heavenly orb, peep-holes of heaven; it is there we worship, and through them we peer in our search for truth.

One great objection made to Spiritualism, is, that we do not disclose all the truth—if true, why not tell all? Are you capable of perceiving the truth? The man has not yet been formed upon the earth fitted to know the whole truth. Immortality is before you! Immortality gleams upon earth—gleams like a lighthouse, like a beacon to you. The future is not even understood by all of us,* but we draw nearer and nearer to God, for here there is no one to hold you back, to say you are mad; peals of angel voices call you onward and upward; cheer you in your struggles, and aid you.

There are great laws of development that draw the organic and the inorganic together; you on earth witness the onward course of all things in the organic world, rising to higher conditions, as, for instance, the development of the child into

---

* The meaning is obscure. The words, "The future is not even understood by all of us; but we draw nearer and nearer to God, for here there is no one to hold you back," evidently refer to spirits, and the sentence should stand: "For here there is no one to hold us back—to say that WE are mad." Substituting the words "us" and "we" for "you," which is evidently improperly used. It is an open question whether the remaining lines belong to the same sentence or not; the context would rather lead me to suppose not. If the lines constitute one sentence with the same train of thought running all through it, then the word "you" should be altered to "us" in the last two lines also, which should read thus: "Peals of angel voices call us onward and upward; cheer us in our struggles and aid us." But it appears to me more probable that the reference to the state of the spirits concludes with line 8, and that the two remaining lines are an aspiration or prayer that "peals of angel voices may call you" (that is, mortals) "onward and upward; cheer you in your struggles and aid you."

manhood. Onward is the progress; onward and upward. Search, —search for truth,—be true, be brave, be prayerful; ye are all children of God created by Him. The time is rapidly coming for a great change in spiritual life; we are nearing the cycle, so near that some of you here present will witness the change, others will have gone to their home, to their rest, to the blessed. Are you weary of life? weary of the earth? The soul tires not, it is only the body. (In answer to question by H. J.) You are right, Henry; your father is clearer in his views now, more to the point, sees things clearer than he did when on earth. Oh, how much he wished to know Daniel; had he but known him! You remember how anxious he was about him."

No. 10 Séance.

Last Monday I was at a *séance* at Mr. Hall's. There were nine present: Mr. and Mrs. Hall, Home, the Misses Bertolacci (mediums), a cousin of mine, two gentlemen whose first *séance* it was, and myself. Almost immediately we felt the sort of phenomena that usually take place first, such as cold currents of air passing over the hands, table vibrating, &c. These ceased, and for some time nothing occurred. Some one suggested that the young ladies should try if anything would be written. They did so with the planchette, both placing one hand upon it at the same time. These words were written, " *By patience, and in the name of Christ.*" We were also told by the same means to sit down again in the same positions we had occupied before. After a time very strong manifestations took place, the table vibrating, tilting, and being raised about a foot off the ground; raps were heard on the table, on the floor, on our chairs, &c.,— nearly every one was touched. I felt a hand between my leg and Home's: I was sitting next to him. There was evidently some very strong influence about Home. After a time a message was given by raps: " *I now know that my Redeemer liveth: have patience and bear all. Daniel, I owe you many thanks.— John Elliotson.*" After this, in answer to some question (I forget what), the table was tilted three times in the four opposite directions, and was then lifted three times in the air. Home's chair was once drawn away a little from the table, and raised off the floor, but certainly not more than one inch. His chair was also turned completely round, so that his back was towards us, his feet during the whole time the chair was moving being off the ground. An arm chair moved of itself a distance of about a yard up against the back of my chair. Home's hand and arm became cataleptic, and were moved about quite independent of his will. His hand was sometimes thumped and beaten violently against the table, but without causing him any pain. His hand was moved to the back of my neck, and pushed me forward in my chair. He then began to thump me violently on the back, and to rub me across the back, commencing at the right side. His hand also stroked and patted my head, and was also moved to my cousin sitting at the opposite side of the table, and stroked and patted her hands and head.

The following message was written by Home's hand, his fingers being so strongly clenched, it was with difficulty that the pencil was inserted between them. " *We know all your discussion about A——— W———; we are the best judges, it was a bad influence. F——— and F———.*" The paper was then pushed across to my cousin to read, neither of us could understand what F——— and F——— meant, although we ought to have guessed, as the same words had been used about the same subject, in a message given us a few days previously. Seeing that we could not make it out the words "*forget and forgive*" were written. Other messages were written through Home and one . of the ladies present. Mr. Holt, a gentleman whose first *séance* it was, became much affected; soon after sitting down, his hands were taken possession of and violently agitated, sometimes on, and sometimes under the table; occasionally his arms were drawn back behind his chair, his hands being all the time violently agitated; a pencil and paper were given him, but though his hand moved over the paper with the greatest rapidity, nothing but scribbling was the result. So strong was the influence over him, that he went and sat alone upon the sofa at some distance from us, to try and diminish it; when he left, the power about the table became sensibly lessened; he continued to be slightly agitated the whole evening. We were all anxious to know who was endeavouring to make him write; two Christian names with the word "*uncle*" between them were written through Home. Home at one time said he felt convinced that a spirit was near him who had passed from this life by being drowned. Some little time after, Mr. Hall was telling us how one of his brothers had been mysteriously drowned at sea, he being a very good swimmer; Home's hand was taken possession of and wrote the word "*Shark*" upon a piece of paper, and then pushed it to Mr. Hall. Home and one of the ladies present went into a trance at the same moment; for some time they sat in their places, occupying themselves with putting their fingers upon the sheets of paper on the table, and then waving their hands about, the paper adhering to their fingers; Home then got up and walked about the room; he took a large sheet of paper off the table, doubled it up and placed it on the piano in the next room; the young lady also got up, and sat down upon the sofa, at the other side of the room.

Home sat down in his chair, and began to talk to Mrs. Hall in a whisper. I could not hear the exact words he used, but they were to the effect that during their occupation of that house, there had been a bad influence present during *séances* twice only. He mentioned who one of the spirits was, and said that the same influence had that evening turned Home round in his chair, and had brought the arm chair up against mine. He also told her that in the house to which they were going, nothing but what was good and holy would come near them. Home was elongated to the extent of, I should say, 6 inches, four times; he walked about, stamped, and shuffled his feet, to shew that he was standing fairly upon them. He went round to Mr. Holt, one of the gentlemen present, and made him place his hand upon his waist that he might feel how he become elongated and contracted. Mr. Holt said that he held his hand flat against Home's side; that the lower edge of his hand was resting on his hip bone; that he felt Home's lower rib pass under his hand, until it was some inches above it; the whole flesh and muscle apparently moving and stretching. On the contraction taking place, he felt the lower rib come down until it pressed against the upper edge of his hand and moved into its proper position. Home said that the young lady had also been elongated, and would be again. She was then standing near the table in a trance, and began swaying herself from side to side; she was palpably elongated to the extent of, perhaps, three inches. About this time a loud knock came at the outside door. Home said, " He must come in—it is the Master of Lindsay." Home then opened the room door, went out into the entry, and took the gentleman by the hand; he led him into the room; made him shake hands with Mr. and Mrs. Hall, with the young lady who was in the trance, and with me, we being all perfect strangers to him. Home then said to him, " You must go out of the room until Daniel awakes, for if he was to awake and find you here, he would be frightened." Shortly after this they both awoke, and the party broke up.

I arrived at home about half an hour before Home. Soon after we had gone to bed we both heard the hall door loudly slammed. I said, " Oh, Dan, you have left the door open, and some one has come in !" He declared he had locked it, and put the chain up; however, we both got up and went down to see what was the matter. I found the hall door locked and the chain up, and the study and dining room doors both wide open. I went into the study and heard raps, I then went out to where

Home was standing in the entry, and we heard raps on the floor. He said, " Oh, I am sure it is dear old Dr. Elliotson," " *Yes*," was rapped. I then said, " In that case I suppose no burglars came in and we may go to bed again?" " *Yes*," was rapped. We went up stairs, Dr. Elliotson following us rapping on the banisters and stairs. After we had got into bed again we heard heavy footsteps walking about the room, and raps in various places. Home carried on a conversation with Dr. Elliotson for a little time, asking questions and receiving answers to them by raps.

He (Dr. Elliotson) told us that he had not suffered pain in passing away, and that he had found the other world very much what he had expected it to be; that he had not intended to frighten us by making a sound as of slamming the door, and that he would be more careful not to make so much noise in future; but that as yet he had only imperfect control over physical manifestations; that he had followed Home to the house, and was glad to be near him, &c. Home and I talked about him for some little time, he joining in our conversation, assenting or dissenting by means of raps.

Two days after this as we were getting up, about 10 o'clock, a bright sun shining into the room. loud raps came upon the floor, &c., and a long message of a private character was given to Home.

No. 11 *Séance—July*, 1868.

Having missed the last train to London I was very glad to accept Mr. Jones's kind offer to remain all night at his house. Home and I carried a sofa upstairs to his (Home's) room for me to sleep on. I did not leave the room after bringing in the sofa. My clothes I placed upon a small round table near the foot of the bed. On a chair by the sofa I placed a pocket handkerchief, two eye glasses, and a snuff box.

During the *seance* in the evening it was said that I should hear music without any instrument that night. Home turned off the gas previous to going to bed. A certain amount of light entered the room from the street, so that it was not perfectly dark. I could easily distinguish Home when he sat up in bed; and could have seen anybody moving about the room.

We had not been in bed more than three minutes when both Home and myself simultaneously heard the music; it sounded like a harmonium; sometimes, as if played loudly at a great distance; at other times, as if very gently, close by. The music continued for some minutes, when Home got up to ask Mr. Jones if any one was playing the accordion. Mr. Jones returned with him, and we all three then heard the music. The usual phenomena of raps and vibrations of the floor, sofa, &c., occurred very frequently and with great power; the raps sounded all over the room; on the floor, walls, even on Home's bed; on, under, and in my sofa. My sofa occasionally vibrated very strongly; the bed clothes on Home's bed and on the sofa were frequently pulled and moved about. We both several times heard sounds such as would be caused by some one in a muslin dress moving about the room, although we could see nothing.

After a short time I heard the chair close to my sofa moving, and a finger touched one of my hands that was hanging over the side of the sofa, the next moment I felt the snuff box on the chair touch me, and found that the chair was moving, I said, that I thought some one had touched me, but that probably I had been mistaken, and that it was only the box; the spirits said by the alphabet that I had been touched. The chair then moved to the foot of the bed, and we heard the various articles upon it being stirred about. I was sitting upon the sofa, with one hand resting on the edge, suddenly I felt something brush across my hand; this was repeated, and I became aware of something swinging in the air. I then heard some object brushing backwards and forwards against the back of the sofa, inside; on putting my hand to the spot, my eye glass was placed in it. I took the glass, and in drawing it away, I felt by the resistance offered, that the cord was attached to something; while feeling the resistance a hand and arm holding the end of the cord became visible. This I saw distinctly for a second or two, it then disappeared.

I now heard a sound near the foot of the bed as if my double glasses were being opened and shut, and I distinctly saw a figure, apparently draped, standing over the foot of the bed; it held, something, I believe the double glasses, and I could see the hand and arm waving backwards and forwards; I could hear the eye-glass swinging in the air, but could not see it; the figure stooped down towards Mr. Jones, and disappeared. A message was then given: " *The figure is not the same as the one that touched you.*"

About half a minute after, I distinctly heard something moving along the side of the sofa, and immediately my double eye-glass was placed upon the back of my hand; I felt the hand that held it push it on, and then stroke and pat my fingers; I took three fingers of the hand in mine, and held them for some seconds; as I increased the pressure upon them, they appeared to withdraw themselves from me; I was again touched, and my hand stroked and patted, the fingers were like a delicately formed human hand, the skin feeling perfectly natural to the touch.

A message was now given: " *We place it there to shew you that we do not wish you to contract a habit, pernicious, and that can be of no possible use to you.*" While wondering what this could mean, my snuff box came right across the room through the air, falling against my leg, where it remained. Home saw it pass through the air in front of him. I asked who had thrown it; and was told " *Grandfather Goold.*" Mr. Jones asked if the snuff had been taken out, " *No,*" was immediately rapped in various parts of the room.

Mr. Jones wished that something might be done for him, and he was slightly touched. He asked also that the chair might be moved round to him. The chair began again to move, but there was not room for it to pass between the foot of the bed and the round table. The table was raised off the floor and moved out of the way, the top becoming slightly luminous. While moving, it suddenly fell to the floor and rolled over. My clothes tumbled off, the money in the pockets rolling about the room. I said, " I wonder how it happened; it is so unusual for them to let anything fall." They answered, " *It happened by mistake.*" I observed, " How kind it is of them to answer questions like this." They answered, " *Would you not do the same for us.*" Mr. Jones said that he supposed the spirits in the room were friends of mine. They answered "*Yes.*" I asked how many of my own family were present. They answered " *Six.*" I asked if they had not come to welcome me home from abroad. They answered " *Yes,*" by rapping three times all over the room.

A message was now given: " *We wish to give you the* ——." ' Here it broke off; and though Home repeated the alphabet three or four times, nothing more would come. While we were wondering at this unfinished sentence my pocket handkerchief dropped through the air into my lap. I took it up and found there was something hard in it. It turned out to be my latch key that I had left in my trowsers pocket, knotted into one corner of the handkerchief. The remainder of the unfinished message was then spelled out: " *Key to the mystery,*" making altogether, " *We wish to give you the key to the mystery.*" Mr. Jones had been telling me that the spirits were anxious to prove to me that there was an actual intelligence at work, and that the phenomena were not the result of mere animal magnetism.

After this, " *Good night*" was spelled out. The last sound I heard was that of the jingling of the money while being picked up about the room I put my eye-glass, handkerchief, and snuff box on the floor. Mr. Jones left the room, and I very soon went to sleep. In the morning I found the things on the floor in the same position that I had left them in, the key being still knotted to the handkerchief. The chair was near the foot of the bed, a blanket that I had thrown off my sofa entangled round it. The table was lying on the ground—my clothes on the floor. All my silver I found in the pocket I had left it in; the gold, consisting of four pieces, I found on Home's counterpane.

These phenomena could not have been caused by any mechanical contrivances. In order to produce the violent vibrations and the raps on the sofa, it would have been necessary to attach some complicated machinery to it; that was impossible, as I-assisted to carry it up from the drawing room, never left the room after we had brought it up, and was lying down upon it within three or four minutes after we had placed it in the room. It would have been also necessary to attach machinery to the chair and table. Articles were taken from the chair, and conveyed to me without any human agency, for I must have seen anyone moving in the room, and the chair was too far removed from Mr. Jones and Home to have been reached by them by any means.

No. 12 Séance—5, Buckingham Gate, August 3rd, 1868.

One day last week Home complained of not feeling at all well, and of being in very low spirits. I did not feel well myself, and lay down on the sofa, where I presently went to sleep. When I awoke, Home told me that there had been raps on the tables, &c., but that instead of cheering him they made him feel more uncomfortable. They had given him answers to several questions. He asked why it was that he felt so low and ill. The answer was, " *There is nothing Spiritualistic in it; it is rather a tinge from the thoughts of Adare.*" This puzzled me very much, as I was quite unaware of anything having taken place that could give rise to unpleasant thoughts. I sat down at the writing table and heard raps on various parts of it. They again said that they showed their presence to "cheer Dan." Home had said that he felt a desire to smoke a cigarette, a thing I have never known him do before. He smoked one, owing to which, I think, a fit of coughing was brought on. Home coughed up a quantity of blood and seemed relieved by it; he then lay down on the sofa. The raps continued for a short time, and I asked if Home's indisposition was anything serious. They answered, " *No.*" I asked if he would be all right soon. They answered, " *Yes.*" This occurred about 3 p.m. in broad daylight.

No. 13 *Séance—5, Buckingham Gate.*

Two or three days subsequently, Home and I having gone to bed after a *séance* here, at which we felt a few movements of the table, we had manifestations in the bed room, consisting of our beds vibrating strongly and of raps on the furniture, doors, and all about the room. Home's bed was slightly moved out from the wall. We both heard something on the dressing table being moved about, and at the same moment we both saw in exactly the same spot, a perfectly white column, it can scarcely be called a figure, as the shape was indistinct. It moved from the dressing table towards Home's bed. Home said he saw a white object about the size of a child floating near the ceiling above his head. I saw it also, but it appeared to me to be in mid air, half way between the bed and the ceiling: it was floating about in a horizontal position; it was like a small white cloud without any well-defined shape. I saw it descend close to Home, who then lost sight of it, but I perceived it come within about two feet of his head. It then slowly floated to the foot of his bed and disappeared. I afterwards saw the same appearance near the door. Home saw it intercept the light coming in from the window against the opposite wall; I did not. We had three messages given us: First, " *We love God best by loving you and seeking to influence you for good.*" Second, " *Seeing that you have been troubled to know what we meant by its being rather a tinge from the thoughts of Adare, we wish to tell you it was owing to something in a letter received from his father.*" The manifestions continued for some time when the third message was given: " *Now sleep.*" After this we heard and saw nothing more. There was sufficient light in the room to distinguish candles, books, &c., on the table.

No. 14 *Séance—August 6th,* 1868.

Present: Mrs. Jencken, Mrs. Hennings, Mr. Jencken, Home, and myself. Very few physical manifestations, Home's hands were taken possession of, and were strongly agitated,* he

---

* I have frequently seen people's hands taken possession of and agitated during *séances* in a somewhat similar way. The same thing has occurred to myself. In my case, my hands were moved about sometimes violently, sometimes gently, without any act of volition on my part; and yet in a manner not entirely beyond my control. In Mr. Home's case the muscles became perfectly hard and rigid; and I fancy he can neither direct nor prevent the movements.

took the accordion and played with considerable feeling, his hands moving and touching the keys independent of his will, during this he went into a trance, got up, walked to the piano and played a piece of music with considerable execution; he then sat down and spoke as follows : (Dr. Elliotson speaking through him the greater part of the time).*

"Henry, do you know that your father met Dr. Elliotson to-day, and for the first time, and much pleased him; they are charmed with each other, he (Dr. Elliotson) is very enthusiastic. Those that are longer away from earth lose their intense interest in it, they have other calls upon them. He, like your father, sought for development and truth, though often wrongly guided; he did not look up to the great sunlight, but doubted and erred. These two, have, as I said, met to-day, just now, according to your mode of computing time. Dr. Elliotson is so delighted to meet your father. 'Why have we not met before?' he says, 'we ought.' 'That was your fault, Dr. Elliotson; not mine.' Then he turns back, shakes your father by the hand and tells him he is so glad to know him. In the state that we live in there are no restrictions; men are drawn together by mutual sympathies. Here is no deception, no saying 'I am glad to see you, my dear fellow,' when the heart does not mean it. Thoughts are seen and read, and those suited to each other are naturally drawn together.

"Dr. Elliotson is full of plans how to operate better, he wants to invent some sort of mechanism to act with the brain, some more powerful battery, he wants to convince the whole world; he is very enthusiastic. There are some Physicists with large brains who strain and wear themselves out with over work. The brain becomes weary, loses its elasticity, disease sets in, preponderosis. This was the case with Elliotson, but it was particularly painful for him, as every morning on awaking he knew what he was, and was aware of the state into which he had fallen, but afterwards his brain failed him and could not act. He is now so delighted,—delighted in studying nature; he is particularly engaged in studying how illness is generated by mere presence without actual contact; he has a theory also of winds carrying diseases, and has found that the south wind carries disease further than any other; he finds that the winds have curative powers, and that the geographical position of winds is important, the currents having different effects at different altitudes.

"We can see all physical changes, and from out of them, the

---

* The following account of what occurred during Home's trance is compiled from the notes taken by Mr. Jencken.

moral changes resulting from them, for instance, the heat and abnormal condition of the atmosphere will in a short time produce a fermentation in the human mind and changes will follow. It affects the human race and must find a vent, in the same way as a heated condition of body will result and find relief in boils and eruptions."

Home here threw himself back in his chair, rubbed his hands together as if very much pleased, and said, " Now, if you wish to ask any questions I am ready to answer them."

Question (Henry Jencken).—How do you make us see spirit forms ?

Answer.—At times we make passes over the individual to cause him to see us, sometimes we make the actual resemblance of our former clothing, and of what we were, so that we appear exactly as we were known to you on earth; sometimes we project an image that you see, sometimes we cause it to be produced upon your brain, sometimes you see us as we are, with a cloudlike aura of light around us.

Question (H. J.)—Do you use actual garments ?

Answer.—Purity is our clothing.   We have no need of garments; but are enveloped in a sort of aura, or cloud of light. Other spirits, more impure and gross, dwelling nearer earth, have need of garments.

Question (H. J.)—How do we appear to you ?

Answer.—Mostly in pure light.

Question.—Can you see our light?

Answer.—We can see all lights; sunlight, and every colour that it is composed of.   We see the most beautiful combinations of light.   Everything has its light.   We see the progress either of growth or decay that is taking place in everything. The table that you are sitting at was once growing.   We could see every particle expanding and increasing; now it is decaying; and though it is so gradual that to you it is not apparent, yet we can see the change taking place in every particle of it.

Question.—In moving among us, do we present an obstacle to you ? Do you avoid us?

Answer.—We do, and must avoid you.   For your ether bodies and the atmosphere that surrounds you is, in many cases, as solid and impenetrable to us as granite is to you.   We can see both the light of your spiritual bodies and of your material bodies.

Question.—Are not the sun's rays composed of something more than light ?

Answer.—Of light only, and an elastic wave of electricity that precedes the light.

Question.—I suppose it is not possible for you to visit the sun?

Answer.—Most certainly we can. Why should we not?

Question.—Does it take time for you to travel?

Answer.—Yes.

Question.—I suppose you move in the same ratio as light?

Answer.—We can travel faster than light.

Question.—What is the appearance of your form or body?

Answer.—Exactly like your material body, only slightly smaller in every respect.

Question.—How do you produce material forms?

Answer.—You produce them with and through us.

Question.—But have you no field for action?

Answer.—You cannot understand us; the material is to us as it were spiritual. Suppose I want a fruit, I cannot create it by thinking of it; I must go and fetch it from where it is: so if I want an idea I must travel into higher spheres, and seek and find it as an actual created thing. Many things are more real than you suppose; thoughts, are they not almost realities? Try and think of a house you knew long ago; you will invariably enter it by the door; you go in by the door in your imagination; were you to enter by the windows or the walls, you would not understand or recognize it. That will tell you that there is something of material reality in the idea of a house in your mind.

Question.—Are then your flowers and fruits as actual and real to you as those growing upon earth are to us?

Answer.—They are as real to us as an apple or pomegranate is to you.

Question.—Have you animals in your spheres?

Answer.—There are animals that give pleasure such as horses and dogs; nearer earth are baser animals, and those that cause pain; some saints and holy men, being in an ecstatic state have at times caught glimpses of what is going on near them, animals and men, strange and curious forms all mixed up together. The only way I can at all describe it to you is to look at a drop of muddy water under the microscope, and observe the strange forms; you will see the tail of one protruding from another, and so on, hence the old ideas of satyrs and creatures half man, half beast, hence the notion of devils with horns and tails, and of a material hell. Other men have seen higher and brighter spheres. All this is but the imperfect imagining of those who see visions: as in Dante's Frozen Hell, he saw the frozen zone and spiritual forms moving about, and mixed them up all together. Bodily suffering produces mental suffering; and mental suffering afflicts the body; need you be told this?

Instance, a case where fright may produce paralysis; or where pain, insensibility.

In answer to some question.—The spirit is always sane; the body makes insane. We can see the spirit like—what shall I say —well—like, to use a very homely simile, a jack-in-the-box; we see the empty, useless casket, and the spirit hovering above it, the spirit bounds forth as soon as liberated by death—by sleep.

In answer to some question.—Some spirits are removed to other planets, in the course of formation, not necessarily as a punishment, but that by trial they may develope and return again at some future time purified. Spirits very often go voluntarily to other planets, until they can fit themselves to be of use to those on earth, or to dwell with other spirits in higher spheres; tell this to Dan when he awakes, as he has often wondered why some of his friends have not returned to visit him?

In answer to a question.—Actual substances are thrown off from the earth and get entirely beyond its attraction; and actual substances are brought from the sun to the earth by means of the rays of light, substances that can be weighed—aye, and that will be weighed some day.

In answer to a question as to punishments.—Why and how are you punished? You punish yourselves if you have broken a law of nature; for no natural law can be broken without amends being made for its violation. Cut a vein and the blood flows, because you have violated a natural law.

Question.—Do you like making manifestations?

Answer.—It pleases us to come to you, and to make manifestations. We get so charged by remaining any time in the earth's atmosphere, that it is a positive relief to make sounds. There is a spirit now come into the room; he is what we call naturally charged. (Quantities of raps heard on the table.) Now he cannot help doing that, and it is a positive pleasure to him. (Speaking to me) Elliotson did not want to frighten you the other evening at your house; he does not know yet how to manage manifestations, hence the noise he made the other night. He wanted to see Daniel and you too, but he did not intend to frighten either of you.*

Question (H. J.)—As to a law of predestination?

Answer.—Yes, there is a law of predestination which is quite true, only you could not understand it.

Question.—Infinite possibility gives freedom of action?

Answer.—Yes, infinite possibility, harmonizing with pre-

---

* This sentence has reference to certain things that occurred at No. 5, Buckingham Gate—mentioned in pp. 23, 24.

destination is the law. Oh, I wish so much some spirits from other planets could come to you, but that is very rarely allowed. When Malle (Mrs. Jencken's servant) passed away, a spirit from another planet passed by the open window, that was all, and yet the room was filled with perfume for days; if you had thought of it, and had gone out into the garden, you would have found the perfume stronger there than in the room.

"Henry, your father was inspired when he wrote his works, remember this (grasping H. Jencken's hand). Act! Do something! it is so very glorious to assist in the search for truth. There are so many stubborn men to be convinced. It is your duty to say that which you know to be true, to utter it. (taking my hand) Oh, my lord, do something! Act! Aid the many beings yet in darkness. There is the truth, it is only hid, it is there nevertheless shining forth in all its splendour."

Dr. Elliotson, through Mr. Home, now spoke at some length on the subject of mental and bodily disease and imperfections, insanity and crime. He said, "It s very wrong to allow persons to marry who are not properly fitted to perpetuate their race. By allowing perfect freedom of marriage, crime and disease become perpetuated, and the lower and imperfect form becomes too permanent. Such as are imperfect should be put aside, cared for, pitied, but not allowed to perpetuate by marriage. Angels standing by at very many weddings, where all is rejoicing, weep and mourn—for they see the poor form that must go out and suffer,—the outcast, the criminal, and the murderer. But, when the soul is released, then a shout of joy goes up to heaven that a spirit has been set free." He then addressed us about the universal justice of God, saying, "You hold up one book, the Bible, and you say that all those who differ from you shall be damned, yet other nations have other books and scrolls, and in their turn say that all those who believe not in them, must equally be damned. There is no damnation in that sense—man is his own damnation; it is the evil that lies in the little troubled heart of ambitious man, whose acts are after all but as the gurglings from the neck of a bottle, signifying naught."

He then spoke of the great mistake parents make in teaching their children religion without appealing to their reasoning powers, and giving them something they could hold on to. "Therefore is it that men are driven to take refuge in a cold barren philosophy. I doubted and told myself that all was not so, that there was no future—no God, then there came this (rapping with his fingers on the table, and being answered by some spirit on the other side of the table,) one, two, three, four, nothing more —and all was changed, and the scales fell from my eyes, and the

c

broad light of immortality shone upon me. I felt that I was immortal; by a few gentle raps only was all my scepticism dispelled." Towards the close of this sentence Home got greatly excited. Suddenly throwing his hand up to his forehead he said, "Oh, Dannie!" in quite a different tone of voice, and fell back in his chair; he presently added, "Do not be frightened, Dan will be all right presently, but we have made too much use of him; take his hands but do not touch his feet, and let him stretch himself out." We held his hands and he became perfectly rigid all over, stretching his legs out to their full length. After a minute he fell back in his chair, then started up and taking Mrs. Hennings' hands said, (Dr. Elliotson speaking through him) "They tell me I have been too violent with Dan, but my dear lady, I must just tell you this. You remember many many years ago you brought me a little girl, a clairvoyant, and I was not good, and would not be satisfied with the tests. I was influenced by the other two girls; they were very jealous. You are not angry now, are you? You know I meant no harm. I mention this to satisfy you of my identity. You have had many such tests,* and are now satisfied.

After this, Home threw himself back in his chair and awoke, he said, "I am wide awake, but I cannot move at all." In a few minutes he recovered, and said that he was quite well; that he did not know what he had been doing; but that he felt as though he had been very happy.

No. 15.—*Séance, 5, Buckingham Gate, August,* 1868.

My dear Father,—While staying at Dunraven the other day I saw announced in the paper the death of Adah Menken, the American actress with whom both Home and I were slightly acquainted. On the following morning I got a letter from Home, saying that she had been to visit him, that she appeared very restless, and that she was very anxious to come when he and I were together. On returning to London, Home, at my request, came to stay at No. 5. All the evening he complained of being very nervous and in an unpleasant state, which he attributed a great deal to her influence. I felt just the same, but put it down to having been out at two fires and not home till six o'clock the previous morning. Almost immediately after we had gone to bed and put the lights out, we both heard music much the same as at Norwood

---

* This scene occurred some 30 years ago at Dr. Elliotson's studio, where Mrs. Hennings attended with a remarkable clairvoyant named Ellen Dawson Dr. Elliotson behaved very abruptly on this occasion, and punctured and injured the child, whilst in the mesmeric state; no one present knew of this incident and it had even escaped Mrs. Hennings' memory until reminded of it.

but more powerful and distinct. Home said that the music formed words; that, in fact, it was a voice speaking and not instrumental music. I could hear nothing but the chords like an organ or harmonium played at a distance. Home became quite excited because I could not distinguish the words, thinking that if I could not hear them, it must have been his imagination. He asked the spirits if possible to make the words sufficiently clear for me also to hear them. They said "*Yes*" (by raps); and the music became louder and louder until I distinctly heard the words, "Hallelujah, praise the Lord; praise the Lord God Almighty." It was no imagination, or the result of anxiety on my part to hear the same as Home did. Every now and then I could not distinguish words, although he said he could; but I repeatedly heard the words above mentioned as plainly as possible. I cannot in the least explain to you how the voice articulated; the words were not separately spoken, neither did it resemble a human voice. The sound was slightly reedy and metallic, not very unlike the Vox humana on an organ. If you can imagine an organ pipe of some rather reedy stop speaking to you, it will be as near it as anything I can describe. Home said he heard the words, "Adah Isaaks Menken" pronounced; I did not. The music or voice gradually died away. We asked if it was Menken's voice, and they said not hers alone. There were loud raps at different times upon the floor and walls, and some article of furniture was moved: I heard the movement, but could not see what it was.

The room was dark, the blind being nearly down over the window. We both saw as it were a luminous cloud about the middle of the room over the table, and another luminous cloud-like body floating in the air. Occasionally, I saw a luminous form standing at the foot of Home's bed which he did not see, and he at one time saw a similar appearance at the foot of mine which I failed to perceive; we distinctly heard the rustling of a silk dress moving about the room. Home and I had called on Menken at her hotel one day last year, and she then had on a very heavy silk dress, it appeared as though she caused the rustling of this dress to be heard by us. At one time I heard some one moving, and on looking over towards Home's bed, I saw her quite plain (as did also Home) as a white slightly luminous body, I could clearly see the folds of the drapery. In passing between him and the window Home said she obstructed the light. She moved up from near the foot of his bed where I first saw her, making as loud a rustling noise as a living woman in a heavy silk dress would do, to the head of his bed, bent over, put her hands upon his head, and disappeared.

Presently Home said that she was slightly taking possession

of him, and I heard his hands moving about on the bed clothes in the curious way that they do under those circumstances. He then sat up in bed involuntarily, and said she was taking possession of him, and asked me not to be frightened at anything he might do. I felt rather nervous at this; and asked him, if possible, to tell me before he did anything. He said nothing, but lay down in bed again. In about a minute, he said in quite an altered voice, "I am coming over to you now," and I saw him get out of bed. I did not feel sure whether he was asleep or awake, and I said, "Can you see your way?" He said, "Ah, I want no light to guide my steps." I then perceived that he was in a trance, and that Menken was speaking through him. He walked slowly over to my bed, knelt down beside it, took both my hands in his, and began speaking.

I shall never forget the awfully thrilling way in which she spoke; the desolation of the picture she drew of her feelings at first. The words I do not recollect—the effect of them I shall always remember. She went on to speak of the wonderful mercy and goodness of God; of the hopeful state she was then in; of the very little we know of the next world, saying that she had thought she knew something of it. She spoke a great deal about Home, of his character, &c., &c., and a good deal about herself, and mentioned a curious fact. She said that at the time Home and I called upon her together, she felt then what she was. "Yes," she said, "what was I but an animal? Yet I felt and knew that I ought to aspire to higher things, and I longed sometimes for it." It appears as if our having called together upon her, had some curious effect, as she said she could not well say what she wanted, till we were together again. She spoke of the intense desire of the spirit sometimes to communicate with, and do good to, those on earth. She spoke in such an humble yet happy manner, of her having been permitted to come that night into a house where so many pure and holy beings had been. She spoke with the greatest pleasure of having been allowed to go into my mother's boudoir, and said that her greatest happiness, since she passed away, had been that evening—in being permitted to make her voice audible to us in praising God. She went on to say, how much she wished to be sometimes near me and near Home to watch over us; and assured me again and again that she would do me no harm or hurt. She then kissed my hand and said, "I must go now; I must not make too much use of Dan." Home then got up and walked slowly away, turning round twice, and raising his hands above his head in an attitude of prayer or of blessing. As he went away from me, his clothes became slightly luminous.

He got into bed and I could hear him breathing regularly as in ordinary sleep; in about five minutes he awoke and asked me if I was asleep, he said he had been asleep and wanted to know whether we had been hearing beautiful music, or whether we had been dreaming. I told him nothing about his having been in a trance until next day. Home said he felt remarkably happy and calm,—probably some reflection of the more calm and soothed condition of Menken when she left us. I was in a queer state, my fingers and feet tingled as if I had pins and needles. Every time I dropped off to sleep I heard, or fancied I heard, the same strains of music. However I slept very soundly.

Now all this is to me far more wonderful than what took place at Norwood. I was, to all intents and purposes, actually conversing with the dead; listening, talking, answering, and receiving answers from Menken. Home's individuality was quite gone: he spoke as Menken, and we both spoke of him as a third person at a distance from us. Menken said something (what I cannot remember) about her having been a Jewess, and that events were tending gradually towards a greater unity of different creeds.

No. 16.—Séance, Homburg, August, 1868.

At Cologne we slept in a double-bedded room. As Home was going to sleep, he said, " How odd." I asked him what he meant; and he said he had heard Menken's voice say, " That is right, Dan," in reference to an observation he had just made to me. She also told him that she was with us that morning when we were talking about the probability of dogs being able to understand each other; that they could communicate with each other by magnetism, by touch, and through the eye; but not at all by sound. She added that she was going with us, and that we should hear her voice.

At Frankfort, Home came into my room in the morning; and on my asking him some question as to how he had passed the night, said that after he had gone to bed he heard Menken's voice say that his sheets were damp, that he had found they were so, and had slept in a railway rug.

On Thursday night, at Homburg, we both heard strange raps about the room. I then felt and heard little gentle taps upon the foot of my bed, by which I recognized the presence of my mother. I asked if it was so, and was answered " Yes." I said to Home that I was glad my mother was there, because I thought that she had not been near me for some time. This message came : " *You must at times be allowed foreign influences; but I do not leave you—I love you too much for that.*" We were talking about this sentence; and Home was saying it was unselfishness that induced my mother to give way to other spirits sometimes, who were very anxious to communicate, when this message was given: "*The love of our great Creator is unselfish.*" We then began speculating as to whether there was a continual contest going on in the next world between good and bad, and I was answered by a message saying that "*there is a contest the same as on earth.*" I made some remark that on earth it was a great deal a matter of physical force, and that a good weak man could not turn a bad strong one out of his house, when this message was given: "*Purity, when freed from the mortal, is strongest, as truth overcomes error.*" Home presently said, "There is a spirit standing in the corner, can you not see it? I can see it as a faint light increasing and decreasing in brightness." I looked, but could not make it out; but I saw a faint light on the other side of the room, and called Home's attention to it. As we looked in that direction, the light in the corner shone out suddenly, like a flash of lightning. It was an instantaneous perfectly bright flash of light, lasting perhaps nearly a second.

No. 17.—Séance.

On the 30th of August we had a *séance* at Mrs. Hamilton's. Present: Mr. Home, myself, Mrs. Hamilton, her daughter, Lady Fairfax, and Mrs. Gregory.

Very soon after sitting down, a strong influence became apparent, and raps were heard upon the table. My hands were a good deal agitated; I felt the cold air very plainly. Home's hands were taken possession of, and he was caused to get up. He went behind Mrs. Hamilton and began tapping her very rapidly with both hands on the ears and back; while doing so, he went into a trance. He continued to tap her ears and to make passes over her. He then walked up and down the room, leaning his head upon his hand as though thinking deeply, and making gestures quite strange to him in his natural state. He went behind Lady Fairfax, stooped down, and holding her shoulders with both hands pressed his head against her back. He then stood behind her, pressed his hand to his side on the region of the liver, and looked as though he was suffering great pain or inconvenience; he then opened the door and went into the other room. From there he said, "Mary (Miss Hamilton) and Adare, come in here." We went in and found Home on the sofa, leaning his head upon his hand. He said, "Adare, take a pencil and paper." I did so, and wrote down what he said.

Home said, " Mary, the drum of your mother's ear is surrounded by wax; the nerve is not paralyzed. Take some plain
sweet oil in a phial, place it in hot water until the oil is warm,
and drop one drop into the ear every night. After some time a
discharge will take place, that is, the wax will become softened
and come away. It is untrue that the nerve is paralyzed; there
is nothing wrong with that, or it would have been cured at
once. You may remember once that the hearing came back;
that was because the wax broke away slightly. Lady Fairfax
has an over secretion of bile—the liver is inactive; this causes
irritation of the nerves, great loss of appetite—in fact, a complete loathing of food. Take in the morning, every other day,
one drop of tincture of digitalis." Home then came to my
chair, sat down beside me, and pressed me close against him.
He sat down again upon the sofa, and said, " You must prepare
some little powders composed of as much cayenne pepper as will lie
upon the point of a penknife, the same quantity of ipecacuanha,
and twice that quantity of carbonate of soda : take it immediately after meals. You could have it made up into pills if you
like, but the powders are best. You suffer from indigestion—
the bile is faulty ; that causes nervous irritability, which extends
to the brain, and causes sleeplessness and other results. You
should avoid heavy suppers and strong drink late at night;
but this, of course, must be left to your own good sense. We
have no remedy for that : lead a plain natural life."

Home then got up, told us to go back to the other room, and
not to tell him when he awoke what he had been doing. We sat
down again, and he placed himself in exactly the same position
behind Mrs. Hamilton as he had occupied when he became
entranced. He then awoke and said, " Is it not funny, all the
power has left my hands!" and sat down. We then had some
physical manifestations ; the table was moved, tilted, and raised
off the ground; my chair was a little moved, as was also Home's.
"*Good night*" was then said. While he was in the trance, some
one asked whether he could see. I said "No ;" but, as if to prove
he did not use his eyes, he took out his handkerchief and blind-
folded himself, and did not remove it until just before he awoke.
e was also elongated while in the trance.

Mrs. Hamilton has been deaf for some time ; the doctors have
declared that the nerve is injured. Mrs. Hamilton told me that
Mrs. Weldon, of London, being in a clairvoyant state, told her
that her deafness was owing to a secretion of wax, and recommended oil. Lady Fairfax is very unwell, and I had been
suffering from sleeplessness, unpleasant dreams, and nervous
uncomfortable nights.

No. 18.—Séance, Homburg, Monday, September 7th, 1868.

Last Tuesday, the 1st, we had a *séance* at Mrs. Hamilton's, but nothing whatever occurred. Home was not well. On Wednesday morning Home picked up a wonderful specimen of the death's-head moth, and brought it home, put it in a drawer and thought nothing more about it. That night I suddenly awoke, Home said to me, " A very curious thing has just occurred. I was fast asleep, and so were you, all at once I turned round, awoke, and saw a spirit—a man, standing by my bedside. He said 'You are on no account to part with that death's-head moth, it is your good genius, you are to give him two louis to-morrow, and he will play with them according to his impressions at a quarter-past twelve, and with the money he wins you will get a medallion to put the moth in. That window must be shut. The spirit also said something to me about Mrs. Lyon, but I cannot remember what. When the spirit had finished speaking, he moved a step towards your bed, stretched out his hand, and immediately you awoke." Home having a bad cold on his chest, I got up and shut the window. (The night before this—Home being much oppressed by difficulty of breathing—a spirit told him through the alphabet, to lay on his right side, he did so, and found relief.) Neither of us could go to sleep after this, and after some time I said " I wish as the spirit awoke us, that he would send us to sleep again." Soon after I felt a most curious influence, my eyes kept shutting involuntary, and squeezing themselves together so tightly that I could not open them. My right leg and arms became occasionally quite rigid; the sensation was not the least uncomfortable. I was quite conscious, and heard Home go to sleep, but could not sleep myself for a long time.

On Thursday, the 3rd, I had fever, palpitation of the heart, and felt very ill. Soon after we had gone to bed, we heard raps, and a spirit said, " *You have both caught cold in that gambling room, sitting at the table in the large room near the door, there is a strong current of cold air there.*" I asked if it had not something to do with Count Ronicker, they said, " *Yes, his influence is too strong, let him make a few passes over you and you will conquer it.*" I asked, should he mesmerise me and send me to sleep, they said, " *No.*" They then said, " *We have already calmed you,*" which was the case. Home then went into a trance; he got up and came over to me and sat down on my bed; he sat for some little time holding one of my hands in his and pressing the other against my heart. I felt very calm and quiet ; he then joined his hands in prayer and began praying, but I could not hear the words. I said, more to myself than him, "I will unite my prayer to yours." He took my two hands, joined them within his and we prayed together; something affected me so much that I burst out crying, and the tears ran down my cheeks. After a minute or two, he passed his hand across my throat, and stopped the crying immediately; he then made passes over my head and down my side, took my hand and kissed it, kissed my forehead and said, "Good night; sleep, sleep—when you fall asleep you will not awake." He then got quietly into bed again; in about half a minute the clock (a very noisy disagreeable one) struck eleven. He got out of bed and went into the next room where he awoke and nearly fell down; he was so much astonished at finding himself standing opposite the clock. The clock stopped at that moment, though I do not believe he had touched it; in fact he could not have reached it without getting on a chair. In a short time I fell into a sound sleep.

The next morning Home gave me two louis to play for a medallion for the moth; I went in at a quarter-past 12 and put one on red—red won; I then put the other also on red—red won again; making therefore six louis. Something seemed to say to me six is enough, and I put out my hand to the rake to take the money; however, when I had my hand almost on the rake, I felt a disinclination to take it. I allowed the money to remain on red, and so lost. I left the table to look for Home to tell him the money was gone; when half way down the corridor I involuntarily stopped, turned round, and walked back again. Something seemed to say, you must use two louis of your own, and take them back afterwards. I did so, and won a small sum. I took back my two louis and handed the remainder to Home.

No. 19.—*Séance.*

On Friday, the 4th, we had some raps in the room, and a spirit said, "*Are you good?*" We both thought, but could not discover that we had done anything particularly wrong that day. I asked, "Is the question for me?" No answer. "Or for Dan?" No answer. "Or for both?" No answer. I said, "Is it not for me?" Two raps came, meaning "*Partly,*" or "*Perhaps.*" After a pause, they said, "*We do not wish to reproach you, but at the close of the day it is always well to review all that you have done, so as to be able to avoid repeating the same things, if wrong, another day.*" The same night we both saw a luminous hand waving in the air at the foot of Home's bed.

On Saturday, the 5th, Home was not well, and a certain circumstance annoyed him. In the evening, I took him up rather sharply about it; telling him it was absurd letting his imagination run wild, and supposing all sorts of nonsense. At night Home was very ill; it was about eleven, o'clock, I was undressing, he was in bed. Count Ronicker came in and sat down. Home became cataleptic or something having that appearance; his fingers were turned back, his arms and his neck twisted round, and his whole body became as rigid as iron—for about five minutes he did not appear to breathe. Count Ronicker magnetized him, and did him a great deal of good. Home completely forgot English, and said he could only speak Russian to the Count. He spoke about me, but I do not know what he said.

After a time he got better, and went into a trance and spoke English; but so low that I could scarcely hear. I asked him to speak louder, he said, "We cannot—oh, do try to hear, we cannot keep Dan long in a trance as we would wish, he is so ill." He said, "When Dan told you to-day that he felt a disagreeable influence, as it were, trying to separate you, he did not tell you all; he ought to have done so; you were too sharp with him; you were too hard upon him also about playing; remember he is very differently situated to you; remember always that his nature is very sensitive, very different from yours. You must arrange your worldly affairs together." He then sat up in bed, and began to talk in French, still in a trance; he smiled and beckoned to some one at the other side of the room. "Ah," he said, "there is such a sweet gentle spirit here; I will tell you her name directly." He described her, and said she had most beautiful eyes; that when she smiled, she smiled with her eyes also. He described the colour of her hair, eyes, &c., minutely. "There is a little child with her—ah, there are two! One passed away at its birth; the other is older." He then shuddered and said, "There is a spirit here who committed suicide. Oh!" he said, and began making passes before him, and drawing himself back as if in horror. Soon he went on in French, and said, "Daniel is very ill: his brain is very bad; the influence about him is mixed to-night. At four in the afternoon he began to be ill, and his friend did not talk to him or understand it, and afterwards his friend was a little cold and hard upon him; he has also undergone a very great trial lately, we cannot cure him of the effects at once. We tell you that you may understand the state he is in." He then lay down, and said to the Count, "It was Sophy who made the raps on the wall of your room last night. She is your guardian spirit, and is always about you and caring for you." The Count asked "Which Sophy?" He said, "Both the younger and the elder." After a minute he sat up again, turned to the Count, and said, "Where then was your faith when you prayed to God on your knees for death? Where

was your faith?—you should then rather have wished to live."
He talked for some little time in French to the Count, and told
him some facts which he (the Count) swore positively to me
could be known only to himself and the spirit that Home had
been describing; he then said, "When Daniel awakes we will
try and make some manifestations for you; but Daniel is so ill
we cannot do much. You will take a chair; but not too near
Daniel, your influence is too strong. Adare will put the candle
out." After he awoke I put the candle out, and we heard
distinct raps on the floor, walls, door, &c., and the Count felt
his head touched. The Count then went away. Soon after he
had gone, the same spirit that had told us the night before to
review our actions said, through the alphabet, "How about
to-day?" Soon after, he said, "Are you happy?" I then heard
that Home was getting some message; but I do not know what
it was. I heard him say, "I cannot do it—oh! please don't;
you know I am so ill?" Directly after he turned his head round
towards me, and said that when he had told me he felt an unpleasant influence as though trying to separate us, he had not
told me all, and he went on to explain about a very extraordinary case of second sight that had occurred to him that day.
After he had done so, he said that he felt quite comfortable
and happy. We talked for some time about second sight, and
he was explaining how one could tell by the appearance of his
eyes when it was likely to occur to him. Suddenly he said to me,
"I am in the Kursaal, in the playing room; I will tell you what
I see." All the time he talked quite naturally, and knew that he
was in bed; at the same time he declared he was actually standing
on the floor of the room, and could observe all that was
going on there. "Oh!" he said, "it is horrible! Oh, it is dreadful! My God, it is so horrible that, if it lasts long, I can never
go into that room again! I see the table, and I see crowds
of hands all about it, flying about all over it,—young hands, old
hands,—hands of men and women,—they are dashing about
over the table, sometimes catching hold of each other, and then
throwing each other off. Oh, there is a hand with blood upon
it! There is an old man's hand, and a woman's hand that
seizes his, but he dashes hers away from him! Oh, it is too
terrible! It is changed now. I will tell you what I see directly.
There are a number of young people sitting round the table, all
young, pretty and pleasant looking; nearly all of them are
women; they are playing, but laughing, talking and thinking of
other things also, not intent upon the game; the others are all
driven back from the table; they are in a varied confused sort
of crowd, there is a regular solid barrier that I can see before
them. Some are leaning over and trying to get across, but they

cannot; now the table is covered with roses: I see that they are playing with roses. A sort of leader among them, a woman, is getting up and says, ' Well, I suppose we must take away these lovely roses with us; it is a pity, but if these poor people prefer money to them, why we must take them away.' Now it has again changed. The table is covered with little children, they are sitting on the table, and most of them look thoughtful; they are such pretty, sweet little children. The crowd is still kept back by the barrier, but some of them look as if they wanted to caress the children. There is one man who is stretching out his hands so eagerly towards such a rosy, pretty little fellow, and wants to shake hands with him, but the child is saying, ' I cannot shake our hand, because we have all just been washed and dressed, and your hands are so dirty from the money that I must not touch them.' " After this he saw nothing more and went to sleep, and awoke the next day wonderfully well, considering how ill he had been.

On Sunday, the 6th, we had a *séance* at Mrs. Hamilton's. There was a strong influence; there were raps on the table, chairs, &c.; our chairs were violently vibrated; Home's chair moved, and there were no messages. The table was tilted, not lifted. Count Ronicker was present, and his magnetic influence was so strong that it made us all more or less ill, and I think stopped the *séance*.

No. 20.—*Séance, Friday, the* 11*th.*

Last Wednesday night, soon after the lights were put out, a spirit asked if our actions during the day had been as they should be? Soon after, he said, " *The atmosphere of this house is not good for either of you; it is very damp.*" I said, " Is that the reason I always awake in the morning with a sore throat?" The spirit replied, " *Yes.*" We asked where we should go; the answer was, " *The Hesse is the highest.*" We accordingly moved into the Hotel de Hesse. The house in which we lodged was, as the spirit said, in a very low and damp situation.

No. 21.—*Séance, Sunday,* 13*th.*

Last Friday, we had a *séance* at Mrs. Hamilton's. Present: Mr., Mrs., and Miss Hamilton, the Baron de Veh and his wife, the Princess Karoli, Mrs. Watkins, Mrs. Gregory, the Count de Mons, General Brevern, Home, and myself. We had physical manifestations, currents of cold air, vibration of our chairs and the table, table-tilting, &c. Home's chair was moved slightly; Mrs. Watkins, who was sitting near him, was moved also. Mrs. Watkins had suffered severely from rheumatism, and was quite bent double by it. Home's hands were taken possession of, and he 'was moved to get up. He placed himself behind her chair and began tapping her on the back and grasping her shoulders; he then sat down and presently went into a trance. We recognized by his manner the same spirit that had prescribed for Mrs. Hamilton, and Lady Fairfax, and myself, on a previous occasion. He walked up and down the room two or three times; then placed his head against Mrs. Watkins's back, and held it firmly there for a minute or two. He then walked into the next room ; beckoned to me and made a sign as of writing. I got a pencil and paper, and went in. He was sitting down, and said, " We wish you to have a compress made—a sort of plaster of tar spread upon a cloth, and covered with muslin, to be placed upon the back; it will give strength to the spine. There is want of action, and no proper re-action ; the blood is very acid—that is the cause of the rheumatism; that will do now." I went back to my place ; he came in and sat down, and began to speak of the different spirits present, telling their names, and describing them, so that their relations present recognized them. He said that with one lady there was a sweet little girl who wanted to play with him, and he went through the form as if playing with a child. He then stood behind the Count de Mons ; addressed him as his father; leant his head against his, and spoke to him for a long time in a most affectionate and touching manner. He said he could become a medium and be able to draw. Mrs. Gregory had been very sleepy for some time. Home turned to her and said, " We wish to take this influence away from you ; it is purely physical—nothing spiritual about it; you live very much with Lady Fairfax; she is very ill; that is what affects you; you must not be too much with her ; you are not strong enough to bear it." He then made passes over her hands for a few minutes. Home then began talking to Madame de Veh, and spoke to her for some time in a most kindly manner ; the words I forget, but they were to the effect that she was on no account to let her heart grow faint; that the future would be brighter than the past; and that there was a new development coming to her (she is a writing medium) ; what it was they would not tell her, but it would cause her great happiness. Home spoke to several others and then said, " Daniel must now come back, as we want to make some manifestations."

Soon after, he awoke. Although we sat for some time longer, we had only slight manifestations. Two or three people got up soon after he awoke, which perhaps was the reason of it. During his trance, Home spoke sometimes in English, sometimes in French. When he was describing the spirits present, he seemed not to be quite certain about the name and relationship of one of them, and said he must go and find out. He rose up, went into the next room, and stood there a short time by himself, and then came back and told us about the spirit in question.

September 15*th.*

Last Saturday night I was very wakeful. Late at night, Home being asleep, I heard raps on some part of the floor near his bed. They were tolerably loud and monotonous, going on with a regular beat, like the ticking of a clock, until I fell asleep.

At dinner last Saturday, Home pointed out to me a young man sitting at the end of the table, and said, "I feel impelled towards him—I have something, I know not what, to say to him, or to do for him." After dinner Home went up and spoke to him, and asked him to come the following evening to Mrs. Hamilton's.

No. 22.—Séance.

Last Sunday we had a *séance* at Mrs. Hamilton's. Present: Mr., Mrs. and Miss Hamilton; Mrs. Mainwaring, Mrs. Spearman, Mr. A——, Home, and myself. Soon after we sat down, there were vibrations of the table, the chairs, the floor of the room, &c., and we felt cold currents of air. However, it soon ceased, and we sat for some time without anything occurring. Some one suggested that we should have tea, and try again afterwards. We accordingly did so; and after the things were cleared away, sat round the table again. We felt the cold air and vibrations of the table. Home suddenly said that he had distinctly seen a figure pass before the window outside. Before coming to the *séance*, Mr. A—— had told us a curious occurrence that happened to him the previous night. He was waiting in a garden to meet a friend of his, a lady; and he saw her, as he supposed, walking towards him. He got up and went to meet her; but when quite close, he looked on the ground for a second, and on raising his eyes the figure had disappeared. He was very anxious to know whether what he had seen was a delusion; and if not, whether the figure that passed the window was the same or not.

Soon after, Home went into a trance, and sat for a little time making passes over his own eyes and head. He then went and stood behind Mr. A——, and looked at him for some time. "Ah," he said, "you are like the simoon—like a wild wind of the Desert." He talked to him for some little time; I cannot remember his words. He then said, "You have many spirits about you who love you, and many who do not. Your atmosphere is very varied; it is like your character, changeable, wild, uncertain. You are pursuing a phantom." Home also said something about marriage, but I forget what. He then sat down. Mr. A—— had been wishing to hear something about the apparition he had seen the previous night, but had said nothing aloud. Home turned to him, and said, " Yes, it had to do with what you have in your mind. You understand very well what I mean. When I said you were pursuing a phantom that ought to have been sufficient answer to you. You will have a vision at a moment when you least expect: it will be a pleasant one. Take care that you profit by it, or you will see one other vision which shall be terrible." Home then got up, went close to Mr. A——, clasped his hands together, and said, " Ah, do think of what you are doing; do reason about it." He then walked up and down the room, raising his hands and letting them fall again, as a man would who had done all in his power and could do no more, and saying, "The ways of God are inscrutable—the ways of God are inscrutable." He then sat down and began explaining to us how God's creatures could only act according to His will; and how spirits, though they could frequently see events coming on in the future, yet could not avert them. "We can see," he said, " the rocks in your path, and can sometimes strew them and cover them with flowers, but we cannot remove them; so, though we may see misfortune—though we may see blood will be shed about it—we cannot prevent: we can only influence, and sometimes warn." Turning and pointing solemnly to Mr. A——, he said twice, " There is danger in it—there is danger in it." He then turned to Mrs. Mainwaring, and spoke to her to the effect that she was never to allow her mind to dwell on a certain subject that had occupied her three times during her life, once for a whole day. " You have got rather a low influence about you," he said, " because you are always expecting and wishing for spiritual interference in the every-day affairs of life. You should take a higher view of it than that. You wonder why the spirits do not help you. Are you not a spirit? You are all spirits, only you have the earthly envelope about you. Rouse yourself, do all you can to rouse yourself, and help yourself; do not expect others to help you if you do not act yourself. It is a common thing for people to say, ' If spirits are about us, why don't they manifest themselves?' Is not God everywhere? Is He not about you? Why then does He not manifest Himself? Yet do spirits interfere in a thousand ways that you little dream of, and never notice. God has so ordained, that though many of you spend your lives looking for evidence of His existence, yet every day you pass by unnoticed the most wonderful and beautiful evidences.

" Do not suppose for a moment that you can do anything in

secret; have no false modesty or false shame, and think not to do that in private which you would not do before the world. If it be not enough for man to know that God is everywhere, and sees all his actions, then let him remember also, that his father, mother, brothers, sisters and all those most dear to him, are continually about him; do nothing therefore in private that you would be ashamed of doing openly." Turning to Mrs. Spearman, he said, "Louisa, when your mother suffers from those acute pains in her limbs, she should foment them with an infusion of hops, just pour boiling water on the hops, and use it as hot as she can bear. Hops are very good; they not only act as a sedative, calm the nerves and mitigate the pain, but they also strengthen and act as a tonic." He then, after listening apparently at Mrs. Hamilton's ear, said, "The oil is too heavy against the drum of the ear, that is why your deafness was increased." Turning to Miss Hamilton, he said, "Mary, you have used more than we ordered; we prescribed one drop only, you ought not to have used more; for the future, drop the oil on a bit of cotton and use a little ether with it."

Home then got up, walked round the table, taking our hands one after the other. He was then twice elongated and shortened to less than his natural height. He made Mr. A—— put his foot on his feet, and place his hands, one on his chest, the other just above his hips, in order that he might be sure that he was standing fairly on the ground, and that he might also feel the elongation and contraction taking place. He then sat down and turned to me, laughed, and speaking in quite a different tone of voice, said, "A. M—— says she will come to you to-night. She says she was with you last night, and made those monotonous taps that you heard; she wanted you to sleep and thought that might send you to sleep. She says she made those slow regular sounds, like as it were the rocking of a cradle, as a sort of lullaby to soothe you. She says she will be able now sometimes to make sounds like that, even when you are alone. When Dan said last night something about having been praying for you, it was she who spoke through him; it was not Dan who spoke at all himself. You had better tell him this as he, has been rather worrying himself, thinking that his mind must have been wandering in his sleep. Dan will come back now; sit for five or ten minutes, and we will try and make some manifestations; we want John to see some." Home then awoke, and we sat for a little time, but had scarcely anything more. We then broke up and a most extraordinary thing occurred. I was standing in the balcony, the rest were about the table; all of a sudden the gas went out and the room was in darkness; the gas was not turned off, but went out. They all declared that no one was near the burner; three people, Mr Home, Miss Hamilton, and Mrs. Mainwaring, said that they distinctly saw a hand and arm stretched out over their heads upon the jet of gas and that at that moment it went out. They said it was so distinct that their first idea was that some one had gone suddenly crazy and must have burned themselves.

Mr. Hamilton told me next morning that he had investigated it, and found that at the same moment eight jets of gas went out in the house, namely one in the room in which we were; two in the next; three, I think, on the landing and stairs, and two in the kitchen. The meter had not been turned off, the meter does not communicate with the street gas, but has a separate pipe leading to the gasometer.

That night we heard raps announcing, I suppose, the presence of Adah Menken; they did not last however. Just as I was going to sleep, Home who was asleep, turned in his bed, and said, " I have been trying but I cannot." He said it in a different tone of voice to his own, and as if he was rather vexed at having failed. I said, "Never mind," which awoke him, and he asked me if he had been talking in his sleep.

No. 23.—Séance, Sunday, September 20th, 5, Buckingham Gate.

Last Friday night, after we had gone to bed, we were talking, and I was saying something about how small and trivial our lives on earth must appear after we have passed away. A spirit joined our conversation by saying " *Yes*," by three very emphatic loud raps. Home presently had a sort of vision; being quite awake, and knowing where he was, and describing to me what he saw, he said, " I am in a desert, that is just at the edge of a great desert—there is a sort of barrier between me and it. The desert is perfectly barren, there is no light of the sun, but a great cross at the far side of it, and the light flowing from the cross is lighting it all up, the cross means truth; there are a number of pigmies all about the cross. Oh, it is so strange, they are all working away as hard as they can, and trying to build up blocks of stone and rubbish and stuff before the cross, but as they build them up, the blocks become transparent, and the light from the cross still shines through them. The pigmies are digging away and working so hard about it, they seem to have made a desert of the place by digging out earth and stuff to hide out the cross." Home suddenly stopped talking, and when he spoke again, was in a trance, he said, " Now that you are quietly at home, we wish to explain to you how it was that Dan was so nervous at Homburg." He then explained some circumstances that had puzzled me a good deal. He went on to say, " After that Dan

D

caught a cold, you also felt the same influence and you caught a chill, then the magnetic atmosphere of that man Romker was so strong, that it irritated your nerves intensely, and on that night you were on the point of having brain fever, but by the foot bath that we influenced Dan to insist upon your having, and by magnetizing you through Dan, it was prevented. It was Adah Menken that influenced Dan in that matter." I remarked how thankful I was. Home said, "Oh, it was not Adah Menken that magnetized you. She made Dan see that vision he told you of, she is very often about you." I said that it was very good of her to endeavour to do us good. Ah, he said, "It does her good! Ah, if bitter tears could wipe away the recollection of what has been, and the knowledge of what might have been; well, it was not to be. It was not, therefore, it was not to be. Adah Menken was the most suited of all the spirits about you to interfere in that matter at Homburg that you know of; her life had made her more capable of it, in fact—as she laughingly says herself—'You must set a thief to catch a thief.' She says that the wish you expressed at Homburg shall be gratified. Get her book. She says, 'If I could send it to you or write an order for it I would, you know; but then I cannot.' However, it is very small and not expensive, and you can very well afford to buy it, so if you will get it, she says she will this winter write her name in it for you. You remember saying that you wished to see an instance of direct spirit writing, she thinks that will be a nice way to do it for you; she will do the same for Dan." I said, "Shall I tell Dan?" "By all means Dan is now coming back to his desert, he will not know anything about this little episode." Having a matter on my mind, I said, "May I ask a question?" He said, "Yes," before I spoke, having read my thoughts and said, "Yes," again, when I asked. I accordingly asked about what I wanted to know, and received an answer and explanation; while he was speaking he laughed, and said, "Some spirits say we should not tell you too much, since this is in the future." Home then awoke and took up the thread of his description of the desert, directly after he said, "It is beginning to fade," the vision then melted away gradually.

No. 24.—Séance.

On Saturday we had a *séance* at Mr. S. C. Hall's. Present: Mr. and Mrs. S. C. Hall, Mr. Humphreys, the Comtesse Medina de Pomare, her son, a boy of about 14 years of age, the two Misses Bertolacci, Home and myself. Before we sat down there were raps all about the room; immediately after we were seated strong physical manifestations took place, violent trembling of chairs, table, floor, &c., &c.; currents of cold air, very loud raps in various directions; the table tilted, moved, and was raised from the ground; some questions were answered. Home was in a very nervous state, presently he went into a trance and said, "We are doing this to calm Dan; talk." He then got up, walked about the room, sat down and played the piano for a little time; he then arose, went to the boy and placed his hands upon his head, patting and stroking it; he then went to the Comtesse de Pomare, but when he came near her he drew back, shuddered, and looked distressed, "Ah," he said, "There is something here the spirits do not like." Some one said, "It is because you are in mourning, and have crape on your dress." "Yes," he said, "We do not like that at all. He, (her husband) has pulled your dress two or three times, as you are aware of, he will try presently and tear a bit of the black crape off to shew you that he does not like it."

We began to talk about the custom of wearing mourning, and the difficulty there would be in breaking through it. Home walked about the room; then sat down and said something to this effect: "If you like to put on some outward sign of woe while those you love are in gloom before dissolution, do so; but to put on mourning after that, when a soul has been set free, and has risen nearer to God—yes, nearer to God—oh, no; rather put on all that is pleasant—all that is pleasing to the eye, and cheerful; but, if you think that soul is not worthy of approaching nearer to God, but must be in darkness and tears, then, if you will, put on mourning; but wear it longer than six months or a year." "Yes," the Comtesse remarked, "but we do not wear mourning because we think that a soul is unhappy; but because we ourselves are unhappy." Home said, "Have you so little confidence in God, that you cannot trust Him to do all for the best?" He then spoke of some of the spirits present, chiefly addressing the Comtesse. He then turned to Mr. Hall, and told him his sister was present; he smiled and said, "She is standing just there behind you—she has a communication to make to you, but she cannot make it now; she seems so gentle and timid." Then he laughed, and said, "She has such a funny habit of shading her eyes with her hand, as if she was afraid the light would hurt them. Of course, it does not; but she cannot get rid of the habit now and then, and the others are smiling at her for it. She is doing like this now," and he shaded his eyes with one hand, and went feeling about before him with the other (Mr. Hall's sister had been quite blind, and had had the habit of shading her eyes and feeling before her, so that was a good test of identity). Home then turned to me, and said, "There is a spirit standing near you that went

D 2

through a great deal of suffering before passing away, her name is V——; she and the other spirit (Mr. Hall's sister) seem so much drawn to each other. They both underwent a great deal of suffering, and that appears to draw them to each other. They are talking about it now, and they are speaking of their suffering, as if it had somehow purified them, and as if they were so thankful for it, and considered it to have been the greatest blessing." He told me that we should see lights that night, and then said " Daniel is coming back now." He then awoke. We had some more physical manifestations, and the accordion was played under the table, Home holding it in his hand. It was then suggested to put out the lights, and try if we could see anything; the candles were accordingly put out, and we should, I think, have had a wonderful *séance*, but that the son of the Comtesse de Pomare got so frightened and nervous we were obliged to stop. We had strong physical manifestations, the table being lifted high in the air; the window curtains were moved, one being carried right across the table, and twined round Mrs. Hall; the other was drawn between Home and me, laid over my shoulder, and across my knee. I had hold of the curtain while it was moving, and felt that there was a hand moving it, but when I tried to touch the hand it slid away. I and several others saw a form moving about behind me and Home, and another form at the opposite side of the room, and we were touched at different times; however the boy got so frightened we had to light the candles, and put an end to the *séance*.

The same night Home had to drop some lotion into his eyes, I dropped it in for him, and then put the lights out. Almost immediately he said, " What a curious effect that stuff has had, I see the most beautiful little lights before me." I said, " That is not the effect of the drops; you said when in a trance that we should see lights." " That may be," he replied, " but, what I see is in my eye," and so positive was he that he came over to me and asked me to look into his eye, and try if I could not see them; of course I could not. He went back to bed, and then I began to see the lights, and he was satisfied that they were not in his eye. I saw the most beautiful little phosphorescent lights moving. I saw as many as three at a time; sometimes there were two together like eyes, sometimes two would come together, and then dart away again from each other. We had no other manifestations.

No. 25.—Séance at Ashley House, October 20th.

Present :—Captain Wynne (Charlie) and his wife, Brinsley Nixon and his wife, Home and myself. We sat at a small card table. There were slight manifestations, currents of cold air, vibration of the table and chairs, and raps. The alphabet was called, and the sentence was given : " *Sit at the other table.*" As soon as the influence became pretty strong, the table was moved towards the card table. After a time we got up, and as they evidently wished to alter the position of the table, we moved it ourselves into the centre of the room, and sat down again. We soon felt violent vibration of the floor, chairs, and table—so violent that the glass pendants of the chandelier struck together, and the windows and doors shook and rattled in their frames, not only in the room in which we were sitting, but also in the next. The card table was moved (no one touching it) up to our table, and the two were pressed hard together. The sofa was, under the same conditions, moved up to our table. A sentence was soon after given : " *We had to overcome the influence of the little table, and we have accomplished it.*" Shortly after we were told to move the table and sofa back to their places. We had raps on both the tables and on the floor, and the spirits joined in our conversation two or three times by rapping " *Yes* " or " *No.*" The following message was then given : " *We have made these external manifestations to convince you all ; Charlie, ask questions, we have a work to do with you.*"

Charlie asked if Augusta would recover ; they rapped " Yes " emphatically. He asked if his sister would, and after a pause they answered " *Perhaps,*" by touching him twice upon the knee. He asked if they could bring us word what Augusta was then doing ; and afterwards asked for the name of the spirit who had touched him. " *Will* " was spelled, and a " W "; but the power then appeared to cease, as we could get nothing more. After a pause, they spelled " Father," but the power again failed. After an interval they said, " *We have not power to do more now ; find violin near,*" referring to the fact, I suppose, that Augusta had her violin near her. We had no further manifestations after this. Both Emmy's and Cadly's dresses were pulled during the evening.

After they had all gone, Home went into a trance. "Ah," he said, " there was nothing wrong ; no evil influence to overcome about that little table. It was rather this way ; you had been accustomed to sit at the other table ; you had eaten off it, and always sat at it, and it had therefore become as it were partially magnetized by you. We were obliged to equalize the power over the room and furniture ; and we therefore brought the two tables in contact, and moved up the sofa to inoculate them, as we might say. There was nothing evil about the card table. There is no such thing as evil in your sense of the word. Evil is but good perverted and distorted, gnarled and twisted out of shape. As a blade springing up through the ground if it meets with a stone that obstructs it, is forced out of its course, stunted and thwarted, so is good changed by circumstances into what you call evil. If evil was as you think, you would have to say that the devil had made the world to answer his purpose, but it is not so; God has made the world to answer his ends. You may not be able to see how all this evil can ever harmonize and resolve into good; but it is nevertheless so. Because the sun rises in the midst of clouds in the morning you do not know that it will be cloudy all day; no; so it is that though all may be dark and cloudy now, it will end in brightness.

It is wonderful to stand as it were above and outside the world, and to watch the great wheels revolving; the cogs look all black and broken, covered sometimes with blood, and disfigured; but yet they all fit in and work on smoothly, though, to you it appears otherwise. Yet a time will come when there will be peace and knowledge on the earth about all those matters that so much distract it now. The world revolves in its sphere, turning on its axis, and will enter upon a region of greater peace and knowledge.

You do not know the difficulties that have to be overcome in communicating with you. Supposing now we want to make manifestations, four spirits would perhaps take possession of the four corners of the room, and would begin, as it were, to throw across to each other, and weave together their harmonizing influence, so as to get everything equalized and prepared for the adoption of whatever they want to do. One spirit will remain in the midst who will manage and direct all that is to be said—of course, if one of the other spirits wish to communicate he would let him do so, they are not selfish, but one must have the direction of the manifestations to ensure unity of purpose. That is why it is so bad to wish for the presence of any particular spirit; that spirit might come, and the others not being selfish would admit him into the circle, and he not being in harmony with the others, would destroy the whole thing. You may often notice, especially at the commencement of a *séance*, a whole volley of taps let off, that is a spirit discharging the electricity, to equalize the current; often until the whole is harmonized we cannot stop ourselves from making raps and cannot control them; so that a spirit might at first, if you wanted them to communicate before they were ready themselves, answer "Yes" for "No," and "No" for "Yes." If you put your ear also against the table while communications are being given by raps, you will generally hear a number of little ticks going on; that is, some spirits are discharging the electricity to keep the current in equilibrium, while the others communicate.

If we did not take all these careful precautions there could be no conversation, nothing but a chaos of sounds and raps. It is this same difficulty—the difficulty of encountering the materialism of all about you, that is the cause of a great deal that you call bad and evil influence. A spirit might be standing near you that loved you very much, that was not the least impure, and that wished to soothe and comfort you; and yet he might only serve to irritate you, and the more anxious he was to soothe, the more he might irritate and distress, because he was not in harmony with you. You can feel that yourselves; you are not always in harmony with your best friends, and sometimes you do not feel as much at ease with them, as you would among strangers, and would have more difficulty in showing off any accomplishment, such as playing, singing &c., &c., to them than you would to strangers. Now, this case of the lady who is said to have had her hair pulled out by the roots; it might happen that a spirit that loved her very much was standing near, perhaps even her own father wished to soothe her and caress her hair, and it might have the effect of irritating intensely ; he could not stop himself, he could not withdraw in a moment the electric current that was set going, and the consequences might be painful ; of course all this applies chiefly to undeveloped and partially developed mediums.

Question.—As it is so difficult to influence men are you not constantly endeavouring to do certain things and failing ?

Answer.—To a certain extent,—yes. But spiritual influence has much more to do with the affairs of the world than what you dream of. All inspiration, poetry, improvising as in the case of the old Troubadours,—all that is owing to it—everything in fact, is set in motion by spiritual interference. To those who pray earnestly for and seek for light and truth, light will certainly be given; our greatest difficulty is the folly of men's hearts, and their blindness. There are thousands of men who pray that rather than that Spiritualism should be understood, men should beleive it to be the work of the devil ; to advance themselves one day only, they would retard the progress of the world for ages. Every prayer has its effect, and every aspiration and wish is a prayer; it is not necessary to go down on your bended knees to pray. Would that you could see as we do the great black cloud (to speak figuratively) of prayers and aspirations that is for ever rising up from a populous haunt of mankind like this great city of London. Aspiration for truth and knowledge will surely bring its answer, and as surely does every prayer to the contrary distort and retard true progress.

Question.—I had a question put to me the other day as regards the comparative truth of different sects, which I answered according to my ability. I should be glad to know if I answered with anything like truth.

Answer.—There is truth in every religion; even the poor Pagan, who bows down before his idol, possesses the germ of truth, inasmuch as he worships something outside and beyond himself. It is very wrong—oh, very wrong indeed, to say there is only one portal to heaven; were that the case, there would be few indeed who would arrive there. You are right in supposing that the form of religion which is best suited to a man, though it may contain a smaller proportion of truth than another form, is yet the best for him; being the most adapted to his character and mind, it is that in which he can expand and improve himself to the best advantage. A good answer for you to have given would be : ' Spirits teach individuality of spirit.' As you leave this world you are apt—oh, very apt indeed—to continue for a long time. Those who seek not to raise themselves, and look not for truth, must continue as they were until they—to use a common expression—find it does not pay; then they will try to improve and will do so. There is this individuality; and a man is apt to get around him an influence agreeing with himself. Like seeks like everywhere—it is a universal law. The crow cannot consort with the eagle, or the magpie with the dove."

Question.—" Have we not better opportunities here than we shall ever have hereafter of forming ourselves?" " Most certainly, this is your time. If you strive earnestly and prayerfully here, you enter your true life in a state fitted for it. Seek for truth and you shall find it."

Account of Manifestations at Stockton.

Little Dannie Cox died in London last Sunday the 11th October, 1868; Home, who was his godfather, and very much attached to him, was extremely cut up about it at first. On the Monday morning, Home breakfasted with me at No. 5. I was reading the *Daily Telegraph* over the fire, waiting for breakfast, and he was sitting at the writing table, we heard loud raps on the floor between us; and the following message was given[*]:—
" *We wish you to take the body to Stockton* (Mr. Cox's place in the country) *to-morrow ; you will place the coffin in the drawing-room ; and at half-past eight we will show you a spiritual funeral. You will take care that all the family are there, and no one else ; if I want Mr. Bat* (family lawyer) *I will send for him. I invite your friend to be present.*" After this, we went to breakfast, and the same spirit rapped repeatedly on the table during breakfast, and answered some questions.

------

[*] Believed to be by the spirit of the late Mr. Cox.

No. 26.—Séance.

The next morning the body was sent down; I accompanied Home and Mrs. Cox. The drawing-room was most prettily arranged, everything being covered with white drapery, and quantities of flowers and ferns tastefully placed. The coffin was open, and the little body entirely covered with flowers, all but the face; which looked very calm and peaceful.

At half-past eight o'clock we all entered the room, and sat down, forming a sort of circle, but having no table. Home went into a trance, got up and fetching a chair sat down close to the coffin; he then took Mrs. Cox's hands in his and delivered a most wonderful discourse, taking as it were for his text, the words, "The Lord gave and the Lord hath *not* taken away, blessed be the name of the Lord." He went through the greater part of the burial service, explaining and expounding; he then spake in the most consoling manner to Mrs. Cox, bidding her have confidence in God and in His goodness, and not to look upon that as a separation which was not so in reality ; told her the little boy would be continually with her, was there even now ; spoke of his purity and happiness, told her to be strong and not to give way to sorrow ; but now that her husband and other relatives, had undertaken the development of little Dannie, she was to devote herself all the more to the education of the two remaining children. He then took Gerrie, the other son, by the hand, and spoke to him for some time in the most impressive manner about his future conduct through life, bidding him be an honest God-fearing man, and to remember that his brother would be cognizant of all his actions and therefore not to do that which he knew would offend or grieve him. He then took the little girl's hand, petting and comforting her, and giving her messages from Dannie about his pet rabbits and things of that sort, and telling her that Dannie would often be in communion with her in her sleep, and that she would dream of going about with him. He then walked round the circle, taking each one's hand and saying a kind word or two, and standing up in the centre, and pointing to each of us, enumerated the spirits present, saying, "Your mother, your brother, and so on." He then made a sign to signify that they were all standing round him, and raising his hands, prayed in the most beautiful and earnest way for some little time, and then sat down again in his place ; he said that little Dannie would make raps, and we heard three distinct little ticks, like electric sparks going off; he said we should recognize Dannie by the peculiarity of his raps. He then said, "We wished to have made physical manifestations, but Dan is spiritually weak and we cannot, but

something will occur to-night." After Home awoke, we went
into the conservatory, and again heard little Dannie rapping on
the floor and on the glass.

At supper, at about ten o'clock, there came suddenly very
loud raps all around on the table, walls, floor, &c., &c. I never
heard them so loud before. Home was entranced, and taking
Mrs. Cox by the hand led her into the drawing-room. When
there, she heard something rustling near the coffin, and immediately felt a little hand touch her, and place between her
fingers a sprig of lauristinus. Home then brought her back into
the supper room; and somebody remarked that lauristinus meant
in the language of flowers—" If neglected, I die." Home awoke
immediately.

He and I slept in the same room. Soon after he had gone to
bed, he went into a trance; and began discoursing about moral
principles, &c. He then said, " You tell his mother in the morning
that Dannie gave her that sprig of lauristinus, which means, ' If
neglected, I die;' because he wanted to show her that if she did
anything unworthy of him it would give him pain. Your greatest
idea of pain is death; you are quite wrong there; but that is your
idea, and therefore he put it in that way." I made some remark
about its being a very wonderful thing his giving her the flower.
He said, " We are going to do something still more wonderful
for you. A little later, when the house is quite still, you and
Dan are to get up; you will take the slippers; we will take
care Dan does not catch cold. You are to go down stairs, and
into the drawing-room; Dan will stand at the door; and you
are to go alone up to that little box you call a coffin, and lift the
lid a little; and then return to Dan—that is all. Little Dannie's
colours are purple and white—signs of the greatest purity;
purple and white are the most perfect colours; remember that;
and after them blue, and so on down to black, which is the
lowest." Home then awoke, and presently said, " I feel impressed to open the door." " Well," I said, " do so if you
like; it can do no harm." He got up and did so; and, on his
way back to bed, I heard some spirit tap him on the shoulder.
He said something in answer, and went into a trance; he picked
up the slippers, put them on my feet, and told me to get up.
" Do not be afraid," he said, " I require no light to guide my
footsteps." He took both my hands in his, and then led me
rapidly, without hesitation, out of the room, down the stairs,
and across the hall, the place being perfectly dark. He conducted me into the drawing-room, and then stood still, saying,
" Now walk straight before you to the coffin, and do as you have
been told." I did so, raising the drapery, and lifting the lid at
the head about an inch. Home said " Raise it a little higher,

about as high as would permit of a hand entering." I did so, and heard something rustle inside. Home said, "That is sufficient." I replaced the lid, and returned to where Home was standing. He, as before, took both my hands in his, led me upstairs, and into the bedroom, closed the door, and put me down in a chair by the window, still retaining my hands in the same position. He said, "Little Dannie is there between you and the light; can you not see him?" "No," I said, I cannot." He laughed and said, "Dannie would make himself appear as white; but he cannot just yet; he has so recently come to us. He will try and make himself visible as a dark shadow to you." I still said that I could see nothing. "Ah, never mind!" Home said; and holding one of my hands in his he stretched it out in the dark, and said, "Dannie will let you play with it first." I perceive a strong scent, as it were, blown over me, and felt a flower touch my fingers and then withdraw itself. Presently, I felt a little soft hand touch mine, and a flower was given me. I then felt a strong tremor run through Home's hands, and he spoke as little Dannie, and said, "You must get into bed quickly; Dan is going to awake; if you would like very much to see what you have got you can make an excuse to light a candle presently." Accordingly, after Home had awoke, I lit a candle, and found I had been given a purple and white petunia that had been placed in one of the little hands in the coffin.

No. 27.—Séance.

The next evening we had another *séance*, this time sitting round a table placed against the head of the coffin. The coffin had been fastened down and covered with white drapery, most prettily arranged with flowers and ferns. We had physical manifestations and some messages from little Dannie, the table on which the coffin was placed was moved about, the drapery agitated, &c. We then heard pieces of fern being plucked, we could distinctly hear the branches broken; a piece of fern was given to each person present, their attention being called to it by being touched on the knee, and the hand being then placed beneath the table the fern was put into it. With the fern presented to me, the following message was given :—"*Birth has given you distinction, let your life be the more distinguished for a prayerful and earnest search after truth ; it is kind of you to have come to the house of joy ; truth seekers are brothers and sisters and should share each other's sorrows and joys.*" Home then went into a trance, and took the lamp out of the room, saying we were to see a manifestation that could only take place in the dark.

We presently saw a brilliant little star, it flitted about with an uncertain-like motion—sometimes approaching, sometimes receding from us. We heard raps come from the star which flashed like an electric spark at each detonation. Mrs Cox suddenly said that a quantity of Eau de Cologne had been thrown over her from the ceiling. Home carried a small flask containing some which the spirits probably made use of. Home, who was standing at some distance from us, said, we should have the odour changed four times, and in effect a totally different scent was blown over us four times on a palpable strong current of air. Home then fetched the lamp back. We heard a knocking at the door, he opened it and appeared to invite some one to come in, but did not succeed; he shut the door, when the knocking re-commenced he opened it again, but was unsuccessful; this was repeated three or four times, at last he went and gathering some ferns and flowers from off the coffin opened the door and held them out; still it was in vain, the knocking again occurred at the door, and this time he took little Ada and led her to the door, when he appeared to succeed in inducing the person to come in. He said, " 'It is ——' (a little servant girl who had died two days previously). " How very curious, she seems scarcely to know that she has passed away, and says, she does not like to come into the room where there is anybody dead. Every time I opened the door she said, 'No thank you, I would sooner not!' But little Dannie wanted her to come in and rapped, or rather got another spirit to rap for him at the door, every time I shut it. I took the flowers and ferns to shew her there was nothing disagreeable about the room, and then I took little Ada with me, and she has come in now and is standing there in the corner. She will move this fern that I have placed here on the table near her." Home placed a fern on the table, and presently we saw it taken up and put down again. He then awoke.

———

The next afternoon the little body was placed in the ground. During the service a slight shower came on; but just at the conclusion, when we had lowered the coffin to its place, a bright beam of sunshine broke out, flooding us with light; and a beautiful rainbow appeared in the heavens. On our way home every one remarked that the burial service, which is in general so impressive, had that day while in church sounded strangely flat and unprofitable. Mrs. Cox asked how it was that the clergyman had not used the words dust to dust, ashes to ashes, earth to earth. We assured her he had; but she declared she had not heard them, although standing as near to him as any of us.

No. 28.—Séance.

The same evening we had a *séance*, and Home was entranced—Mr. Cox speaking through him. He turned to Mrs. Cox and said, " I was there with little Dannie to-day, but I did not like to take him into the church; we waited outside. The reason why the service did not impress any of you is, that there was no spiritual presence inside the building—nothing but the bare rafters. We magnetized you to prevent your hearing the words—dust to dust, ashes to ashes, earth to earth. Now, if you had been consigning to the earth this day the body of some celebrated mediæval ecclesiastic or great saint, those circumstances of the shower of rain, the bright gleam of sun, and the rainbow, would have been considered miraculous. Of course they were not so; it is unreasonable to think that God's great laws should be interfered with to give you a rainbow. Yet was it the result of interference in this way. We knew by our superior knowledge of meteorology, and the laws that govern those things, that at that hour on Thursday, there would probably be a combination of circumstances that would produce those effects. We therefore very strongly impressed Dan to insist upon having the funeral on Thursday instead of Friday, which was the day you had fixed upon; and we impressed him to make you all hurry. You remember how he did hurry you all on your way to church. As it happened, you arrived at the right time, and everything occurred just as we expected. That is all the interference there was." He then spoke for some time to Mrs. Cox, exhorting her to have patience and courage, and to trust in God. The "Nameless Doctor" then took possession of Home; who after walking about the room thinking, took little Ada's hand in his, and said to Mrs. Cox, " This child's stomach is of more importance now than her brain; do not push her too much in her studies." Dr. Elliotson then took possession of him, and he spoke for some time to Mrs. Cox. Then turning to me he said, " I suppose you have found out, if not you will—I know I did when on earth—that if you try and climb up one rung higher on the ladder of knowledge than others, the world will scream and say you are going to tumble down and break your neck; but when they find you stick there pretty safely, they will try and scramble up after you, and endeavour to get ahead of you. Provided your own conscience does not reprove you, never mind what the world says. As my friend, Mr. Cox said to you yesterday, ' Be constant in a prayerful and earnest search for truth; seek truth, and you will find it.' " He went on speaking for some time, describing different phases of worldly ambition, and warning us against them.

No. 29.—*Séance, November 3rd*, 1868.

In the account of the phenomena that occurred at Homburg, mention is made of Home finding a death's-head moth; of my being told to play with two louis, and with the proceeds to buy a locket for it. I took the moth to Tessier's, and ordered a crystal medallion to be made for it. In due course it was sent home. While Home was sitting with little Dannie Cox, during his last illness, the locket in his pocket was broken by a blow from some invisible hand, or other agency. We speculated as to the reason for this, but came to no satisfactory result. The day before yesterday I asked for the locket, in order to get it mended. When I saw it, I thought that the material was glass and not crystal. I took it to my optician, and found I was correct. I then took it to Tessier's to have a proper crystal made. Yesterday, while washing my hands before dinner, I said to Home, " I now know why the locket was broken; it was to call attention to the fact that glass had been substituted for crystal." Immediately a spirit rapped " Yes," very loudly, on the dressing table. About nine o'clock I was reading; Home lying on the sofa. He said, " There is a strong spirit standing near you; he is nicely made, and appears to have nice features, but I cannot see them clearly. His hair is cut very short indeed, and has a sort of mark, not amounting to a scar, upon his cheek bone." I could not think who it was, when it seemed to flash upon me that it was A—— B——, though I could not recognize him the least by the description. Home said, " His name begins with an A." I said, " No; with a B, if it is the person I imagine." " His name begins with an A," he said, " that is, of course, his Christian name." " Well," I said, " that would be right." " Yes," Home said, " his name is A——; he says he will come to us to-night." Home said it was a case of second sight, and asked me to look at his eyes to try and discover the film that is said to cover the eyes of a person during second sight. I could see nothing abnormal about them, except that the pupils were much dilated; on applying light near them they contracted naturally. The vision had nearly faded when I examined his eyes.

Later in the evening we had a *séance*. Present: C. and E. Wynne, C. and B. Nixon, James Gore-Booth, Home and myself. We sat for about an hour, and scarcely anything occurred. We then went into the dining room to have a cup of tea, and raps came upon the table. We returned to the other room and sat down, but had only very faint indications of spiritual presence. Home said to me, " Let you and I and

Charlie Wynne go into the bed room by ourselves for a minute, perhaps they would tell us the reason why we have no manifestations." We did so, and put our hands upon a small table. The table tilted itself into Charlie's lap; and we had messages given by tilts of the table, by raps on the table, and on the floor.

Message to Charlie.—" *We are developing you. You heard sounds like drops of rain upon your pillow; you will soon be able to have raps; persevere in sitting as you have done at home: you will be rewarded by manifestations.*" Charlie asked, " Was that shaking of my bed anything spiritual?" " *Yes, like this table is shaken.*" Charlie: " Yes, that is like it exactly; but I do not like to be shaken in bed." The table was shaken more violently, as if to say that perhaps he would be shaken again. Charlie: " Who shook me?" " *Grandfather William. We took away the pain from Emmy the other night.*" In answer to a question, they said there was nothing antagonistic in any of the party, but that Dan was not in a good condition. We joined the rest again, but had no further manifestations.

———

After we had gone to bed, Home went into a trance; for some time he spoke with difficulty. He asked me who certain people were. " Who is Willoughby Wynne? Who is Emily?" he then said something about a pretty little child and two Amys; and also there was an uncle of mine there who used to give me apples out of his pocket. I asked " Wyndham?" he said " No, Goold." "Francis?" I asked; "Yes," he said, "Francis." He then began to speak quite clearly, and said " We would often like to tell you who we are, but our opportunities of communicating are so rare and so short, that we cannot generally do so. There are so many difficulties in the way, it is like sending messages along wires that are continually breaking and getting out of order. We could scarcely do anything to-night. Dan ought not to have drank a second cup of tea, or that second glass of sherry at dinner; the slightest thing is sufficient to prevent anything occurring. Ah, A—— has just come in; he has come bustling into the room; you heard him.' I said, ' Well, I heard a noise as if the door had been opened. ' Yes,' he said, ' that was him; you will always know when A—— comes; he will make a sound like that at the door. He is standing close to you now, looking straight at you. He does not quite understand his position yet, poor fellow. He cannot disabuse himself of the idea that he is going to be punished. He does not think that according to the life that he led on earth he ought to be in the company of those who are here in the same room. He says, ' I am going to help you out of a scrape, old fellow.' He has a

strange regret at having left the earth ; he was in love ; he will
of course soon cease to regret it ; but he does not quite
understand himself as yet. He asked us why you had put your
glasses there close to you ; and when we told him in case he or
any of us made ourselves visible to you, you wished to be able
to use them, he could not understand that he could possibly
make himself apparent to you. He was a bit of a fop ; fond of
being neat and tidy, and very careful of his hands ; he had very
nice hands."

(In answer to a remark of mine). " He says he has nothing
to forgive. He has been a good deal with your mother ; she is
fond of him ; he is very truthful. He is very fond of his father ;
he says that his father is honest in his belief, and that is more
than he can say for most people. Your mother and he, and all
of us have been consulting about you, as regards a question you
promised your father that you would ask. You had better
absolve yourself from that obligation, for your mother would
not like you to ask her about any single or particular dogma

That religion in which God's created creatures worship him
in spirit and in truth, forgetful of self, and casting aside worldly
ambition is a true religion, nor does it matter by what title you
choose to call it. There is too much of worldly ambition and
love of power mixed up in religion." Home then spoke to me
about some purely personal matters, and then for some time on
the subject that atonement must be made for all wrong done on
earth. " Ah," he said, " Many that are very high and mighty
when with you, must become very humble indeed when they
come to us ; you would scarcely think that Alexander the Great
is yet, as it were, in the position of the lowest servant ; he did
certain things on earth that he knew to be very wrong, and he
was a very powerful man—powerful, I mean magnetically. Every
great general, statesman, or orator, is full of magnetism. The
power of an orator, the way he draws his audience to him, is
mainly due to his magnetic attraction. We sometimes magnetise
you, and you are not aware of it. You were magnetised just
now, and you heard a spirit shout." I said, " I am not aware
that I did." " You did not notice it ; you did not know what it
was, and you did not pay any attention to it ; but you heard it.
The spirit wanted to come into the room, but he knew he could
not. He was not worthy to come into the presence of those who
are in the room, no one said anything to him—no one rebuked
him ; but he felt his own unworthiness, and rushed away screaming, as you would if suffering pain ; as you, if some one were
telling you some dreadful harrowing story, would cry out to stop
them, thus he felt what he was, and fled away. Now some men
would call him a devil, but he is not ; he will try and make

amends, and eventually all will come right. God could not create what you call a devil."

Home then began talking about dreams. He said, "You may think it a very curious theory, but it is true, that we are sometimes in communion with your spirits when we cannot even see your bodies. In sleep, sometimes, your spirits are, as it were, nearer to us, more open to impression. Of course, as you all know, it is the mortal body only that requires sleep; the spirit is always awake. Now, with you, your stomach is so much out of order, your digestion so hard, and in such a bad state, that any impression upon you in sleep takes a fleeting and painful nature."

(In answer to a Question). "Yes, you can take it with other medicine. Take it for a fortnight, then leave off for a fortnight, then take it again, and in two months or so we can judge of the effect. We can only tell these things by watching the effect." Home was then silent for a short time. When he next spoke, he spoke as little Dannie Cox. He said, "Oh! I say! now look here (two expressions Dannie habitually used when on earth)! I like you to pray, it does good, and I am fond of you. Never you mind about that fern, you shall have another one. Perhaps you will find it yet, for I am not sure that it is destroyed; at any rate, never you mind about it; if it is, you shall have another. Dan is going to awake now. When he has awoke, if you will go and sit down on his bed for a minute I will come." I did so, telling Home that I wanted to see if we should have any manifestations. We heard a spirit come in and walk about the room; and perceived a light near the ceiling. Little Dannie Cox then came and moved away a pillow that Home had over his feet. He stroked and pulled my feet, and sat on them; and when Home asked him if his mother was asleep, he bounced up and down on my feet, feeling just as heavy as a child of his age would if in the flesh. We also saw the same sort of little star we had seen at Stockton. He then said, "Now, good night," and stood upon the foot of the bed. I saw him distinctly as a shadowy figure, of the same size as his mortal body, with apparently some loose drapery on. His hand was stretched out towards us waving about. The hand and arm were directly between me and the window, and interrupted the light as palpably as if made of solid flesh and bone.

No. 30.—*Séance held at Mrs. Hennings' House, at Norwood.*

Present: Mr. Home, Mrs. Hennings, Mrs. Jencken, Mr. Jencken, Mr. Saal, Mr. Hurt, and myself. The peculiarity of this *séance* was that the manifestations appear to have been conducted with a view rather to convince the spirits present, than the mortals.

Mr. Saal is a medium, but has been accustomed to make a joke of the whole thing; and has latterly been a good deal troubled and annoyed by the spirits. We had physical manifestations—tilting and raising of the table, movements of the piano, currents of air, raps, &c., &c. A series of messages were then delivered to Mr. Saal. He was told that he should not treat spirits in a manner that he would not dare to exercise towards mortals. Good advice was given him, and he was told to submit all to his reason, for it was given him for that purpose. Suppose, they said, a spirit were to tell you to put your finger in the candle, you would be very foolish to do so; you would be burnt; but if a spirit was to tell you to do this, and then magnetize you, causing you to feel that some substance, as it were, had been placed over your skin, you might reasonably think means had been taken to prevent your being burned, and then you would be right to try. Home then went into a trance. He walked about the room, opened the door, and appeared to welcome a number of people. He then seemed to be explaining to them the different phenomena that had occurred in that room. He showed how the table had been raised, the piano and the furniture moved, &c.; and apparently explained the process of elongation, pointing to certain marks on the wall that had been made on a previous occasion to record the height to which he had attained. He then went to the fire-place; stirred the coals into a blaze, and seemed to recount how he had handled hot embers. He sat for some time on the hearth, and then got up and walked about a little while, and taking up from the other table Glanvill's book on Witchcraft, he appeared distressed. He brought the book to me, and placed my right hand flat upon the cover, supporting it himself underneath; raps came upon the book. He gradually withdrew his hand until the book was supported by one finger only; lastly, he withdrew that also, and the book was suspended in the air, or rather adhered to my open hand. My fingers were not near the edges, my hand was extended flat upon the cover; I could not have grasped and retained the book in any way; it simply adhered to my hand. Home seemed pleased at this, and laughed, and turned round to the (to us) invisible spectators, as much as to say, "Do you see that?" He repeated this experiment, making me place my left hand upon his, which he placed underneath the book, in order, as he said, that I might feel that his hand left the book. When he withdrew his hand, there was a space between it and the book of, I should say, three inches. The book felt to me as though supported from beneath by a cushion or column of air. He then placed *Glanvill on Witchcraft* on the table, and, leaving the room, brought back with him a large volume on Mythology, which he had taken from a perfectly dark library; he also brought his own book, *Reminiscences in My Life*, and laid them both upon the table. He then walked about the room, and appeared to be expostulating with the spirits, then sitting down he placed the three books before him, in the form of a cross, and began speaking about them. "This," he said, placing his hand on the mythological book, "is pure Materialism; This," touching Glanvill, "Religion materialized; and this," taking his own book, "Materialism spiritualized. The first, blood to appease a God; the second, blood to appease mankind; the third, the blood of the soul to appease mankind. Though you boast of your civilization, and though there are no longer persecutions of fire and blood: yet is there a moral persecution, and, in many respects, your age is as dark as any. Who will dispel this darkness? Who is bold enough to take the broom and clear away the cobwebs? It must come from the material side—from your side—we cannot do it." He spoke for a long time, more than half an hour I should think. He likened different men's ideas of God to the different attempts we would all make to delineate the highest peak of the Himalayas. "None of you," he said, "have seen it; you would all draw a different form and none of you would be right."

He was very sarcastic about the wise men of the day, who he said, were afraid to investigate for fear of discovering something beyond their own philosophy, and which they could not account for; and yet, not one of them could tell you why one man's hair is light and another's dark. "You are much puzzled," he said, "about many things. Know that the highest angels also are lost in wonder and awe at many things." While talking, he appeared to become uneasy and getting up, said, "There is a spirit here that will go on arguing with Dr. Elliotson, so that he cannot attend to anything; I must really interfere," and he walked to the other end of the room, where he seemed to expostulate with some one. Coming back he said, "Dr. Elliotson and Dr. Jencken have invited a number of spirits here, they did not know the nature of manifestations, and were anxious to see them. Owing to circumstances not being favourable at first we failed to do what we wished and they are not satisfied, we will try again now." He went to the fire, poked up the coals, and putting his hand in, drew out a hot burning ember, about twice the size of an orange; this he carried about the room, as if to shew it to the spirits, and then brought it to us; we all examined it. He then put it back in the fire and showed us his hands; they were not in the least blackened or scorched, neither did they smell of fire, but on the contrary of a sweet scent which he threw off from his fingers at us across the table. Having apparently spoken to some spirit, he went back to the fire, and with his hand stirred the embers into a flame; then kneeling down, he placed his face right among the burning coals, moving it about as though bathing it in water. Then, getting up, he held his finger for some time in the flame of the candle. Presently, he took the same lump of coal he had previously handled and came over to us, blowing upon it to make it brighter. He then walked slowly round the table, and said, " I want to see which of you will be the best subject. Ah! Adare will be the easiest, because he has been most with Dan." Mr. Jencken held out his hand, saying, "Put it in mine," Home said, " No no, touch it and see," he touched it with the tip of his finger and burnt himself. Home then held it within four or five inches of Mr. Saal's and Mr. Hurt's hands, and they could not endure the heat. He came to me and said, "Now, if you are not afraid, hold out your hand;" I did so, and having made two rapid passes over my hand, he placed the coal in it. I must have held it for half a minute, long enough to have burned my hand fearfully; the coal felt scarcely warm. Home then took it away, laughed, and seemed much pleased. As he was going back to the fire-place, he suddenly turned round and said, " Why, just fancy, some of them think that only one side of the ember was hot." He told me to make a hollow of both my hands; I did so, and he placed the coal in them, and then put both his on the top of the coal, so that it was completely covered by our four hands, and we held it there for some time. Upon this occasion scarcely any heat at all could be perceived. After having replaced the coal in the fire, he went and held his hand—the fingers being extended downwards—about nine inches above a vase of flowers, " You will see," he said, " That I can withdraw the moisture and scent from the flowers." He came over to me and rubbed my hands, imparting the odour of the flowers to them ; his fingers were quite moist as with dew; he also flipped the moisture, and with it the scent from his fingers to each person. He now appeared quite satisfied, and after speaking a little to the spirits in the room, opened the door and bowed them out, and then resumed his seat. "Now," he said, "Do you all realise that you have seen what is called a miracle, yet in reality it is no such thing. All these phenomena only shew our superior acquaintance with natural laws, and our power over material substances. Mankind ought to have the same power over the material world in which he lives; you little know the power that is in you; had you faith, you could do things you little dream of." He spoke some time in this strain, and then said, "Dan is going to awake now, do not tell him what has occurred, but let him wash his hands." When he awoke, he was much exhausted, but after washing, appeared quite refreshed. We examined him closely; there was no sign—not even the smell—of fire about him, neither was a hair of his head singed.

No. 31.—Séance.

The other night, having been unwell for some days, I went to bed very uncomfortable, and agueish; I could not get warm. Home's bed was rocked about, and he said, "I do not know who you are, but unless there is some object in it, I wish you would leave off rocking my bed, for it makes me dizzy. The bed left off shaking and a spirit spelt out "*Adah.*" She said, "*I am here, and seek to do you good ; can you imagine my inexpressible joy, your angel mother has taken my hand in hers.*" Home went into a trance, got out of bed, wrapped a fur rug round his middle, then warmed his hands at the fire, and commenced shampooing me over my chest, stomach, legs and feet. He then took off my fur rug, warmed it at the fire, and put it on again, and made passes over my head, retreating as he did so to the further side of the room. He then got into bed and awoke. I fell asleep soon and slept soundly.

No. 32.

Last night, the 11th, I had gone to bed about nine o'clock, and Home an hour later. Charlie Wynne happening to look in, he sat down in the bed room and smoked. We were talking on serious subjects, and a spirit joined in our conversation. Home went into a sort of half trance and spoke for a short time. After Charlie had gone, Home had a second-sight vision. He said that he saw a wonderfully beautiful flower, the stem purple, the leaves the purest white, the flower the deepest crimson, turning to purple, each colour emitting a light of the same tint. As he looked it changed and he said it had reference to what we had been talking about, namely, whether there was change in the next world. It was to shew that there is. "You were speculating," he said, " as to whether spirits could visit planets. They can visit them, planet after planet, star after star, world after world, through infinity, through space. Without change and progression they would not be happy." He then said, "The tobacco smoke is very bad, I was going into a deep trance, but that prevented it; I see it, not as a cloud of smoke, but as material particles."

ADARE: "But it could not be helped, I could not have stopped him."

HOME: "You might, it was only false modesty, Charlie would not have minded."

ADARE: "But if I had stopped him when I saw you were going into a trance it would have been too late."

HOME: "Yes, but you might have prevented it at first, it was at any rate very bad for you." Home was at this time only as it were half entranced, he became quite entranced and said, "Tell Dan in the morning that a Turkish bath will be good for him." He then got up and began blowing as if to dispel the smoke, and agitated the window blinds also, for the same purpose. He said, "You have a stiffness about the head yet." He got out of bed, came to me, and began rubbing and kneeding the back of my head, and the upper part of my spine, occasionally extending his hand behind him, and obtaining some moisture upon his fingers. I thought at the time that he was using a phial of spirits of camphor, that had been on the dressing table, but I discovered afterwards that I had been mistaken. He finished by vigorously rubbing my feet and legs; he then got into bed, rubbed his own chest, legs and arms, and soon after awoke.

No. 33.—Séance.

Last Sunday we had a *séance* at Norwood. Present: Major Drayson, Mr. Collins, Mr. and Mrs. Jencken, Mrs. Hennings, myself, Home, Charlie Wynne, and a Prussian. We had strong physical manifestations, but none of the higher sort, as two of the party were occupied in investigations. Charlie happened to mention to some one a rather curious reason that a lady of his acquaintance had given for not believing in Spiritualism, namely, that she had lived 50 years in the world without hearing of it, and that therefore it could not be true. A spirit said, "*She forgot that people had lived before her, and would in all probability live after her. Fortunately all have not her organism.*"

About ten days ago we had a *séance* at Ashley House with Henry and James Gore Booth. We had good physical manifestations, which I think satisfied James.

No. 34.—October 27th.

Last night I was saying to Home, that it was curious my meeting him in such an unexpected manner at Malvern, and wondering why it was that after having known each other in Paris, we should have remained entirely separated for so many years. I said that there must of course be a reason for it. "Perhaps,"

I said, " my mother might not have liked my investigation of Spiritualism." Immediately a spirit rapped on a table by my bedside, " *Yes*," meaning that she would not have approved of it. Recognizing the raps, I asked if my mother was there, and was told, " *Yes*." Home asked, " But do you now object to it?" Answer, " *No, it adds greatly to my happiness.*" After a pause, " *My boy; now more than ever, my own boy.*" We then heard one of the ornaments upon the wall being moved, and judged by the position of the sound that it proceeded from a benitier that was suspended over Home's head, the benitier consisted of a flat slab of marble, with two guardian angels represented on it, and a vessel for holy water. We heard the benitier removed from the wall. My mother spelled out, " *I bless you not with water, but by the pure presence of a spirit;*" and I then saw a hand and arm extended over me, between me and the light of the window. The fingers were stretched out, and the hand descended towards me, waving in an attitude of blessing until close to my face, when it disappeared. Home then said, " I see my Sacha (his wife); she is standing near the foot of the bed, and has got the benitier in her hand." I could see neither the spirit nor the benitier. He said, " She is bringing it over to me; it is pressed against my forehead; she is making the sign of the cross with it on my face." Directly after I saw the benitier in the air, near me; it came quite close, pressed against my face, and made the sign of the cross. I could see no figure or anything supporting it. Sacha then said, " *I bless you both.*" The benitier was placed on Home's bed, near the foot, and left there. Home said, " Do tell me, Sacha, for otherwise I would not feel comfortable about it; did you take down the benitier because you do not like it to be there?" Answer, " *No.*" " Do you then like it?" " *Yes, because it is a symbol of guardian spirits*" (referring to the figures upon it). She then said, " *And now a fond good night;*" and my mother added, " *God bless you both.*"

No. 35.—Séance.

We had a very pretty *séance* at Mr. S. C. Hall's, the beginning of last week. They had just come into their new house at Ashley Place. There were only Mr. and Mrs. Hall, Home, myself and one friend present. Home went into a trance, and as it were, consecrated the house. He prayed most earnestly and beautifully at the threshold, at the hearth, at the dining table, and at Mr. Hall's writing table. It was very striking. Dr. Elliotson then spoke for some time through Home, and said, " I am waiting for Dr. Ashburner, it will not be long before he joins us, and right glad I shall be when he does."

No. 36.

Last night Home went into a trance, and spoke about two strange spirits that were present. "Oh, there are a number of men here, they are standing in a ring, and are writing in little books: every now and then they dash them down; but they are compelled to take them up and go on; they are very angry with each other, for each one thinks that he has found out something much to his advantage, and then he is disgusted to find that the others know it. There is Fred Goodwin and a man called Campbell among them, and there is one who seems in a sort of mist, he says, 'You may put me down for what you please.'"

ADARE: "Why they must be betting."

HOME: "Yes, they are betting, and they must go on although they hate it. There is a regular barrier between you and them, they would be disagreeable to you if they came too close. It seems as though your mother had by her love woven a sort of net between you, so that you may see how horrible it is; but still may not be hurt by them."

I now heard a sound as of a horse galloping in the air.

HOME: "Do you hear that horse? You will always know that C—— D—— is near when you hear that noise. He did not now make it himself; he cannot; other spirits made it for him."

ADARE: "Will C—— D—— have to keep the company of these betting men?"

HOME: "Yes, he will for a time, and it will be painful to him, for he was not by nature coarse; all his coarseness was put on for bravado."

ADARE: "Will he have to attend races?"

HOME: "Yes, he will; and will see all the evil, all the rascality and misery resulting from them. He will not wish to go there; but he will be compelled by an irresistible impulse to do so until he becomes purified, and fitted for better things."

ADARE: "I hope that may not be long."

HOME: "It does not appear to me that it will be long; his nature is good; he was very kind and did many good actions. Many old and poor people to whom he was kind, and some of his friends also who went before him, are very anxious about him, and pray earnestly for him. Altogether it does not seem that it will be long. C—— D—— does not quite understand himself yet; he is conscious, but he does not know whether he is dead or not. His mother is near him, and will be of use to him. She was a very worldly woman; she would be higher than she is were it not for that." Home was then silent for a short time, he became much agitated, and said, "Oh yes, I am sure we are very much obliged to you indeed, are we not, Adare? We mortals are very much obliged to you. Oh, please don't; Oh, don't strike him! Oh—(and there came a noise in 'the corner of the room like a blow struck)—did you hear that? he hit him. Ah, they have all gone. Our mothers would not let them come any nearer—they have gone now—they would have been disagreeable if they had been nearer—they were so very rude and coarse—they were boxers—they made the noise like of a horse galloping, and then they said they had made a cursed row for us, and that we were not thankful enough; and they were angry. One of them said, ' Come away, and let the chaps go to sleep; ' but another got very angry, and got him in a corner and hit him; you heard the blow." Home afterwards said, "Of course he could not hurt him; all these things are done to shew you that perfect individuality exists in the other world." Home soon after awoke.

No. 37.—Séance at Ashley House, November 20th.

Last night the Master of Lindsay dined here. About an hour after dinner, the drawing-room being very full of tobacco smoke, we went and sat down at the table in the dining-room. Immediately we had decided manifestations. The table was strongly moved; my chair was rocked about; Lindsay and Home heard a voice; and we all heard a spirit moving about the room. We were told to go back into the other room. Nothing occurred at the table. Home got very drowsy—half unconscious. He said he could see the table covered with light, and light coming from my hands. He said, " How very curious, I can see these words quite plain : ' Some one in a high position will commit suicide. He said he had taken an overdose of medicine and drugged himself.' " After a short time he roused himself, and got better, and presently went into a trance. He said to me, "There are a great number of Roman Catholic spirits about you." I asked if I knew any of them. " Yes, there is one you knew, a priest, a very tall man. There are a great many of them. It is curious, they seem to be going through some sort of ceremony." He began speaking of the strange and horrible influences about the Tower (Lindsay is quartered at the Tower). He said, " They are very dreadful, but can do no harm; they are obliged to remain at the Tower; they could not even make manifestations, were a séance to be held there. There is one among them, could he manifest himself, it would be by a most horrible stench, as of corrupt flesh." He described him as having elevated eyebrows, pointed beard, and wearing a ruffle.

We asked if he had been a torturor, or anything of that sort. "No," he said, "but an instigator of those things. His tools and accomplices have all gone. He is left alone—quite alone—walking always round and round." "How unhappy," I said, "he must be." "Unhappy," he replied, "Oh, he bears a weight of misery upon him that would crush mountains. Oh, those who perhaps here have worn upon their heads a crown, when they appear before God and before His throne, have to exchange it for a weight of woe upon their brows that would seem insupportable." He described several spirits at the Tower in most graphic language. At last he appeared to see some spirit that he could not endure. "Oh! go away! Go away!" he said, "You must go away!" He sobbed convulsively; tore open his coat and waistcoat; took off his cravat and collar, and appeared to be suffering very much. Presently he got better, and we enquired who the spirit was; he shuddered, and told us not to seek to know. I asked why these influences were suffered to come about us. He said, "It is good you should know that there are two sides to the picture, for fear that you might bring upon yourselves such suffering as these feel." He then got up; pulled off his boots; took a rose from a vase, and walked into the centre of the room. Presently he came close to me, and apparently spoke to a spirit. "Yes," he said, "Thank you." Then turning to me, said, "When Dan went into the middle of the room, they took him by the throat, and tore this button off his shirt; they threw it at you, and you heard it drop; and then they tried to throw it in the fire, but they had to bring it back to him." I asked, "Why did he take off his boots?" "Just to typify his defencelessness; that is why he took the rose, to shew his goodwill. It is thus that right overcomes wrong. Why, even if a beast were suffering pain, and you went up and threatened it, you could do no good; but if you went soothingly and gently, though at first it might resist, not knowing you, yet it would soon become passive. Ah, the influence is all changed." Turning to Lindsay, he said, "You will have a curious manifestation at the Tower, quite alone." Lindsay asked him about it. "I must not tell you anything about it. Adare, perhaps, may be informed; but if you were, your mind would become too positive, and that would surely stop it." He got up; walked about; patted me on the shoulder, saying, "You are all right, you are going to get quite well soon." He sat down and said, "I see an old man with silver locks; he has on a mantle, covered with stars." "Who is he?" I asked. "Pythagoras. He is much interested about winds and tides; he has been studying the passage of the Red Sea. He says it was quite a natural phenomenon, and has occurred three or four times before the Jews crossed, and once since. It is a curious circumstance, owing to a combination of wind and of tide." I said, " Was it observed when it occurred since ?" " He says, No, he thinks not," Home replied, " But when it occurs again, men will observe it." " Are we about correct as to the spot where the Jews crossed ?" " Oh, yes, tolerably correct. He (Pythagoras) was correct in his theory, that man should never wear the skins of beasts ; there is an influence in them that is never lost. He was right ; but he exaggerated. You must, for instance, wear leather for your feet, the influence is so slight and so easily counteracted by other influences that it does you no harm. Cagliostro is often with Lindsay, because he takes an interest in freemasonry. You may tell Dan that he has not been to him for a long time; but he will come again to him. C—— D—— is very anxious to come to you, but he cannot to-night. I see a woman, she represents Fate, she has in her hand a rosebud, it contains a worm that has eaten it to the core, she is fastening it to a horse—the horse is galloping off—oh, he looks as if he must break his neck. Ah, the rosebud has fallen off now. Every-body was anxious, before it was fastened to the horse, to get at it, see it, and sniff at it ; but now there are only two or three who have a good word to say for it." " Is this emblematic of C—— D——?" "Yes it is. The same spirit is here that foretold all those earthquakes and convulsions of nature, he is standing a long way off ; but he seems anxious to say that there will be a great war, or plague, or some national disaster of that sort before long." " In Europe ?" " Yes." " In England ?" " No ; it seems rather that it is to be in France." " Is it a war between France and Prussia ?" " No ; it does not seem to be." Home got up, walked about, sat down again, and turning to me, said— " The doctor is pleased with you, boy." " What doctor ?" I said, " Why, Dan's silent doctor ; he says you will get all right, the sooner you go away for a little change the better ; but you must not take a long journey, or cross the sea, it would be very foolish to do so, a chill might strike in again upon your stomach. He says that the other night, when he rubbed the back of your neck, he did not make use of any liquid, as you thought. If Dan's fingers had been wet, they would have felt rough to the skin ; but they did not." I said " No ; they felt oily." " Exactly ; like oleaginous matter ; still it was in reality nothing but very strong influence. I cannot explain this to you, you would not understand it. He saved you from very acute suffering, from violent pain in your head ; he cut it off from your head, and confined the disease to your stomach." Home laughed and said, " Some of your relatives think that you have made yourself ill by being at so many *séances*." " What am I to do to dispel that idea?" " Why, do just what you are doing; get well to be sure, that is the best thing." Home then awoke.

No. 38.—Séance.

Last Monday we had a *séance* at Mr. S. C. Hall's—which was a failure. We had scarcely any manifestations. At the close, the spirits asked for a decanter of water, they directed Home and the two Misses Bertolacci to stand up and hold their hands in a certain position above and below it; and we were directed to stand round. They held the decanter for some time, magnetizing it, and were then told by the spirits to place it upon the table. The spirits said, " *Adare is to take a wine glass full night and morning, and with the blessing of Christ, he will be cured in six days.*"

No. 39.—*Séance at Ashley House, Tuesday, November 24th.*

Last Sunday Home went to Norwood; Lindsay accompanied him. They had a *séance*, but scarcely any manifestations. Lindsay came back here with Home about eleven o'clock. We three sat round the table and had a very curious *séance*, the room being nearly dark. Lindsay and Home saw spirit forms. I did not; but I saw, as did also the others, phosphorescent lights about the room; balls of light would move along the floor and touch us, feeling like a material substance and highly electrical. Adah Menken was there, and spoke to us a good deal. She removed her book from the table, turned a leaf down, and brought it back, putting it in my hand, and telling me that she had marked a certain place. Little Dannie Cox's spirit came and moved a small chair from the wall, and placed it near the table. He lifted the chair (no one touching it), up in the air, brought it to me, then carried it over the table to Home who was sitting at the other side. He tried to materialise his voice so that we might hear it. We heard the voice distinctly, and he articulated the words " *Uncle Dan.*" The spirits gave one message in a curious way. Lindsay was anxious to be touched. They said, " *All in good—*" and then turning the hands of a clock that was not going, so as to make it tick and strike, finished the sentence, " *All in good time.*" The table we were sitting at was twice raised in the air so high that we could see under it without stooping. It was altogether a wonderful *séance*. We had a number of messages, but I forget them.

No. 40.—*Séance.*

Last night Lindsay called; he said that he had had strong manifestations that evening when alone, and had been told to go to Ashley Place. About 11 o'clock Home came in. We sat round the table and had a most wonderful *séance*. The room was nearly dark. We had physical manifestations. Home went into a trance; he walked about the room for some time, arranging the light, and talking to himself; he then opened the window, drawing the curtains, so that we could see nothing but his head; and got outside the window. This frightened us, and Lindsay wanted to stop him, but did not. Presently, he came back and told us that we had no faith whatever, or we would not have been alarmed for his safety. He went into the next room, and we saw him pour out from a bottle on the table about half a large wine glass of brandy. He brought the glass back with him; then partially covering himself with the window curtains, but holding the glass with the brandy in it above his head, between us and the window, so that we could see it, he was lifted off the floor about four or five feet. While in the air, we saw a bright light in the glass; presently, he came down and showed us that the glass was empty, by turning it upside down; he also came to us and turned it upside down upon our hands; then going back to the window, he held the glass up, and we heard the liquid drop into it. He began talking about the brandy, and said "It is under certain circumstances a demon, and real devil; but if properly used, it is most beneficial." As he said this the light became visible in the glass, and he was again raised in the air; "But," he said, "if improperly used, it becomes so," (the light disappeared) "and drags you down, down, lower and lower;" and as he spoke he sank gradually down till he touched the floor with the glass. He again raised the glass above his head and the liquor was withdrawn. He then told me to come and hold my hand above the glass; I did so, and the liquor fell over and through my fingers into the glass, dropping from the air above me. I sat down and asked him where on earth the liquor went to. "Oh," he said, "the spirit that is making the experiment is obliged to form a material substance to retain the fluid. He might drink it, or hold it in his mouth; in this case he held it in his hand."

ADARE : "When you say his hand, do you mean his own hand, or that he created a substance like a hand to hold it; was he obliged to be there to hold it, or could he have been at the other side of the room?"

HOME : "Of course he must be there; it was his own hand made material for the moment to hold the liquid, as a hand is made material when you touch or feel it."

ADARE: "Then that story in Howitt's book of a spirit drinking a glass beer may be true?"

HOME: "Oh, yes; certainly it may."

ADARE: "But could he swallow and retain it?"

HOME: (laughing) "No, he could not retain it long, he must have held the beer for a time, but it must have been spilled outside If the doors and windows had been shut, so that he could not carry it out of the room, it must have fallen upon the floor."

ADARE: "He could not then transport it through a solid substance?"

HOME: "Oh dear no, certainly not! If, when the liquid in that glass was retained in the air, you had put your hand there, it would have fallen to the ground." He then said, "I am going to take the strength from the brandy," and he began making passes over the glass and flipping his fingers, sending a strong smell of spirit through the room; in about five minutes he had made the brandy as weak as very weak brandy and water; it scarcely tasted at all of spirit; both Lindsay and I tasted it, at the moment, and also some time after the *séance* was over. Home then began to walk about and talked, or rather some spirit talked through him; he turned and said to some spirit, "Well, really I think you had better not, we don't know you, or know anything about you; thank you, yes, that will do quite well." A chair then moved up to the table between Lindsay and me, and Home said that the spirit who had tried the experiments with the brandy was sitting there; Lindsay could see him, I could not. Home, or rather a spirit talking through him, then began speaking about manifestations to this spirit, but in such a low tone, I could only now and then catch what he said. This spirit appeared ignorant of how to raise a substance in the air, and the spirit who was talking through Home seemed much amused at what he said. He tried experiments with my chair, but could not succeed, and Home laughed. He then began talking about lifting him (Home) up, and after speaking for some time in a low tone, apparently suggesting different ways, he said, "Well, then, I will lift him on to the table and sling him right off into the air." "Oh, yes," said the other,* "and perhaps break his leg, that will never do." They then arranged that he was to try by lifting him first on to the back of my chair. Accordingly, in about a minute, Home was lifted up on to the back of my chair. "Now," he said, "take hold of Dan's feet." I took both his feet in my hands, and away he went up into the air so high that I was obliged to let go his feet; he was carried

---

* Apparently two spirits were at this time speaking alternately, through Mr. Home, so as to let us know the meaning of what they were doing with him, and what the subject of their conversation was.

along the wall, brushing past the pictures, to the opposite side of
the room; he then called me over to him. I took his hand, and
felt him alight upon the floor; he sat down upon the sofa and
laughed, saying, "That was very badly done, you knocked Dan
up against the pictures." Home got up, opened the door, pulled
up the blind and made the room much lighter; then sitting
down, said, "We will lift Dan up again better presently,
and in a clearer light so that you can see better. Always
examine well, never forget to use your reason in these matters."
He was not however raised again, for some other spirits anxious
to communicate came, and those who were experimentalizing
gave way. "Ah!" Home said, "There is an unadvanced
spirit here; you perceive the earthy smell?" We both noticed
it, and asked if he had long left this world. "No, only a
short time." We then heard the noise like of a horse galloping,
and I knew C—— D—— was there. I said, "Is C—— D——
here?" "Yes," he said "he is." Home got up and said
(C—— D—— speaking through him), "I suppose you would
think me a brute because I ask for brandy." He took the glass
of brandy, walked about with it, and then put it down and
sat down, and in answer to Lindsay said, "For some years,
with whatever medium it may be, you will always know him by
the sound of the horse. Turning to me, "You did not do as
much as you might for him. You might have advised him and
spoken to him." I said I was truly sorry; I had not thought I
could have done him any good. "Well, he thinks perhaps you
might, but he is not sure that you could; but you might have
tried; he was really attached to you, and is so still. He says as
regards all this (Spiritualism), if you had spoken about it, he
would have called it all damned nonsense; that is what he
would have said then. He wanted to see if he could taste brandy,
but the others would not let him." I said, "Has he any desire for those things now?" "Well, he never did care for brandy;
he was fonder of champagne. He does sometimes think about
those things, but he will soon cease to do so; his desire for
them was produced by bodily weakness, and when he finds
himself suffering no longer from that feeling, he will not want
them. Ah, poor fellow, poor fellow, he is crying; he says
he was not what he ought to have been, but he was not as bad
as he has been painted. He is unhappy; something is weighing
on his mind." I asked questions and received answers, giving
me much information as to the cause of this spirit being
unhappy. He mentioned facts that I knew to be accurate,
thus affording a satisfactory test of identity; but, it being
undesirable that the identity should, in this case be known, I
refrain from mentioning what passed. I then asked, "Can I be

of any use about it?" "He says if the real person is not found out, he will try and manage to impress you—to give you some clue; so that without your name coming forward, you might be of use." (*After a pause*) "Adare, He says, that he would not come back to earth if he could; he feels that he has a better chance of improvement as he is. All will come right, he says, in time; he feels as if he had been ploughed and harrowed, and torn to bits, and may now bring forth fruits. Ah, he is off; restless, very restless. He turns back to say, 'Adare, I would not come back if I could; I know that all is for the best.'" We waited in hopes of Home being lifted in the air again; but the power was expended, and he presently awoke, and we went into the next room. After Lindsay had gone, Home went into a trance for a minute or two, and spoke to me. He said that C—— D——'s coming had prevented them doing what they had wanted. He said, "We were in the room when Dr. Hawkesley was talking to you yesterday, and we much approve of his suggestions. It is the quinine that caused those unpleasant feelings in your head; there was nothing spiritual about it.

No. 41.—Séance at 5, Buckingham Gate, Wednesday, December 16th.

On Sunday last, Charlie Wynne and I went over to Ashley House after dinner. There we found Home and the Master of Lindsay. Home proposed a sitting. We accordingly sat round a table in the small room. There was no light in the room; but the light from the window was sufficient to enable us to distinguish each other, and to see the different articles of furniture. Immediately on sitting down we had physical manifestations and messages, chiefly from Adah Menken. Lindsay saw two spirits on the sofa, and others in different places. Home went into a trance. Adah Menken spoke through him, to what effect I do not remember; also little Dannie Cox. The latter having in speaking to Charlie Wynne called him Charlie, turned to me and said, "Please tell him that we always call people by their Christian names." Home suddenly breaking off in the middle of a sentence said, "Who is this man, E——? What does he want? Do you know him?"

CHARLIE: "Yes, I knew him, he came to me at Lissadell, and told me a variety of circumstances connected with his death."

HOME: "He is come about that. Do you object to his doing so?"

CHARLIE: "Certainly not; I am glad of it."

HOME : " Then he will sit down beside you."

A chair moved of itself from the wall up to the table between Home and Charlie. Charlie said he could feel that there was some one there, but he saw nothing. Lindsay perceived the figure in the chair, and said he was leaning his arm on Charlie's shoulder. The upstart of a long conversation between Charlie and E——, speaking through Home, was that he, E——, would on no account give any information that would lead to the prosecution of . . . . . . That Charlie had been told at Lissadell to let the matter alone; that he had not given the information at Lissadell; that other spirits very anxious on the subject had done so; that they had made some mistakes, and that owing also to the imperfect development of the medium other mistakes had occurred. That some of the information was incorrect he said could be proved by his writing to certain places, when he would find that no person of the name given had been there. He had not been allowed to discover what became of a certain man after his, E——'s, death. God's justice was very different from man's; and God's justice would find him out. He could not and would not have anything to do in the matter.

ADARE : " But you do not object to human justice taking its course?"

HOME : " Oh dear no; it is necessary for the well being of society that it should do so; in human affairs let human justice proceed; but we cannot interfere; God's justice is so different from man's. It is obvious also that were we permitted to continually interfere in these matters, the result would be extremely bad."

Home became much agitated; " Ah," he said, " he has something weighing on his mind; poor, poor fellow !" He laid his head upon my hand on the table and sobbed violently; two or three tears fell upon my hand

HOME : " Do you feel how hot his tears are?"

ADARE : " Yes, I do."

HOME : " They will leave a mark of blood upon your hand."

CHARLIE : " But at Lissadell he told me he was quite happy."

HOME : " So he thought perhaps at the time ; but do you think that a man can be cut off in a moment in that way, leaving his family, who were dependant on him for daily bread, almost totally unprovided for, without a pang of regret and sorrow? Poor fellow, he seems to want to speak about something that has been lost."

CHARLIE : " Is it about some missing papers?"

HOME : " Yes, that is it."

CHARLIE : " Can he tell me where they are?"

F

HOME: "He says that unfortunately most of them were destroyed, but some were sent to his lawyer. He does not tell me the name of his lawyer, but the family will know; he says you will find several among some receipts and other papers in a small box over the door of his study; there are two or three small boxes there. 'Oh! I wish R—— was here. I could tell him things about my affairs that I cannot tell you, Charlie.'"

ADARE: "If R—— comes to London would you like him to meet Home?"

HOME (excited): "Oh, yes; oh, dear yes. Ah! he has gone, poor fellow; he is rather abrupt in his manner, is he not? He does not brook much delay." Home told me to go into the next room and look if the tears had left any mark upon my hand. I perceived a very slight red mark. When I returned he told me to stretch out my hand. I did so, and Dannie Cox touched it with the tip of his finger and said, through Mr. Home, "You will see the marks plainer in the morning." They were rather plainer, but still indistinct, when I awoke the next day. Home then got up and walked about the room. He was both elongated and raised in the air. He spoke in a whisper, as though the spirits were arranging something. He then said to us, "Do not be afraid, and on no account leave your places;" and he went out into the passage. Lindsay suddenly said, "Oh, good heavens! I know what he his going to do; it is too fearful."

ADARE: "What is it?"

LINDSAY: "I cannot tell you, it is too horrible! Adah says that I must tell you; he is going out of the window in the other room, and coming in at this window." We heard Home go into the next room, heard the window thrown up, and presently Home appeared standing upright outside our window; he opened the window and walked in quite coolly. "Ah," he said, "You were good this time," referring to our having sat still and not wished to prevent him. He sat down and laughed.

CHARLIE: "What are you laughing at?"

HOME: "We were thinking that if a policeman had been passing, and had looked up and seen a man turning round and round along the wall in the air he would have been much astonished. Adare, shut the window in the next room." I got up, shut the window, and in coming back remarked that the window was not raised a foot, and that I could not think how he had managed to squeeze through. He arose and said, "Come and see." I went with him; he told me to open the window as it was before, I did so: he told me to stand a little distance off; he then went through the open space, head first, quite rapidly, his body being nearly horizontal and apparently rigid. He came in again, feet foremost, and we returned to the other room. It was so dark I could not see clearly how he was supported outside. He did not appear to grasp, or rest upon, the balustrade, but rather to be swung out and in. Outside each window is a small balcony or ledge, 19 inches deep, bounded by stone balustrades, 18 inches high. The balustrades of the two windows are 7 feet 4 inches apart, measuring from the nearest points. A string-course, 4 inches wide, runs between the windows at the level of the bottom of the balustrade; and another 3 inches wide at the level of the top. Between the window at which Home went out, and that at which he came in, the wall recedes 6 inches. The rooms are on the third floor. Home presently got up, again, told us not to be frightened or to move, and left the room. Adah Menken told Lindsay that they were going to shew us the water test; but for some reason or other I suppose they were unable to do so, for Home came in again directly, sat down and said " Dan must awake now, he will be very nervous; but you must bear with him, it will pass off." I asked Lindsay how Adah had spoken to him on the three occasions. He could scarcely explain; but said it did not sound like an audible human voice; but rather as if the tones were whispered or impressed inside his ear. When Home awoke, he was much agitated; he said he felt as if he had gone through some fearful peril, and that he had a most horrible desire to throw himself out of window; he remained in a very nervous condition for a short time, then gradually became quiet. Having been ordered not to tell him, we said nothing of what had happened. We now had a series of very curious manifestations. Lindsay and Charlie saw tongues or jets of flame proceeding from Home's head. We then all distinctly heard, as it were, a bird flying round the room, whistling and chirping, but saw nothing, except Lindsay, who perceived an indistinct form resembling a bird. There then came a sound as of a great wind rushing through the room, we also felt the wind strongly; the moaning rushing sound was the most weird thing I ever heard. Home then got up, being in a trance, and spoke something in a language that none of us understood; it may have been nonsense, but it sounded like a sentence in a foreign tongue. Lindsay thought he recognized some words of Russian. He then quoted the text about the different gifts of the spirit, and gave us a translation in English of what he had said in the unknown tongue. He told us that Charlie had that day been discussing the miracles that took place at Pentecost; and that the spirits made the sound of the wind; of the bird descending; of the unknown tongue, and interpretation thereof, and the tongues of fire : to shew that the same phenomenon could occur again. He spoke at length on the folly of supposing that

God had long ago written, as it were, one little page of revelation, and then for ever shut the book, and turned away his face from mankind. Charlie asked questions relative to the nature of God; the doctrine of the Trinity; and God's having once been on earth. Home spoke at great length, and with much eloquence. I cannot remember the exact words; but the substance of it was, that it was impossible for us to comprehend it; that nearly every man had really in his mind a different idea of God; that whether our conception of Him was as a unity, duality, or a trinity, it could not be of much consequence, provided that we recognized Him and obeyed His laws. He spoke much of the immensity of God, and our almost utter ignorance of Him and His works. He described the geometrical forms and attributes of a grain of sand, and asked us if we understood anything of that; and then pointing to a star, he asked us what we knew of that. He commented upon the very slight knowledge that the most scientific men had; mentioning that not long ago the spots on the sun had been considered to be mountains; then water; then faculæ: but that now they knew them to be great chasms. "But what they do not know," he said, "is, that the sun is covered with a beautiful vegetation, and full of organic life."

ADARE: "Is not the sun hot?"

HOME: "No, the sun is cold; the heat is produced and transmitted to the earth by the rays of light passing through various atmospheres. As to God's having been once on the earth, He has never left it, but is everywhere."

Charlie also asked about the divinity of Christ, and said he wanted to know the truth about all those matters.

Home spoke to the effect that even if they could tell us the whole truth, our minds could not understand or bear it. He said that spirits had different views on these subjects, and that they could not and might not unfold the truth. "You are taught," he continued, "as much as you can bear. A common theory, speaking figuratively, is that the heavens and earth are two cones; and that Christ is, as it were, the two apexes, joining and connecting both." He recommended Charlie, if he did or could, to hold the doctrine of the divinity of Christ in its usually accepted form, saying that it was better for him to do so, if it led him to a more religious frame of mind; but added, "Follow His teaching and carry out His mission. His mission was one of peace; do not then cut your neighbour's throat because he differs from you." Home then launched out into a tirade against intolerance and persecution, lamenting over the wickedness of mankind in supposing that bloodshed and persecution could be pleasing to God. He spoke at great length on this subject.

ADARE: "But if, for a time at least the whole truth about such important doctrines as the divinity of Christ is not perceived, do not the differences of opinion among spirits who are much together, lead to bad results? For instance, my mother was very religious; and especially upon that subject of the divinity of Christ. She may be frequently with spirits who do not hold the same views, or hold them in a modified form. Do they still differ? Do they talk about it?"

HOME: "It cannot lead to dissension; they know that they are not perfect, and that they have much to learn. The sort of conversation you have imagined to yourself has actually taken place. A spirit has asked certain questions such as: 'Can you shew me that there was a necessity for it?' 'Can you actually prove it?' &c., &c. And your mother always, as you know, kind and gentle, only says, 'No; perhaps not; but I do not see any reason why I should change the belief I always held about it.'"

Home then turned to me saying, "You have been much troubled and disturbed; you have a difficult and tortuous path before you, and you have thought that if there was anything in Spiritualism it ought to be of use and comfort to you. We know all your doubts and difficulties, and sympathize with you. Be patient and prayerful, and all will be well. Have you had a dream?"

ADARE: "I believe I have dreamt something curious; but I am unable to remember what it was."

HOME: "Adah has been trying to impress you in your sleep. Your mother allowed her to do so; but she has not quite succeeded; she will try again. What you dreamt, you could not remember, it was this: You thought you were journeying along a tortuous, difficult path full of obstacles; at the foot of a mountain you saw two angels; the one very bright and pure, the other rather darker and more earthly. You were in doubt which to choose; but thought the darker one, being most material, would be of most use. You trusted yourself to him; but as you ascended the mountain, the path became more and more difficult, and the angel that guided you became himself weary and confused; could not conduct you any further, and at last you were obliged to stop. You found then still greater difficulty in retracing your steps than you had experienced in going up; but at length, you arrived again at the foot of the ascent; and you then trusted yourself to the other and brighter angel, when the road became at once easy, and he led you up without doubt or difficulty."

No. 42.—Séance at No. 5, Buckingham Gate, December 20th.

My dear Father,—Last Tuesday we had a *séance* at No. 7. Present: Home, Charlie Wynne and his wife, Augusta Gore, the Master of Lindsay, Arthur Smith Barry, and myself. There appeared to be great difficulty in making manifestations; indeed, the spirits said that Home was ill and therefore that they had no power. We felt strong vibrations of the table, which was moved about. Augusta's couch was moved, (no one touching it) as was the screen, at the head of her couch, (no one touching it.) The spirits also answered, and gave messages by rapping on the couch; altogether it was not a bad *séance* for convincing sceptics. Arthur was touched, as was also Augusta, and the latter told me afterwards, that she had seen spirit-forms in the room. Home was taken possession of, his hands and arms became partially cataleptic, and he made passes in this condition over Augusta for some time, then stooping down he made passes under the couch; which Augusta said she felt distinctly.

Charlie Wynne, Lindsay, Arthur and I, adjourned to Ashley House, to smoke a cigar. We sat for a short time in the little room, and had manifestations, but Home was too weak for anything very wonderful. He was elongated slightly (I think), and raised in the air; his head became quite luminous at the top, giving him the appearance of having a halo round it. When he was raised in the air, he waved his arms about, and in each hand, there came a little globe of fire (to my eyes, blue); the effect was very pretty; Adah Menken and Dannie Cox were the only two spirits that I recognized by Home's manner.

No. 43.—Séance.

Last Friday, I went to a *séance* at Mrs. E——'s. Present: Home, H. Jencken, Mrs. E——, Mrs. Honeywood, Captain S——, General ——, and myself. This *séance* was in many respects the most wonderful that I have ever witnessed. Home was in a trance the greater part of the time; the information that he gave was of a very private character to Captain S——; it was given in pantomime, not a word being spoken, in order that some of the party should not understand. Captain S——, for whom it was intended, understood it, and I fancy so did I; but as it was quite private, and for some reasons very fearful, I do not feel at liberty to mention about it. I have since found I was mistaken. Home, before he went into the trance, said that there was a very strange influence about me. He partly made him out, but by degrees, and said that his name (surname) was Thomas. Thomas of *some* place. That he had been a friend of my father's and of my grandfather, in fact a greater friend of the latter than of the former; that I also had known him, that he used to have conversations about religion with my father. He said that he was a very strange spirit, abrupt and yet undecided in his manner; "He wants to say something to you, but when I am going to speak he stops me." "Ah!" he said, "He is going, he says he will come again to-night." Besides the strange story that Home in a trance acted for the benefit of Captain S——, he also took Captain S—— and Mrs. E—— (brother and sister) into another room, and spoke to them in private for some time. We had at different times, pretty strong physical manifestations, table lifted, &c., &c. When Home was acting the story, it being most necessary that not a word should be spoken, his jaws were locked and as rigid as steel; I felt them, as did others.

No. 44.

That night I slept in Home's room at Ashley House; we had a very beautiful manifestation. Home had been giving a public reading the day before at Croydon, which had been a failure, and he was much dispirited about it. A spirit (his mother I think), said, "*Do not be cast down, Dan; serve God truly, and his holy spirits will guard and protect you; fulfil your mission in life, and He will not forsake you,—be not cast down.*" We then both heard, as it were, a bird chirping about the room, and the spirit added, "*For He careth even for the sparrows.*" The spirits conversed with us for some little time by raps. My mother spoke more to me than she has ever done before; Home being in a trance. He made use of the same expressions my mother would have done, in a most affectionate manner. He talked of her happiness, partly on account of an immunity from physical pain and weakness, partly owing to the blessed calm and peace of her existence, and her knowledge that the hearts of those she had loved still beat with love for her, and that soon they would all be united again together. He told me not to think that it was through want of affection that she so seldom communicated with me, and gave me certain reasons for it, and recited two verses of beautiful poetry relative to a mother's love. He mentioned a painful peculiarity of a spirit who had taken part at the *séance* that evening; a peculiarity that I also have, and told me to take warning, and try and break myself of it. He said that her great wish was to see me lead so pure and elevated life, that I might make my existence here a stepping stone to a far higher state of existence in the next life. He told me not to be discouraged by failure, but to strive to do what I knew was right. The spirit calling himself Thomas of (name of place unknown), came and

began to talk about himself. He said that since he had entered
the spirit-life, he had very much changed his views on religion.
He broke off suddenly and said he would tell me all about it
another time. It was then late, past three a.m., and my mother
said, " I will request the other influences to leave you; you
should sleep now."

No. 45.

Last night I slept in Home's room at Ashley House. I did
not go to bed till past three. Soon after I was in bed, there
were evidences of a very strong influence in the room; and we
saw lights and heard sounds, as if some one was endeavouring
to make their voice audible to us; and we heard a sound like
footsteps. We then had a very beautiful manifestation. There
is a plaster of Paris crucifix, about one foot in length, hanging
on the wall over Home's bed. We heard something being moved
on the wall, and presently saw this crucifix waving in the air
between us and the window. I could see nothing holding it;
it appeared to move of itself. A spirit then said, by raps on the
cross, " *It is to shew you that we do not fear the symbol of the
cross; we should like you to kiss it.*" The crucifix was then
brought, or, as it appeared to me, moved of itself, close to my
face and was placed upon my lips. I kissed it, and it was
then taken away to Home's bed and placed upon his lips. He
did the same. They then said, " *We also will now kiss it.*" The
crucifix was moved away some distance, and we heard a sound
of some one kissing it three times, but saw nothing. They then
said, through the alphabet, that they had something to tell me
next Sunday; and that the same spirit that had spoken to us,
through Home, the Sunday before, would come again; that we
were not to interrupt him by asking questions, but just to listen
to what he said, as he had something of importance to tell us.

No. 46.—*Séance, Saturday, December 26th.*

Last Sunday, Home and Lindsay went down to Norwood to
have a *séance*. They returned about 11 o'clock. Charlie
Wynne and Captain Smith came also to Ashley House. After
Home and Lindsay arrived, we went into the small room and
sat round the table; the room was dark. We had strong
physical manifestations; we were all repeatedly touched by
hands coming from under the table. Our hands when touched
were *on* the table. A hand took Charlie's hand, and the
moment he felt it he exclaimed, " This is 'F——'s hand; I could
swear to her peculiar touch." The same hand also touched me;

playfully pinching and patting the back of my hand; it felt old and wrinkled. A spirit said by raps, "*Yes, it is F——.*" The hand again touched Charlie; he also remarked the wrinkled feeling of the skin. A spirit then said, "*Yes, it feels to you as it once was ; now it is no longer aged ;*" and a hand feeling young and soft placed itself in Charlie's hand, taking his in the same peculiar manner, but patting him briskly as if to shew that it was full of life. G—— H——, an uncle of Smith, and H—— J——, told us by raps that they were present. I asked if it were true that uncle Robert was conscious of their presence near him at night, and if he had real manifestations. They replied, "*Yes, it is true, and not imagination on his part.*" I asked them if Emmy had been touched on the shoulder the morning before, or whether it was as I had declared, her imagination. They replied, "*She was touched.*" Charlie asked if what had happened to him in church was spiritual? They said, "*Yes, certainly, it was.*" They entered a good deal into our conversation. Lindsay fell into a trance; at first he could not speak, but after a time in answer to a question, they said through him, "Yes, he can see sometimes; he will not remember anything of it, we cannot talk through him much yet, he is not fully developed, but he will be in time." Lindsay when awake saw spirit-forms, I saw lights occasionally, faint flashes and sparks. Home went into a trance; he walked about the room apparently settling what was to be done, then sat down, and turning to me, told me to go into the next room, and place outside the window a certain vase of flowers. I did so, putting the vase outside on the ledge, and shutting the window. Home opened the window of the room in which we were sitting. The flowers were carried through the air from the window of the next room in at our open window. We could all hear the rustling, and see the curtains moved by the spirit standing there, who was bringing in the flowers; Lindsay saw the spirit distinctly. A flower and sprig of fern, or something of that sort, was now given to each of us; in some cases it was placed upon the hand on the table; others were touched, and on putting down their hand, the flower was placed in it. I was touched strongly on the knee, and a sprig of box was given me. Afterwards, little Dannie said, "*I will give you another piece of fern in place of the one you lost ; but you must take great care of this ; it is only a very little bit.*" In answer apparently to some question, Home said, "Oh yes, certainly, give it to him yourself." Home told me to hold out my hand—I did so, rather behind me; and I felt Dannie's soft little fingers touch mine, and pat my hand, and place a little bit of maiden hair fern in it. Home then made some very curious experiments with flowers: he separated the scent into two portions—one odour smelling exactly like earth; the other being very sweet. He explained what he was doing; and how there came to be the two principals, as it were, in the flower. I did not clearly understand his meaning when he spoke; and I forget now what he said. While the flowers were being given to us, Home said, " Listen; we did, and all heard the sprigs being broken in the next room. While we listened, the sound ceased. Home said, " You see the effect of the concentration of your thoughts. It is hard for you to understand; but I assure you that the fact of your all directing your thoughts to a certain object there, sent a solid column of polarized light right through into the other room, and completely changed the condition of the atmosphere there for a time, so that they could not continue to do what they were about." As soon as we had all been given our little bunches of leaves or flowers, Home told me to go into the next room, and examine the vase. I did so, and found the window closed as I had left it; I opened it and found that all the tall sprigs of fern, &c., &c., had been taken away. Home never left the room we sat in after I had placed the vase outside the window, so that even supposing that the branches we received had been concealed by Home on his person, still the sprigs in the vase must have been broken off and removed somehow outside the window. Home now left the room, saying, " Do not be frightened; Dan is not going out of the window or anything of that sort." He returned, holding in his hand half a lemon, freshly cut; he handed it to each of us to taste. He laughed and said, " Yes, it is very good, is it not? so refreshing." He then held it up above his head, and said, " We will withdraw all the acid flavour from it." A yellowish light came over the lemon; he held it up for some little time, and said, " Now taste again." He held it out to me; but the room being rather dark, I bobbed my nose against it, and therefore tasted nothing. All the others tasted it, and described it as most disagreeable, having no odour, and the flavour being a sort of mawkish alkali; some describing it as like magnesia; others, as like washing soda. Home laughed and said, " We will take the nasty taste away presently." He then described what had taken place, I cannot recollect what he said, but the substance of it was that a purely natural process had been gone through. " If you were to eat the lemon," he said, " or swallow the juice, the same thing exactly would occur by natural decomposition, all the acid flavour would be freed, and would pass through the pores of your skin into all sorts of forms, &c., &c., while the residuum would be a substance, such as you now tasted. It resembled soda; it is of that nature, and that is why lemon juice is so good for acidity of the stomach and blood." We have done nothing miraculous; by our knowledge of natural substances and laws, we were able to hasten as it were, a natural process, and withdraw at once the acid, instead of its being diffused into various forms: we have retained it in the air, and will now restore it to the lemon." He held the lemon up and a rose-coloured flame, or rather light, came over it. After a little, he gave it to those who had tasted it the second time; they said that it was quite good and fresh, and that all the natural scent and flavour was restored to it.*

Home sat down and said, "It would be very nice if the same party that are here to-night, could sit occasionally together. You are all sympathetic, and in a very short time you would all of you see not only sparks and flashes of light, but the whole forms distinctly of the spirits in the room. I want also some time or other to talk to you on a very interesting subject, namely, when it is that the soul enters the body of an infant; at what period of its existence it becomes a living soul. It appears a difficult subject to you; it is really as simple as the scent of a flower or its colour." Charlie then said something to him about the origin of man. "Oh, yes," said Home, "that is a subject I want to speak to you about; some day I will, and of the difference in the existences of different creatures. No creature that crawls—that is unable, as it were, to do anything to preserve its life here—has immortality." "Do you mean," I said, "that they have no future?" "Oh, yes, they have indeed a very important future before them; I mean they differ from you as regards their individuality." I said, "Can you tell me where the line is drawn?" "There is no exact line; some creatures are endowed with a greater amount of what you call instinct than others that are apparently much above them in the scale of creation: like, for instance, ants and bees. I cannot tell you about it now. We have not been able to do at all what we intended this evening. Dan must awake now, and you must not sit any longer." Home awoke, and we went into the other room.

No. 47.—Séance at No. 7, Buckingham Gate, Monday, December 21st.

Present: Emmy Wynne, Charlie Wynne, Augusta Gore Booth, Home, and myself. We sat at a large square tea table, one side of it being placed against Augusta's couch. Almost immediately on sitting down, we felt a strong vibration of the

---

* I believe I am correct in this account of the lemon, but I cannot swear that Home did not leave the room after, as he said, restoring the acid principle to the lemon, and before he gave it to them to taste.

table. The alphabet was called for, and the following long message given; the first part having reference to me and something that had occupied my mind; the latter part intended for all of us: "*A perfect submission to the crosses of earth life only works out for you a purer and higher life, when freed from the mortal and nearer the Divine. You, my darling boy, did not observe that the little branch we gave you last night was in form a cross. It has a deep significance. There are six leaves at every point; these, too, have a meaning, which you will one day understand. Meanwhile, bear all; God's truth will overcome error. Be patient, my darlings; I am indeed happy that you have been led to investigate.*"

We had all the usual physical phenomena, though not very strongly; the chief feature of the *séance* being the amount of conversation carried on through the alphabet; and by spirits assenting or differing from what we said by rapping "*Yes*" or "*No*" upon the table, furniture, &c. Raps came on Augusta's couch, and it was moved about, and the head part raised a little. After these manifestations a message was given: "*Darling, this is G—— H——;*" and immediately afterwards: "*We all wish to see you thus,*" and her couch was again raised at the head, completing the sentence: "*We all wish to see you thus raised up.*" The table moved about, and was tilted up sometimes to one side, and sometimes to another. A whistle that was on the table did not move when the table was tilted in any direction, except towards Augusta; when it was tilted towards her the whistle rolled. In answer to a question as to the cause of this, they said, "*From a want of influence on that side.*" They told us they did not withdraw any influence from Augusta, as it would weaken her. They afterwards turned the table round, so as to have the side at which Emmy had been sitting next Augusta; the side which had been next to Augusta came opposite to Home. This equalized the magnetic influence round the table. At the same time we were told that they were desirous of showing their presence by messages rather than by physical manifestations. The table was raised in the air about 18 inches, and remained poised for some little time. Emmy's dress was pulled and shaken; Home's chair was moved. Having been told, through the alphabet, to put the white cloth on the table, we did so. We saw, and were touched by hands moving under the cloth. A flower in Home's button-hole was taken away, and carried underneath the table; I heard it moving there. Presently the same flower was thrown from behind Augusta's couch; it touched her face, and then fell upon the floor. It was taken up, and a hand and arm came from behind her couch, and placed it gently against her cheek, and gave it to her. Emmy said, " I saw the hand and arm." A message was given "*A hand, with the flower from K——*." Home also saw the arm; I did not. Some other manifestations were made about Augusta's couch, and the words, "*It was G—— H——*," given. We then heard a sharp noise that we took to be the chirping of a bird under the table, and we heard something moving underneath the table. The message was given—"*We hope soon you will not require ＊ ＊ ＊*;" and at the same moment a heavy handle, used for winding up the couch, was raised from under the table, and placed in Augusta's hand, implying that they hoped soon she would be able to raise herself. The name "*G—— H——*" was given to shew who had made the manifestation. We found that the chirping sound we had heard was caused by the handle of the lever turning while being moved under the table. This chirping was imitated exactly by a spirit at some distance behind us in the centre of the room. We now had a very wonderful manifestation. We were merry about something or other, and we all distinctly heard a spirit voice joining in our laughter; it sounded quite clear and loud. Home asked if it was to shew that they liked to see us happy and were happy themselves; the answer was "*Yes; God is so good.*" Soon after this the message was given—"*Daniel is exhausted,* and all manifestations ceased. During the *séance* Emmy and Augusta saw shadowy forms, hands, and arms.

After talking a short time we went into the next room (Uncle Robert's study). We were at supper eating, drinking, and chatting very merrily, not talking of, or I believe thinking about, Spiritualism, when there came a knock at the door. Charlie turned his head, and said, "Come in.' The door did not open; but the next moment there came knocks upon the table and a chair glided out from the wall to the table (no one touching it), and placed itself in the most natural manner between Emmy and Home; it then moved up close to Home, and the alphabet was called for by the chair tilting (no one touching it). The following message was given—"*I like you because you do good to those I love.*" Home asked who the spirit was; "*G—— H——*" was answered. Emmy's dress was pulled, and dragged strongly under the table, and a hand was twice put into hers beneath the table. Charlie was touched on the knee. Several questions were answered and another message, which I forget, was given by raps on the table, as loud as if some one had struck it underneath with a hammer. The table was moved and tilted, and once raised completely off the ground for a second or two, so slightly that I did not perceive it, but the others did, and the spirits afterward said that it had been off the ground. It must have required great power even to move and tilt it, for the table was a heavy dining-room table covered with plates, dishes, and decanters. Home was told that Augusta had also had manifestations; and when we returned to the other room, we found that she had heard raps in her room, while we were at supper in the other. She also heard the raps and the movement of the table in the study.

No. 48.—*February 8th*, 1869.

Last night I slept at Ashley House. Home was at a party, and did not come in until very late. Soon after he had gone to bed he went into a trance for a short time. He was far from well, and the spirits said they could not make any use of him. In the morning, about 11 o'clock, Sacha, Home's wife, said to me, through the alphabet, " *Will you from my part give to Florence something ?*" I said I should be delighted. She said to Home, " *Dannie, my broad gold Russian bracelet.*"

No. 49.—*Séance, February 9th.*

In the evening of the 8th, Dr. Gully came in. As we were sitting by the fire talking, Home went gradually into a trance. He examined Dr. Gully's heart, gave him some directions as to treatment, and told him that his head and brain were all working beautifully; that his head had not been so clear and in such good order for some time. He walked about the room conversing, sometimes with us, sometimes with the spirits in the room. He asked me to fetch an accordion from Mr. S. C. Hall's rooms; I did so. He then said that Captain Smith was coming, and that he had just then left his house. He became rather impatient at his not coming quicker; he was aware when he did arrive, and told me to go out and meet him, which I did, informing him that Home was in a trance. When Smith entered, Home introduced him in a quaint style. Taking Dr. Gully's hand, he said, " This is James—James Gully; and this is William—William Smith. You are to shake hands. They call him a doctor—there is some sense in that; and they call you a captain, which means nothing at all."

Home said to me, " Turn off some of the gas, it is too heavy on Dan's brain—light is a regular weight upon the brain, that is why a strong light prevents our making manifestations; the brain of the medium cannot act. It is through your brains that the atmosphere we make use of is thrown off. For the same reason, manifestations occur more readily at night, when there is an absence of sunlight, than in the daytime. From a similar cause, a strong light upon the platform, as at Miss Hardinge's lectures that you were speaking of this afternoon is very bad. Light is a ponderable substance. There is much that scientific men do not yet know about the nature of light; there is a material natural light, and a spiritual light. When men know all about material light, they will then turn their attention to the much greater subject of spiritual light. Everything has its light." We now, at Home's request, went into the next room and sat round the table; the room was dark with the exception of the light from the window. Home had that morning given me the bracelet as a present from his wife to Florence;—I had left it in the drawing room.

After we were seated in the small room, the attention of the spirits appeared principally directed to Dr. Gully. Home explained something to him about the muscles of his left side, and they gave him several strong electric shocks. Home seemed much pleased at this. " Oh," he said, " that was so beautifully done, they managed it so well, and it has answered admirably, and done you a great deal of good." Dr. Gully had also some messages from his daughter. I then felt that some one was standing near me, and I heard something moving about my head, and presently felt a substance brushed across my hair, and then placed upon my head. I asked if I might put up my hand and take it. Home said, " Wait a moment." The substance was then taken from off my head and passed across my hands on the table; and finally I distinctly felt a hand place the bracelet given to Florence by Sacha into my fingers. The hand pressed and patted my fingers. Sacha, speaking through Home, then addressed a few most touching and appropriate words to me, on the subject of marriage; after which we all heard a spirit move from beside me over to the window. Home got up, placed himself close to the window and said, " Sacha will try and make herself visible to you." Her form gradually became apparent to us; she moved close to Home and kissed him. She stood beside him against the window intercepting the light as a solid body, and appeared fully as material as Home himself, no one could have told which was the mortal body and which was the spirit. It was too dark, however, to distinguish features; I could see that she had her full face turned towards us, and that either her hair was parted in the middle, and flowed down over her shoulders, or that she had on what appeared to be a veil. She said, through Home, that she would try and appear to us as white light, and she did so, but the form was not nearly so distinct as when she stood as a dark substance against the window. Captain Smith asked me had I not intended to have been travelling that night; I told him that such was my original intention, but that I had changed my plans some days ago. He said, " I know that, but it was not intended that you should travel to-night. I have no idea why you were prevented, but some day probably you will know. I was obliged (by his hand being taken possession of) the other day, to write down some questions; I sealed them up and sent them to Dan; some day you are to open and answer them, I think you will find something in them about it; I have no idea what I wrote." Home also told me later that the spirits had not wished me to travel that night. Smith began talking to me about the *seance* in which the lemon was used, and said that he had been thinking deeply over it, and believed that there was an allegorical meaning attached to it. Home said, "Yes, there is, and in many things that we do, we frequently symbolise; and are content to know that you will, by thinking for yourselves, find out the meaning: it is better so. We sometimes also do things the meaning or object of which we ourselves do not know; we have our impulses the same as you. What meaning do you attach to the story of the lemon?"

SMITH: "I consider the lemon to have represented human nature, and the yellow flame that surrounded it our evil passions. The yellow flame devoured and destroyed all that was good in the lemon—the juice and the fragrance, representing all that is good in human nature; and it left the lemon vile and worthless. The red flame that then covered the lemon and restored it to its former excellence represented the Holy Spirit of God, by which alone our human nature, debased and destroyed by evil passions, can be restored to its natural purity and beauty."

Home appeared much pleased, and said, "Yes, you have read the parable aright: the yellow flame was the fire of evil passions, and the pure bright red flame was the Spirit of God." He then talked about the various colours in, and virtues of, different crystals, diamonds, rubies, sapphires, emeralds, &c., and what they symbolized. Adah Menken came and said through Home, "Many would think it horrible of such a one as I am to come to you now; but you, I know, think otherwise about me, and I must speak a word to you relative to the very important step you are about to take." She spoke a little about my marriage, and said, "I will come again to-night; I want to have a long chat with you, and tell you some curious things that occurred at Adare." When Home awoke he was rather astonished to find himself sitting in the small room, and Smith one of the party. He was entranced for nearly two hours, and was much exhausted. After the others had gone, my mother spoke to me through the alphabet about my intended marriage. She also spoke about Home going to Adare, one message I remember being: "*Mortals seek for knowledge; but when we*

*give them the fruit of our studies, if it does not coincide with
their preconceived ideas, we are classed as devils."* Home was
so weak that she could not make much use of him, and Adah
Menken could not say anything that she had intended. The
last message was: *"Dan, you are very weak; you must not sit
for at least a week. We take away all power from you for that
time.".* I forgot to say that on Monday night Home spoke in a
trance to me about the difficulties in the way of mediumship and
communicating. As well as I can remember, he said: "Very
strange occurrences often take place with undeveloped mediums;
and you are naturally much puzzled by them. These things
are allowed sometimes as wholesome trials, in order that the
person may see how necessary it is to use judgment and reason,
and to approach the subject with the greatest care. Mediumship is of very slow growth; people are too hasty, and expect
to get everything at once. They are often also told things to
make them persevere, spirits are so anxious to communicate,
and it is such a joy to find people to communicate through, that
they rush in, as it were, and try to encourage the medium by
promises that apply rather to mediums in general, than to any
one individually; promises also which may take years in their
fulfilment, instead of days, as mortals in their impatience suppose. You think too much of the individuality of mediumship.
Supposing a person is told that he is to be a great healer, that
he is to go forth teaching the nations, and to be as a king
among men; that person would consider it all as applying
solely to himself: it applies rather to the whole subject, to
all mediums. Mediums should be as kings, in the true sense of
the word; they have a wonderful gift, a weighty responsibility,
and they should, if possible, set themselves apart, and lead pure,
simple, unworldly lives, that they may use their gift to the
best advantage. This mistake as regards promises, *viz. :*
supposing them to apply to a single individual instead of to
mediums in general, is an important fact, bear it in mind. The
discerning of spirits is important. Now if a dark, cold, low
spirit came into the room Dan would know him and he could
not stay; he would feel mean and out of place, and would have
to go. Another person might not perceive what he was—to use
a homely simile, it is something like a man making faces at you
behind your back; he would not do so if he knew there was a
mirror in which you could see him; when St. Paul spoke of
discerning spirits, he did not mean seeing them only, but
discerning the differences between them, judging between the
pure and the impure. Living in any way in an atmosphere of
deceit, holding *séances* on the sly, and having anything whatever
underhand about it, is very bad and is certain to produce a bad

influence. Mediums while being developed must be very cautious, very prayerful, very guarded against deceit; very patient, humble, and quietly receptive of what may come to them; very careful and pure in life, for a calm and prayerful state of mind is necessary for the influx of a high spiritual influence, while lower influences can more easily impress themselves—are more in their element, as it were, with natures more disturbed, and less exalted and pure in mind and body. If those who are being developed as mediums will remember and act up to this, they will arrive at a state in which they will know at once the pure from the impure, and be able to judge of the influences about them."

[The following *séances* occurred at Adare Manor, and at Garinish, a cottage of my father's, on the coast of Kerry. For the sake of uniformity, I think it best to follow the same familiar style, using the first person, as in the previous communications. The *séances* recorded by my father are signed " D."; those by me, " A."]

No. 50.—*Séance at Adare Manor, February, 27th,* 1869.

Mr. Home arrived yesterday, and this evening our first *séance* took place. We sat in the gallery; the party consisting of my sister-in-law Mrs. Wynne, and her daughter, Major and Mrs. Blackburn, Hon. F. Lawless, Captain Wynne (Charlie), Mr. Home, Adare, and myself. During the *séance* there was a strong gale of wind, with heavy hail showers, and flashes of lightning. After a short time, vibrations and slight movements of the table occurred. Presently Mr. Home and Adare went to the end of the room, and sat at a small table and asked what had best be done. They received the following answer: " *The external atmosphere is not good. We are not sure that this room will be conducive. We wish all who remain in this room to be in the circle. Go with your father and Fred Lawless to try another room.*" As Mr. Home and Adare were walking up the gallery to tell us, Adare said " I wonder if Charlie (Wynne) may come with us ? " " *Yes,*" was rapped on a table which they were passing at the moment.

We went to my study, and sat at a small table. Raps were heard, and Mr. Home soon went into a trance, and immediately rose up and walked about the room, seemingly in an uncomfortable state; his eyes were shut. He took the green shade off my reading lamp, and then bandaged his eyes; and after a few turns about the room, he came back to the table. He seemed attracted to Lawless. He placed his hand against the back of Lawless's neck, and pressed it. Lawless felt a sensation as if a hot stream flowed into him. Mr. Home then sat down; and, pointing emphatically at Lawless, said : " You have considerable powers : you have (or ought to have) large healing powers." He again walked about, and seemed very uncomfortable, conveying the impression that there was something unsatisfactory about the state of the room. He said : " The gallery is too large, and full of different influences, the chairs even have different influences ; and then this room is too full of business and of figures." He went out into the hall ; came back, and then went into the vestibule. On returning he took Adare out, and asked him to come and try the dining room. Adare said : " Why not try the room at the end of the passage ? " (his mother's sitting room.) They went down in the dark, Mr. Home finding the door, which Adare missed. They entered the room, and immediately Mr. Home said : " This is the room." He then quitted it, returned to where we were sitting, and taking me by the hand, he led the way rapidly back to the other room, and walked into the middle of it, Adare coming with us. It was pitch dark. " This," he said, " this is the room." We heard raps in different places. He then took my hand, returned to my study, and sat down. He addressed me in a loud whisper : " That is the room ; you will put some flowers there in the morning, and have a fire in the afternoon. There will be a remarkable manifestation up stairs ; you will not know when it will happen. You may go to that old ruin on Wednesday night, or not later than Thursday. The men only are to go, the ladies would be frightened.* When Daniel comes back, go and sit up stairs." Mr. Home soon after awoke. At one time during his trance he was either elongated or raised off the ground, for, while standing close to the table, opposite to me, his head and the upper part of his figure were rapidly elevated several inches ; the lower part was concealed by the table ; this lasted only a few seconds.

As directed we went up stairs, and sat at the large table in the middle of the gallery. Miss Smith joined the circle ; she became slightly hysterical and left the table, but soon returned. Fred Lawless became nearly similarly affected. Vibrations of the tables and chairs occurred, and the usual cold currents of air were perceived. Mr. Home and Adare felt some strong influence between them ; the chair of the former was pulled back from one to two feet, and Mrs. Wynne's was half turned round. The table was tilted in different directions, and was at last raised about one foot off the ground. After this nothing more occurred.   D.

---

* We had been previously talking about going to the Abbey.

No. 51.—*Séance, February 28th.*

As directed last night, we sat in Lady Dunraven's sitting room :—Present, Mrs. Wynne, C. Wynne, Lawless, Adare, Mr. Home and myself. The table was unsteady and creaky; we had very slight manifestations. After some time Mr. Home went into a trance; he seemed uncomfortable, and walked about, altering the position of the different chairs and articles of furniture; he objected to the large stuffed chairs on which we were sitting, and changed them: saying, that the springs in them had a bad effect. He drew down the blinds, and made movements with his hands and arms as if magnetizing about the room. He sat down near the fire, then taking out a coal, partly red and partly black, he brought it and held it between Mrs. Wynne and me, as if showing it to us; then, without making any remark, he put it back in the fire. He held the coal by the black part, which, doubtless, was tolerably hot; yet, still the experiment could hardly be called an example of the fire test, such as was exhibited at Norwood, and is mentioned in No. 30. After this he rubbed and patted several of us on the back, and he pressed his head against me between the shoulders; I felt a warm current flowing from it. He then sat down, and said that the room was now in a much better state. After making a few observations he awoke. Raps were heard, and we were told to go and look for another table; Mr. Home, in order to know who should go with him, pointed to each in turn, and Adare and I were chosen. We went to the hall and the library, trying different tables without any result; on our return through the hall, we heard raps on a table as we were touching it, as we passed; so we took it with us. We sat at this table; but had only slight manifestations. We received this message, " *We are doing our best; we hope you will be patient.*" We asked, " How many spirits present ?" and were told " *Nine.*" " How many that we have known ?" " *Two.*" I expressed a hope that Dr. Elliotson would come, and we were talking about him when the following was given, " *He will visit the Abbey.*" After a short pause we received this message : " *The influence is against us ; we mean the external atmosphere.*" And soon after the following: " *We think you had better try the same table you had last night.*" Upon this we adjourned to the gallery. We were joined by Miss Wynne, Miss Smith and Major Blackburn. The table vibrated, and raps were heard ; but nothing remarkable took place.

During one of the periods when the table was vibrating, the manor clock struck twelve; the continuity of the vibration ceased, but at each stroke of the bell a vibration took place.

When the last stroke had sounded, the continuity of the vibrations recommenced. Soon after this, the following message was given: " *We have done our best ; but find it in impossible. May God bless you all.*" The word God was spelled by strong vibrations of the table; we then adjourned.   D.

No. 52.—*Séance, March 1st.*

We had a *séance* at five p.m.:—Present, Major and Mrs Blackburn, Mrs. Wynne, Miss Wynne, Miss Smith, Captain Wynne, Mr. Lawless, Home, and myself. Tolerably strong physical manifestations occurred. No messages were given, but the spirits present occasionally joined in our conversation by rapping " *Yes* " or " *No ;*" and they answered a few questions as to the number of spirits in the room, whose relatives they were, &c., &c. The table at which we were seated was moved, and raised in the air. A good-sized table standing at some little distance behind Home moved of itself; and a chair behind me moved up to me of itself. Some one asked, " How many spirits are there present?" Twenty raps were given. Miss Smith, having been requested to do so, asked if any of her relations were in the room. " *Yes ;*" was answered. " But," she said, " there are no relations of mine alive here ; no one is related to me." The answer was " WE ARE *the living.*" When leaving the room, Home told me he had a strong impression that Mrs. Wynne and myself were to sit with him alone sometime in the evening ; after dinner, accordingly, we three went and sat in my room round a large and tolerably heavy table. Immediately the influence became apparent by strong vibrations and raps on the table and floor. The room was at this time lighted by a bright fire and one candle. The following sentences were given with short intervals between them, there not being apparently sufficient power to enable the spirits to spell out by raps many words in succession : " *We are pleased to have you thus.*" " Alone ?" I asked. " *Yes.*" " *Emily welcome.*" Home's hands were influenced, and he patted and stroked his chest.

The names were then given : " *Richard,*" " *James,*" " *John,*" " *Robert.*" " Is it Gore Booth ?" I asked. " *No.*" We were speculating as to who these spirits could be, as only one name was recognized by Mrs. Wynne, and none by me, Home began describing them ; but Mrs. Wynne, not knowing that it was of any consequence, interrupted him, and he could not tell us who they were ; he said however that we should know later. We now heard persons moving in different parts of the room. In order to be certain that we were not deceived, we asked that the sounds might be repeated three times ; it was done as we requested. Home also said he saw various figures, but not with sufficient distinctness to be able to describe them. Raps were constantly heard on the table, floor, and furniture, and the spirits occasionally answered our questions. The table was moved about slightly, and raised off the ground. Home went into a trance, got up and walked about without speaking for some little time; by the attitude he assumed I perceived that "the Doctor" was influencing him. He came up to me and whispered, "Tell Dan not to eat so much sweet." Another influence then came over him; he walked about briskly, and seemed happy and pleased; he spoke in a loud voice somewhat to this effect: "As regards the *séances* you have been holding, it is most difficult for us to succeed. In the first place the external atmosphere is most unpropitious, neither have you approached the subject in a proper spirit and frame of mind. In whatever way you regard the subject, it is a most important one, and should not be treated with levity, but should be approached quietly and with earnest prayer. You are not sufficiently serious. Some are actuated by curiosity, some are wishing for one thing, others for something quite different; the aspirations are so various, it is almost as though you were praying to different gods: the influences are consequently all opposed to each other. You should come prayerfully, earnestly, not hoping for, or expecting, anything in particular; above all without levity. It is a solemn subject if you consider it to be a great discovery, calculated to throw light on hitherto hidden subjects, to overthrow many errors, and to be of great benefit to the human race. If you do not believe that we are what we pretend to be, and even consider us to be evil, still it is a subject to be treated with solemnity, for you are communicating with beings or intelligences external to yourselves, different from you, and beyond your knowledge or control. The external influences also are very numerous and strange, and are all, as it were, touching and fingering Dan—wondering at him. It is quite new to them; they have never seen anything like it before, and they do not understand it. Some of them are so intensely anxious to communicate, to say something, others again do not at all approve of it, and would wish to prevent anything of the sort."

ADARE: "That is curious!"

Mrs. WYNNE: "Surely it would be more curious if they were all agreed."

HOME: (laughing) "Why, Adare, your aunt's notions are more correct than yours, although you have been at it so long; but then you spoke without thinking. Oh yes, indeed, some of them are very much opposed to it."

ADARE: "Will you give us any directions about our *séances?*"

HOME : "That is what we have been trying to find out, but it is difficult. You see if we pick out a few, then those who are left out are annoyed, and those who are chosen are sorry for the others who are disappointed, and are affected by their influence. It would be much better if you would settle among yourselves for some to sit one night and the others the next; we can tell you what combination answers best; we would sooner you settled it among yourselves, then there will be no unpleasant feeling." Home then put out the candle, and told me to help him to move the table; we placed it near the window and sat down. Soon after he awoke. There was a strong influence about the table, it vibrated and was lifted in the air, the cloth was raised apparently by hands moving under it, and I was touched on the knee by a hand; Home said he saw hands and figures. A hand came out from under the table, covered by the cloth and touched my left side, it remained there a few seconds and was then withdrawn. This message was given, "*I took it from my own dear boy to give to you my dear sister, take it.*" We none of us understood to what this referred, till I noticed that a rose bud had been taken from my button-hole, however I made no remark. We heard something moving under the table, and the cloth was raised, as if by a hand, near Mrs. Wynne. At Home's suggestion, she put her hand down, and the rose was placed in it. A flower in Home's button-hole was then jerked out across the table, and fell by me. I asked who it was for, the answer was, "*For you to give to your father with love.*" This message was then given, "*Your happiness is ours.*" Then this, "*We would fain manifest ourselves more powerfully.*"

While this last message was being given, the table was raised gently off the floor and moved up and down three times in the air, then raised again a little higher, and again moved up and down; in this manner it was, without ever touching the floor, raised six or seven times, a little higher on each occasion, until it was about three feet above the floor. I have never seen a table sustained in the air for so long a time. Mrs. Wynne remarked that it was delightful to have no bad influence present, when we had this message : "*Prayer to God will protect.*" The table then began moving on the floor in a circle, and the following was given: "*The love of God encircling you round and about.*" Subsequently this was spelled out: " *We love the symbol of faith ;*" and the table was raised in the air, and twice made the sign of the cross. A perfume, as of dried rose leaves and some aromatic substance, was wafted across us and the message given: "*We must now go.*" Nothing more occurred   A.

No. 53.—*Tuesday, March 2nd.*

On the afternoon of the 2nd I was seated by the fire in my room reading, Home was writing at the long table. Suddenly the round table, starting from the window, moved a distance of six or eight feet, and placed itself against the end of the long table. We both heard a sound as of a bell tinkling. Home began speaking about the spirit present, and while doing so went into a trance. He said, "Oh, he is very strange and restless, he is a monk." I asked, "Is that sound of the bell the same as I heard last night?" "Yes; he was here last night, and says you ought to have heard him. He has never been here before, that is, not since this house has been built. The sound of the bell is the same also as you heard outside the house to-day with Dan, only it is more concentrated now." I asked what the meaning of the sound was, "Ah, he was a monk. He seems to have committed some crime and then to have said mass, and the crime weighed heavier on his conscience in consequence." A dagger was then violently knocked off the table to the other side of the room. I was not looking at Home at the moment and cannot say whether he struck it or not. "Oh," he said "he cannot bear the sight of that." A large pair of scissors were then dashed on to the floor from off the round table, no one being near it. Home said, "He cannot bear anything sharp and pointed; Ah, he is trying to pick up the scissors, but he cannot touch them because they have, as you see, fallen in the shape of a cross. Ah, poor fellow, he says he will not hurt you, he would not stop a minute here, but that he sees you do not hate and despise him; he will do you no harm, but you must not mind his being rough and abrupt in his manner. He does not wish you to speak about this to the others, but he wants you, Charlie, and Dan, to come here to-night; he has something to say; he does not like those *séances* down stairs, he is not pleased. He cannot speak to you himself, he can scarcely make manifestations; he talks old Irish. He is the same spirit that Fred saw,* he was stripped of his gown and appeared to have on a blanket."

———

On the same afternoon, or the day before, I forget which, Mr. Lawless, Home, and myself were seated on the bed in my room; Charlie Wynne was sitting by the fire. We heard raps on the table, and a sound as of a hand brushing on the wall, and the bed vibrated.   A.

---

* This alluded to Mr. Lawless, having told us, while on a visit here last winter, that he had seen a ghost or spirit in the castle. I did not pay much attention to his statements, supposing it to have been some illusion on his part.

No. 54.—*Séance, March 2nd.*

Present:—Mrs. and Miss Wynne, Mrs. and Major Blackburn, Miss Smith, Captain Wynne, Mr. Lawless, Home, and myself. This evening we sat at a table in the gallery; very slight physical manifestations occurred, which soon ceased, and after waiting some time, the party broke up. Mrs. Blackburn, Miss Wynne, Captain Wynne, Mr. Lawless, and Home went up to my room to try there. I followed them in about a quarter of an hour. Before I arrived they had a message to the effect that the spirits would do more if they could; afterwards we had the usual manifestations, currents of air, vibrations, raps, tilting of the table, which was on two occasions also raised in the air. At one time, Miss Wynne, Home, and I heard a very singular rumbling and rolling sort of sound in the air behind us, which was repeated three times. We saw hands (apparently) moving under the table cloth; and Mrs. Blackburn, Home, and I were touched. Mrs. Blackburn's dress was sharply pulled two or three times, as was also Miss Wynne's; we all saw and heard it. Mrs. Blackburn was slightly under influence, and became a good deal agitated. Home went into a trance; walked about, and described to Mrs. Blackburn two spirits that were standing behind her magnetizing her and causing the agitation she felt. He said, " They will do you no harm, but on the contrary what they are about is for a good object; one of them magnetized you in the same way this afternoon, but there are now two, and it is consequently stronger. The influence about you is very good, but very strong, you could hear raps at night now." Mrs. Blackburn said, " Oh, please don't !" Mr. Home replied, " Oh, no; don't be nervous, they will not do it; they know it would frighten you, and they will never do that; but the time will come when you will not be frightened at it." Going to Mr. Lawless, he said, " You really must have more command over your nerves, if you cannot control them you must not come to *séances;* you will get more and more hysterical, and it will do you physical harm; you had better go away for a few minutes." Then turning to me, he said, " You did not do what you promised last night. He is here; you know who I mean." I replied, " Yes, I know; but Dan said last night that he had an impression that Mrs. Wynne and I were to sit with him; and I could not do what I promised." Home said, " You might have done so afterwards; however it is perhaps as well that you did not, for you might have attributed Dan's illness to that. He is still here; he is not pleased." I asked, "Would it do as well to-night, or to-morrow?" Home replied, " No; he says he will come unexpectedly again as he did the first time. Oh yes, he knows that you did not forget, he does not blame you, but he is not pleased; he is very much annoyed at these sittings down stairs." Home then opened the window, and appeared to be debating as to whether he should go out or not. He shut the window and said, "You will not let us do it; you have not sufficient faith." He then sat down and awoke. We had a few more physical manifestations, the last being that Home's chair was drawn away from the table.   A.

No. 55.—*Séance, March 3rd.*

This *séance* was held in Adare's room. Present:—Mrs. Wynne, Adare, Mr. Home, and myself. Soon after we were seated, Mr. Home went into a trance. He got up and walked about, remarking that the influence was good, and that Mrs. Wynne's influence was very pleasant. He went to the door, opened it, and said, "Ah, here is that strange spirit that came to Ashley House—Thomas, your father's friend—he is very eccentric; he says he wants to recall some conversation to your father." I said, "I hope he will do so." Adare observed that if he exhibited the same curiously abrupt and undecided manner that he did at Ashley House (*vide No.* 44, *p.* 87), he would probably say nothing, at any rate this night." Home said, "Oh, that was his manner; he is very eccentric." He then walked up to Mrs. Wynne, and made passes over her head, and held it between his hands, and told her that her circulation was bad (which it is), and that her liver was out of order.

He pointed to me saying, "Your influence is very good for physical manifestations; you must not think that you are any impediment to their occurrence." I had been fancying that probably my presence was rather adverse, and consequently I was unwilling to attend the *séance;* but I had not mentioned this to Home. He then gave Adare directions about the table. "You will place it near the window; your father will sit next to Daniel, you on his other side, then Mrs. Wynne, leaving a vacant space next to the window." We then commenced talking about his having had apparently some idea of going out of the window last night (*vide No.* 54), and were discussing as to whether there was any real danger in his doing so; some saying they would be nervous, while others, myself among them, said we should feel no anxiety whatever as to his safety; upon which he remarked, "They will take care and see when the conditions are right; there need be no fear." He then spoke about one of the *séances* which had been held when he was not present, and said, "We do not approve of it at all; it is all wrong; the whole thing is in confusion. That sentence about B—— and the wicked devil is not right; there is no wicked devil in that sense. We do not wish to enter into any explanation, we only tell you that it is all wrong." Turning to Mrs. Wynne, Mr. Home said, "John says he is coming to you to-night, and that he wants to try and put his hand in yours." Soon after this he sat down and awoke. He spoke during his trance in a loud whisper.

We took the table over to the window and seated ourselves as we had been directed. We soon heard a number of very delicate raps, like a continuous stream of little electrical sparks, which lasted for a short time; they were barely audible without placing the ear close to the cloth which covered the table. We then felt vibrations, and heard raps of different kinds, chiefly on the table, but some dull sounds like knocks, occurred elsewhere. We had extinguished the candles, but the fire gave sufficient light to see near objects well, and distant ones faintly. In the recess of the window was a large box or chest with papers and other things laying upon it; one could see them, without being able clearly to distinguish what they were. The alphabet being called for, the following messages were given, with short intervals between them, during which there were frequent raps : "*God be with you. Your father Thomas Goold. You must not think we fear the cross, we love it, we also love God.*" "*We are allowed to pray for you and watch over you.*" Soon after several loud raps or knocks were heard, and the name "*John Wynne*" was spelled out. About this time there were movements and sounds about the papers on the box, and Mrs. Wynne's dress was touched. Presently we had the following message : "*Could you but know the reality of my identity, and the unaltered and unalterable love I bear you, I well know it would be a source of joy to you. I have not sent you messages, for the reason that you could have no means of distinguishing the certainty of my personality.*"* I then said, "To whom is this message sent," and the answer was, "*You, my own.*" I added, "I should like to know the name of the spirit," and was answered, "*Augusta   .*" At this point some interruption seemed to occur. Mrs. Wynne's dress was visibly and audibly moved about, and Mr. Home several times saw a hand; the slight sounds about the papers on the box recurred. Presently, Mr. Home's feet were moved and placed upon mine; strong

---

* This message clearly referred to my having several times lately remarked upon the fact, that no message had, I believe, been sent to me on any occasion during the previous *séances* in London or elsewhere, by the spirit who would most naturally under the circumstances have done so—which fact I had used as an argument bearing upon a particular view of the whole subject.

movements of his arms and legs took place; his hands appeared to be drawn about in different directions, and rather violently agitated. After these movements had ceased, he said, " I feel a hand on me, pressing against my chest; and now it has, I think, taken the flowers from my button-hole." The idea came into my mind that perhaps these flowers were intended for me; I quietly laid one hand open upon my knee. Almost immediately a flower was placed very delicately in it. I then felt another flower, and tried to grasp the hand holding it, but did not succeed; it seemed to vanish, leaving the flower in my hand. Some curious manifestations now took place. The cloth on the table was lifted up, fully six inches, as by a hand. This occurred along the side next the window several times. Mr. Home saw the hand. Mrs. Wynne became nervous, which was to be regretted, as she might probably have felt the hand as had been told her at the commencement of the *séance*. There were vibrations and tiltings of the table, and various kinds of raps. Presently, the alphabet was called for, and the following given: " *Even should we be taken to a distant heaven, would it not be our greatest joy to fly as the——*" Here the message stopped; and we heard a rustling sound about the box in the window, which lasted two or three minutes. Adare said, "I am sure I know what this means." My hand was on my knee. I suddenly felt something touch it, which I laid hold of, and drew out from under the table; it was an arrow. We then re-commenced the alphabet; and the word " *descends* " was given, thus finishing the sentence: " *as the arrow descends.*" During this manifestation, as also when the flowers were being placed in my hand, Mr. Home was sitting quite still, with both his hands on the table. A sheet of paper was lying on the edge of the table next the window, on which a pencil was placed. We presently saw the pencil moving about on the paper. Mr. Home saw the fingers holding it. Adare noticed it also, more than once, but of an undefined form.

We now heard something moving upon the box by the window, and a heavy substance fell near Adare's feet. Some of us at the same moment perceived a decided smell of brandy. Adare said, " I know what it is." The following message was then given: " *You must not take for your cold stimulants.*" Adare asked if he was to take none at all. The answer was by two raps, meaning, "*perhaps,*" or " *a little.*" We afterwards found that it was Adare's flask which had been thrown under the table. On examining it no brandy appeared to have escaped. Soon after this a curious manifestation occurred about the table, just like the sound and motion of the vibration on board a steamer. This was succeeded by the following message: "*We*

deeply regret, but we have no more power. God abide with you."
During this beautiful *séance*, which lasted nearly two hours, the
table was twice raised up from a foot to eighteen inches. The
messages were spelled partly by raps and partly by tilts of the
table. I was touched on two occasions, rather delicately, on
the knee. The whole *séance* was quiet, soothing, and very
impressive.   D.

No. 56.—Séance, March 4th.

Present :—Major and Mrs. Blackburn, Miss Wynne, Lawless,
Charlie Wynne, Home, my father, and myself. We sat in my
room, which was lighted by one candle and the fire. After
sitting for some time without any movement of the table or
other indication of influence, Home went into a trance. He got
up, said in a low voice to me " We have put Dan into a trance
to try and equalize the atmosphere, we wish to make manifestations," and after walking about the room magnetizing it
commenced speaking in a singularly soothing tone of voice,
his conversation being principally addressed to Mrs. Blackburn.
" There are two Elizabeths—who are they?   And Isabella—
she seems to have taken care of you John, when you were
young.   There is a spirit present with whom you were acquainted,
he is lame; you do not remember the name now, but you
probably will hereafter. Who was Margaret Henderson? (no
one answered). Ah, your mother would know, ask her;
she will remember about her. Talk, go on talking to each
other, your minds are much too positive ; the human mind is
like a barrier to us. Your minds now are all intent, and it
makes such a confusion that I cannot see and find out what I
want ; it is like looking through a shrubbery with all the
branches in motion : I cannot make out clearly what there is on
the other side." Mrs. Blackburn becoming slightly under
influence and agitated, he stood behind her and calmed her,
saying, " You must not mind it, they will do you no harm;
when on earth they would not have hurt you, why should they
now ? You must have trust ; but even if you have not confidence in them, you know that God protects you from all evil—
have trust in him. Should it seem unpleasant and even evil to
you, remember that God's ways are not our ways ; and out of what
is apparently evil, much good may come ; that which you might
at first consider bad, may turn out to be the greatest good to you.
It is the influence that came over Dan when we put him into a
trance that affected you ; it was so strong—that is all." Standing
near Miss Wynne he said, " There are two Windhams here, two
young men, Windham Goold and Windham Quin." Touching

Charlie Wynne on the shoulder he said, "Charlie, Robert says he has not forgotten his promise, he will keep it, but he has not been able to do so yet; he is going to Emmy." Home then walked about the room and said, "When Maria has sufficient faith and is willing to be developed for the good of others, she will go into trances." Mrs. Blackburn requested my father to ask Home if it was necessary that she should be willing, Home said, "Do not be frightened, nothing will be done to harm you, when you have sufficient faith in God's protecting power,—when you can say, 'Thy will not mine be done,'—when you are anxious for it for the benefit of others, and to advance the truth, then it will come to you; until then the fact of your being unwilling, of your mind being opposed, would prevent it. Oh, there is a Mary (or Maria) here, I like her so much. Dear me! she has such a curious way of smiling—she smiles with her mouth only, she is very timid. There is also a man who appears to have been shot; who can he be? Was he your grandmother's uncle? He seems to have been in a naval engagement. Although Mary is so timid Maria, she is your principal guardian spirit; there is a miniature or portrait of her, with some peculiarity in the dress, do you know it?" Mrs. Blackburn replied, "No." Home said, "Ah, well there is one, at any rate there is a black cut profile of her. There is an Alexander present." Home went on for some time speaking about the spirits in the room, and then stood behind my father and told us all to talk; while we were talking, he whispered to him, "You should not fast much." He said, "I do not really fast at all." Home added "Your brain is very active and is wearing the vital powers, and you should take nourishing food—fasting materially would be bad, but spiritually would be good for you." Home soon after awoke.   A.

After this we remained sitting for an hour and a quarter without any manifestations whatever. Mr. Home said several times, "I feel a strong influence all about me; it is strange that there are no physical manifestations." At last I proposed that some of the party should leave the room, being certain that something must be wrong. Blackburn and I went away. Mr. Home remarked, "A few moments will shew whether their presence was the obstruction." Still no manifestations. He then said, "Charlie, do you and Lawless go, and send the others back." Lawless went with the greatest reluctance. The door had hardly closed when there were cold currents, vibrations, and raps. I returned, and was scarcely seated, when the alphabet was called for, and this message given: "*We love Freddy, but he is not in a state of mind or body conducive to manifestations.*" Wynne fetched the accordion. Mrs. Blackburn was very soon after touched on the dress, and something became plainly visible moving under the table cloth, along the edge of the table, raising up the cloth several inches, as would be done were a hand and arm. The hand was visible on the cloth to Mr. Home, and I once faintly perceived it. It touched Mrs. Blackburn's hand. This manifestation was repeated different times. I was touched on the ankle, and several times on the knee. Miss Wynne's dress was strongly pulled. The table was beautifully raised in the air, by three successive lifts, to the height of eighteen inches or two feet. Mr. Home then took the accordion, holding it under the edge of the table with one hand, the other resting on the table; soon after it began to sound, it played with considerable power as well as great delicacy, something like a voluntary, with airs introduced. Then there were sounds like echoes, so fine, as to be scarcely audible. The accordion was drawn out towards Mrs. Blackburn, but not put into her hand. I expressed a wish that it might be played without being held by Mr. Home, upon which he withdrew his hand, placing it on the table; the instrument was just touching the under edge of the table, where it remained, as it were, suspended. It began playing very gently. He clapped his hands several times to shew that he was not touching it. The playing soon ceased, and he took it again. Some notes sounded out of tune, and I said, "either wrong notes are played in the chord, or the accordion is out of tune. "*Out of tune*" was rapped out on the instrument. It played again very finely, and with the tremolo effect, which struck me exceedingly. I asked, "Will you tell us who is playing;" two raps were given, implying doubt. Presently the alphabet was called for, and the following given: "*Remember that;*" and then "Oft in the stilly night" was softly played. When one recalls the words:—

> Oft in the stilly night, ere slumber's chain hath bound me,
> Fond memory brings the light of other days around me, &c.

how touching the message becomes, and how beautiful the mode of representing it.* I then again asked, "Will you not tell us the name of the spirit who has been playing." The letters "*a-u-g*" were rapped out by my being touched delicately on the knee. I guessed the completion of the word, saying, "Is it Augusta?" and I was touched, "*Yes.*" I then asked whether it would be possible for the organ to be played if the bellows were filled, and the reply "*Perhaps,*" was given. I said, "I can identify the player from a particular circumstance." Some one remarked, "Is it from what was played, or by the expression?"

---

* This air was, long ago, one of my greatest favourites.

" No," I replied, when Adare said, " Is it from the imitation of the tremolo?" " Yes," I replied, " that reminded me immediately of the organ;" upon which the following was instantly rapped out, by my being again touched on the knee : " *You are right my own.*" Soon after this we all heard strong sounds which proceeded seemingly from a large oblong writing table, which stood several feet from us; we could perceive it moving; it stopped within a foot of our table, which then moved up to it. We heard first one and then another drawer opened, on the side of the table farthest from us, and a rustling sound as if stirring papers. After a short pause, the following sentence was given, partly, if not wholly, (I forget which) by tilting the table: " *We must cease, but not before praying God to bless you.*" We then adjourned. During the sitting the table was again lifted in the beautiful manner before mentioned, reminding me very much of the action of the bellows of the organ while being filled; and it is very remarkable that this occurred, as will be seen in the foregoing description, just before the playing commenced.

D.

Having left my room, Home and I went down to the smoking room. While he was speaking to me he broke off suddenly in the middle of a word with a violent start and went into a trance. Major Blackburn at that moment came into the room, and witnessed what occurred. Home jumped up, caught me by the hand, beckoned to Major Blackburn to follow, and led us up to my room in a great hurry. On opening the door, he said (apparently to some spirit in the room), " Oh, please do not do that!" He then drew out the long writing table, placed it near the window, put two chairs in front of the fire, and hung a blanket over them to exclude the light; then placed a chair at each end of the table for us, and one for himself at the side of the table opposite the window and the drawers. He drew out one of the drawers and placed a piece of paper and a pencil in it; then sitting down, he said, " Listen!" I listened, and distinctly heard the sound of a pencil writing on a piece of paper in the open drawer; the word written was finished by three dots. Home then threw himself back in his chair and said, " Oh, she is so thankful that your father has seen what he has!" He began to sob violently, and calling me over to him, he grasped my hand, and said, " Oh, my darling I am so glad that he has seen something; I wish he could have been here now, but the conditions happened to be favourable at this moment, and we could not wait. You will give him the paper on which I have written, and the pencil; the pencil must be kept; it may be used again, but only at Adare. There was a spirit here when you came in, who damaged the conditions a little, and the writing is in consequence not very firm; the pencil point also broke, and the last letters are not quite distinct; the colour of the pencil is typical of my love—pure, deep, and everlasting." The pencil was a red one, and the word written was "*Augusta.*" Home, on being asked afterwards about his going so suddenly into a trance, said, "I can remember being in the smoking room, and seeing two spirits enter by the door; rapidly approaching, one of them stretched out his hand towards me, and I immediately lost consciousness." A.

No. 57.

It was now nearly 10 p.m., and my father, Charlie Wynne Home and I went to the Abbey; we walked up the church, and stood near the altar. Home shortly went into a trance. He took off a white comforter that he wore round his neck, and tied it over his head, and began walking with rapid measured strides up and down the church. By the expression of his face, by his gestures, and by his moaning, he appeared to be in great agony of mind. As he walked he made (with his mouth, I think) a sound that appeared to us closely to resemble that of a man walking in sandals or wooden shoes, upon a tiled or stone floor. His head became luminous, as did also his hands. This occurred twice; the second time more faintly. An owl flew round the church screeching; I attributed the noise to Home, but as he passed me he said in a most awful voice, "No, it is not so;" and as he repassed, he added, "You were mistaken." He kneeled upon the ground occasionally, waved his arms above his head, and appeared in great distress. He came up to us and, in a frightened tone of voice, said, "Oh, come away—come away!" and led us down to the other end of the church. He walked about a little longer, then, taking my father's arm, he said, "Do you see that tomb-stone with the light shining upon it? It would be better, aye, ten million times better, to lie there in the cold dark clay, than to spend years upon years, every moment of which is an eternity, in wandering here. Raising his hands above his head, he added, "oh, I am so weary—so weary!" Soon after this he awoke. He was rather nervous, and said to me, "Who is that man standing by the window? Is it Lord Dunraven?" He seemed quite astonished when he found we were all near him, and that none of us could see the figure.

During the rest of the time we remained in the Abbey, Home was entranced, I suppose, four or five times, and even in the intervals, when he was awake and knew where he was and what he was doing, he was under a very strong influence. He

H

stood talking to us for a few minutes, and then said, " The figure is beckoning to me, I am quite awake and not the least nervous; I must go." He accordingly moved towards the window and we followed him at a short distance. He left the church by the choir door, and went beyond the low broken wall, saying that he saw the figure standing against a portion of the ruins, at some little distance from where we were standing. I saw a dark shadow against the wall, and I saw a light flash from it as distinctly as if some one had struck a match there; Charlie Wynne said he saw the light flash at the same moment that I did; my father saw the light also, but faintly. Home walked towards the spot where he said the figure was standing, he went behind the wall, and remained out of sight for some minutes; when he reappeared there was somebody, or something with him, that is to say, I could clearly perceive some substance moving along side of him as he walked. Presently we all saw him approaching, and evidently raised off the ground, for he floated by, in front of us at a height which carried him over the broken wall, which was about two feet high. There could not be a better test of his being off the ground, for as he crossed the wall, his form was not in the least raised, but the movement was quite horizontal and uniform. The distance that we saw him thus carried, must have been at least 10 or 12 yards.

He then came back to us and we found he was in a trance. He directed our attention to an old doorway near us, saying, " He is there; he is laying a stone; you will hear the sound of a trowel." We listened and heard indistinct sounds; I cannot say that they resembled the sound of laying a stone. Home then awoke, and said that he remembered that, before he went into the trance, he had been walking about with a man dressed like a friar in a brown gown; that they had been talking together, but that he did not know what he had said to him; that this spirit (the friar) was unable to leave the earth; that he and the spirit had both been raised in the air by some other strong influence. He described the spirit as leaning on his shoulder. He soon left us, and apparently was again engaged in conversation with this spirit. He then returned, and spoke to us. This he repeated two or three times, being sometimes in a trance and sometimes awake when he addressed us. Finally, while in the trance, he led us back into the church, kneeled on the ground, apparently in prayer, two or three times, and then began walking up and down the church, raising his hands above his head, and saying, " Oh, how good! Oh, how good!" He then came up to us, and told us that the spirit would be better and happier for something that he had said or done that night, after which he awoke. He said that he saw a figure in the air between us and the window. Charlie Wynne and I both saw a shadow move across the window. We then returned home.

It is a fact worthy of notice that although the night was perfectly calm, the birds appeared to be in a singularly disturbed state; owls were flitting about, and some other bird flew several times round the church, screaming harshly. Besides night birds, ordinary birds (judging by the sounds) were flying about; and at one time, just as Home said he saw the figure enter a clump of trees at some distance from us, a bird seemed to fly out, chirping. We heard in the church a sound as of a bird flying round whistling, and Home, being then in a trance, appeared as if following it about, and endeavouring to catch it. I could see nothing, and do not know whether it was a real bird or not.

A.

———

Accurate as is the foregoing account of this strange scene, it would be difficult, indeed impossible, to convey by any description, a just idea of its solemnity. When we entered the ruins the night was quite dark and very still. We walked quietly up the nave and choir, and stood for some little time near the east window. Scarce a word was spoken. We had not the least idea what sort of manifestations were likely to occur. While Mr. Home was walking about, what with the deep tones of the voice so utterly unlike his own—the occasional moans and utterances of sounds of pain or distress—his disappearing in the gloom and reappearing again—the light shining around his head and upon his hands, which were occasionally lifted as if in prayer, and were thus visible when the rest of the figure was lost in darkness; his attitudes, sometimes kneeling, at others as if searching for something near the ground—the strange sounds which we heard, particularly a sort of chirping or unearthly whistling, which seemed to proceed from him, and the startling screams made by some bird, but what bird we had not light enough to identify; the effect produced upon us was most thrilling, and one which we are not likely soon to forget. Before leaving the Abbey the light from the moon, just about to rise, enabled us to see objects; the sky too had become clear, and the stars shone out, while an air of calmness and peace pervaded the scene, producing a most soothing effect upon our minds.

D.

———

We had supper in the hall upon our return. While talking, a curious rushing or rumbling noise was heard that we could not account for, and my father felt his chair vibrating. Home went into a trance, and told us to follow him into the gallery. We did so, and at his request stood near the piano, while he sat down at the instrument. The piano vibrated strongly. Home played a powerful and impressive chant, and then commenced speaking of the joys and sorrows of our life, telling us how they (the spirits) sympathized with us. He described what he was speaking of on the piano, playing discords for the sorrows and trials of life, and harmony for the joys. He said, " There is a merry spirit here who rejoices that you have done good," and he played a lively air. He added, " They made that rushing noise you all heard down stairs, to testify their happiness that you have all done a good action in going to the Abbey to-night" (turning to my father), " It was your father and your brother who shook your chair in the hall." He then began speaking about the immeasurable goodness and greatness of God, and finally rose up, stood in the middle of the room, and delivered a very beautiful prayer in the most impressive and earnest manner. He then awoke. It was past three o'clock. A.

No. 58.—Séance, March 5th.

This evening, one of the ladies who had previously been much interested in the subject of Spiritualism, was seized with a sudden and unaccountable idea that the whole thing was either demoniacal in its origin or imposture, and that it was her duty to denounce it. She did so in such unmeasured terms that she suc-ceeded in thoroughly disquieting the minds of more than one of our party. After dinner we had a *séance* in my room : present, Mrs. and Miss Wynne, Major and Mrs. Blackburn, Charlie Wynne, my father, Home and myself. We had scarcely any physical manifestations, but shortly after sitting down we received the following message :—" *The conditions are not so favourable this evening ;*" my father asked if the conditions were affected by any one in the circle, the answer was, " *No.*" We soon after obtained the following communication, having reference probably to a conversation that had taken place that afternoon on Spirit-ualism, and its effect upon religion :—" *We do not bid, or even wish, you to have faith in us, we only come to proclaim immortality, and the reality and nearness of the spiritual world.*" * Home soon went into a trance, and walked about the room, magnetizing it ; he stood by Mrs. Wynne, and said, " Your brother Windham is near you and wishes to kiss you, his mouth is close to your forehead, but you are nervous and that prevents it ; he will come again presently and will do it if he can." Home now sat down and spoke somewhat as follows :—" The conditions are not affected

---

* Some interruption occurred, which prevented the words after "*immortality, and,*" being written down ; the remainder is supplied from memory, and is believed to be correct.

by any one in particular in the circle, but by the disturbed and agitated state of your minds; a good many unpleasant things have occurred to-day and have caused this. The possibility of our communicating with you is much affected by the condition of your minds; a calm and prayerful state is absolutely necessary for the approach of a high spiritual influence, while in an unsettled and irritated condition you become easy of access to the lower and less pure influences.

The human mind in its natural beauty is calm, and casts a holy and peaceful influence on all near it; it is then like a lovely flower, not only beautiful to the eye, but affecting all around with its delicious fragrance. But, when disturbed and terrified by fears and doubts, the beauty of the mind and its fragrance are destroyed, resembling the same flower crushed and unable any longer to shed abroad its sweet and natural odours. The present disturbed condition of some among you has a much wider effect than you would suppose; as, if you drop a stone into the placid waters of a lake, the ripples will spread out gradually widening and widening until they have passed over a large portion of its surface; so, in like manner, the waves emanating from your minds have a wide-spread influence upon the atmosphere around you." Home spoke to us for some time very beautifully in a soothing tone of voice; he deprecated the idea that spirits wished to interfere in matters of religion. "Do we," he said, "set ourselves up as teachers, or tell you to love God less, or to be uncharitable? Do we interfere with the every-day walk of life?" He spoke in this strain for some little time, then saying, "the conditions are getting a little more favourable," he arose, went to the door, opened it, and appearing to invite some one to enter, led the person up to Mrs. Blackburn, saying to her as he did so, "He cannot come fast." During the address Mrs. Blackburn had become slightly under influence; Home took no notice of it at the time, but he now stood by her making passes, and calmed her. He spoke to her very beautifully and earnestly on the subject of the power she possessed of being developed as a medium. He entreated her to have trust, not in them (the spirits) but in God; he begged her to repeat after him "Thy will be done," and he seemed much pleased when she did so. He said, "Do you remember to whom these words apply? 'And he did not many mighty works there because of their unbelief!'" "Yes," she said, "they refer to Christ." "Then, if the highest and mightiest power had this difficulty to contend with, namely, their unbelief, how much more must it affect us. Oh, have faith and trust." Home then sat down and addressed us on the same subject of mediumship, drawing a simile from an account my father had been giving us of a fortnight he had spent in Quarantine, in a place just like a prison. He spoke somewhat as follows : " Dunraven has been telling you how he spent some time shut up, deprived of the society of his friends.   Now if you were in prison, knowing that your friends were without, separated from you only by a great impassable wall, would you not yearn—oh, so earnestly—to send them a few words of love ; then if you found some one who was capable of carrying a message for you, would you not think it a little hard if that person refused.   Although you might know that your message would be distorted and confused by passing through the hands of a third person, that you could not possibly say all that you would wish; still would you not be intensely anxious to send—if only one word—to testify of your existence to your sorrowing and weeping friends.   It is so with us; there is between us and you a great barrier, through the portals of which we have passed; we yearn to send a few words of love to the dear ones we have left beyond it, and when we find some one who could carry that message, is it not just a little hard that they should be unwilling to do so."   (Turning to Mrs. Blackburn), " Do you not love your children?   Will you not ever love them, even when you have passed away?   Think then of others—be not selfish—God is not selfish in his love for us, trust in Him." Home got up and whispered to my father, " You ought to have taken some nourishing food to-day," (the day was Friday).   He then came to me and said, " Go to the Castle to-night, we may not be able to make any manifestations, but it will do good; you will go to the Abbey to-morrow night—ah, but it will rain!" he went to the window, looked out and said, " No, it will do, you will go after twelve o'clock, do not have any *seance* before you go ; the external influence is not very good for your nerves." Home now walked about the room making a sound as of kissing some one, he then sat down and awoke.   Subsequently the manifestations were slight, and we got the message : " *We think it better to reserve the power till later.*"   We then adjourned.

Soon after, we proceeded to the Castle, Home and I walking a little in advance of the others.   On the way he became under influence.   As we neared the Abbey I saw a whitish shadow pass from the ruin into a clump of trees, Home said, " That is the same spirit you saw there the other night, you observe that he is much whiter."   Home ran forward on the road jumping apparently with delight, and when he came back said, " I was made to do that to shew you that he is much happier."   When we were about half-way between the Abbey and the Castle, Home said, " It all looks peopled, they are more real to me than those," turning and pointing to the rest of the party, who were a few yards behind.   He now became completely entranced, and said, "Spirits are sometimes compelled to revisit places that they were much connected with when on earth. It may not be exactly a punishment; they may be occupied about many other things, but at certain seasons they are drawn by an irresistible impulse to revisit such places. Now, supposing you had an estate, and the people on the neighbouring property differed from you in opinions or belief, and you gathered your people together and fought against them, destroying property and even life; that would be all very well for a time, but then you know there comes the passing away, and you see clearly all the evil you have done, and the misery you have caused. Such a man was Oliver Cromwell. Of course, where a man errs through ignorance, and acts up to the best of his knowledge and ability, it is a different thing, but so many men are actuated by a desire for renown and singularity; there is as much pride in wishing to appear different from other men, as there is in being over anxious to conform exactly to them, the Quaker, who puts on that peculiar costume is in reality as vain as the fop who dresses himself in the height of fashion." We now entered the Castle, and Home led us over the drawbridge into the inner court, being still in a trance. He bandaged his eyes with a handkerchief, saying, "There is too much light." My father observed, "Yes, it is brighter than it was at the Abbey." Home replied, in rather a sharp tone of voice, "Oh, not that sort of light; but there is too much for Daniel's eyes." He walked about, and up and down the steep slope leading to the vaults without any difficulty, and then went into the vault, where it was quite dark. We heard a noise; I was at some distance from him, but my father, thinking that he had tumbled down the steps, and hearing the splash of something in the well, went forward to the door feeling for him, and touched his hand. Home said, "You think that Daniel fell and was hurt, oh, no; he would not be hurt even were he to fall from the top of the tower; they are here, and want to make themselves visible." My father heard raps under his feet which I could not hear, as I was several yards distant; he also heard a sound like drops of water falling, and on two occasions observing that three consecutive drops fell, sounding like three raps, he said, "That is water." Home replied, in rather a contemptuous tone of voice, "No; does water answer questions." Charlie Wynne asked if Dr. Elliotson was present; and three heavy thumps were heard above, as if on the ground over the vault. Home then came out, climbed up on the parapet wall, and remained there some time, being generally concealed from us by the ivy; when he returned, he led my father a little in advance of us, saying, "He is trying to speak to you." My father could neither see nor hear anything; but I saw a faint light against the wall, and heard indistinct sounds as of some one trying to articulate. Charlie Wynne also saw the light. Mrs. Blackburn asked Home if the spirit was happy. " No," he said; " but unhappy in a way you cannot understand, he is in a kind of way, happy in his unhappiness; he is not exactly going through a punishment, but he has a great work to do—a work that he can—(drawing himself up, and speaking in a proud determined tone of voice)— aye, and that he *will* accomplish; he says he wishes to like you, Dunraven, and to be of service to you; but he does not quite feel as if he was worthy enough." Home now walked about the inner yard and stamped upon the ground all about a particular spot, then calling me and my father, he said, " There must be a well here; I saw a blueish light over it." We stamped upon the place, and it had a hollow sound. Home having awoke we left the Castle, he and I walking on before the others; we passed through the Abbey, but saw nothing. Home went into a trance, and said, " You have been thinking about the lichens on the trees, you may draw a parallel between the condition of those trees and that of the human race. Those lichens resemble the pernicious influences that check and retard the race from its natural progress towards perfection, as a time comes when the trees are thus affected, so are there ages of advance and ages of retrogression among men. It does as you say seem hard for those who live in a period of retrogression, but God's ways are not our ways, and the progress though it may be slow and checked, is yet inevitable, and sure to prevail in time; nations may pass, and their civilization fade away, but it will be taken up elsewhere; the creation is but in its infancy, man is very far removed from the perfection to which he ought—aye, and to which he will—arrive. These lichens do not appears to have been caused by the excessive dampness of the seasons, they seem to be a deep-rooted blight that has not originated even, on the earth, but has come over it in some sort of cloud; it is like a contagious disease: thinning, and giving them air, would do good. We think that in about two years they will get long, and the wind will blow them away to a great extent—we mean the white ones; the green ones are flatter, and their roots sink deeper; some of us seem to think that a belt of tar round the trees might do good,—the experiment would be worth trying." Home now awoke.

We had a little supper after we got home, and then Home proposed that we should go up to the gallery. We all did so and sat at the large centre table, the room being lighted only by a glimmer from the fire. Vibrations commenced immediately. Home went into a trance, walked to the piano, and played the same fine chant as on a previous occasion. He called my father over, made him stand near him, and said, "I wish one of you could note down this chant; do you hear the harp?" We all heard the chords very delicately and faintly swept, the harp being covered at the time; Home then removed the cover and my father heard some noise or movement about the harp and Home added, "They are trying to tune it;" they then returned to the table, and Home awoke. We had strong vibrations and raps, and Charlie Wynne asked whether Dr. Elliotson was present. This was answered by three very loud raps. Miss Wynne said to my father, "Did you know him?" "*Yes,*" was answered in the same manner. The alphabet was then called for, and the following message, evidently referring to my father's mesmeric experiences, was given. "*Be as true in this cause as you were in bye-gone days for another great truth, John Elliotson.*" After this, raps of different kinds were heard, and soon the following message was given by very loud ones. "*I do not ask you to promise, but expect you to be earnest in working for God.*" Some one remarked, "Who is this message for?" "*I speak to you,*" was answered. "But, who do you mean by 'you?'" was asked. "They mean me," my father said, "for I was touched three times on the knee." Charlie Wynne having brought the accordion, it was played in Home's hand in a different style from the previous evening. My father held the accordion, and it was pulled about and played faintly. Home again took it, and the alphabet being asked for by five notes, the following was given—the letters being indicated by notes: "*We will give you a hymn of praise.*" A slow measured sort of air was played. My father was talking about Dr. Elliotson, and observed that he had been very kind to him. This message was immediately given: "*You mean you were kind to me.*" A sofa was now moved near the table, the table also moving towards it, but evidently with much difficulty; which is not to be wondered at as it was very heavy and standing on a thick Turkey carpet. My father's chair was moved nearer to Home, who said, "I can see Dr. Elliotson standing behind your chair, he has both his hands upon the back of it, and is causing it to vibrate." My father's chair was in effect vibrating at the time; he inquired if Dr. Elliotson had been at the Castle. "*Yes*" was answered by three raps or rather thuds exactly similar to those he had heard at the Castle. Soon after this message came, "*We must go soon.*" My father asked, "Will Mesmerism make progress? it appears to be rather in abeyance at present." "*Yes*" was loudly answered; he added "I should like to ask Elliotson some questions about Mesmerism," and this message was given, "*By the sea I will come*," alluding I suppose to our projected visit to Garinish, on the coast of Kerry. In one of these messages the letters were indicated by touching my father strongly on the knee. Mrs. Blackburn was also touched on the knee. Soon, "*Now, God bless you all*," was given, the letters being indicated by most beautiful chords upon the accordion—the name of God being, as it always is, spelled most softly and reverently. This sentence was then given, "*You will sleep all the more peacefully for knowing that you have done good.*" The raps were much gentler and fainter, apparently made by quite a different spirit. My father said "What does this message refer to?" Mrs. Blackburn remarked, "I suppose to what happened at the Castle." "*Yes*" was answered. Nothing more occurring we left the room. The raps made by Dr. Elliotson sounded as loud as if they had been caused by some one under the table striking it with a hammer.   A.

No. 59.—*March 6th.*

Adare dined in Limerick: after the ladies left the room Major Blackburn, Mr. Home and I commenced talking of the *séances* which had been held here last winter. I remarked that probably L—— was connected with the unsatisfactory occurrences that happened, and that I should be very glad if the matter could in any way be cleared up. We heard raps at the north side of the room, and Mr. Home went over to a side table near where the raps had sounded, and sitting down said, "I wish, dear spirit, you would tell us about it." "*No*," was answered. He added, "Lord Dunraven would be gratified if you would tell." The alphabet was called for, and this message was given, "*Don't ask.*" Raps were then heard near the table in the bay window; Mr. Home sat down at this table, calling us to join him, which we did. On the table were three flower pots or vases with flowers, in one was a good-sized azalea; the table vibrated so strongly that the azalea shook most visibly. We soon received this message: "*Place the flowers under the table, near John.*" We put down, as directed, one of the flower pots which contained cyclamens. Raps were heard upon the table. I said to Blackburn, "Get under the table and hold Mr. Home's feet." He did so, and we heard the raps distinctly over his head. Mr. Home suddenly said, "Oh, look at the hand near me holding a flower!" Twice he said that he saw the hand. I, somehow, instinctively, put my hand under the table, and immediately felt a flower placed very gently in it. The following was then given:—"*The flower is from Augusta, with fond love.*" Then another sentence was begun, which I could not well make out, and then "*a. d.*" No more raps occurring after this we left the table. On bringing the paper to the candles on the dining table I found that the word I had not recognized was (as written) "*Augutsta.*" I had made a mistake, inserting a *t*. The *a. d.* were, I presume, initials.

In accordance with what we were told last night, we had no *séance* this evening, but, as directed, we went to the Abbey. Soon after arriving there, Adare joined us on his return from Limerick. Mr. Home was very lively, and not at all impressed. He remarked that the influence was quite different to-night. He shortly took Adare and me to the kitchen, and after a few turns up and down, he went into a trance. I walked with him, holding his hands. He said he was being touched, and so was I several times, very palpably on the back. He said that there were no spirits belonging to the place present, only those connected with us; we soon turned our steps homewards. Mr. Home and Adare walked together, and before awaking, Mr. Home spoke something to this effect, "You remarked how different everything felt in the Abbey to-night, to what it did the last time we were there. To-night, although the elements were disturbed, and the wind blowing, everything was quiet; no birds were flying about; the whole place seemed peaceful, whereas the other night, although it was perfectly calm and still, yet the birds, not night birds only, but seemingly others, were flitting about, and the whole place seemed filled with an unquiet influence. It is changed now; he (referring to the monk) is in a happier state, he can speak to those about you; he has no objection to your mentioning what occurred in your room when he first came. Oh, he does not the least mind now."

We were sitting in the hall after taking a little supper, when Mr. Home went to the piano and played, and asked Adare to come and sit by him. Adare now called me to join them. Mr. Home remarked that the piano had been off the ground, which Adare affirmed, stating that he had passed his hand under the castors; I felt it vibrating very strongly. His playing became fainter and fainter, and he went into a trance. He got up, said to Adare, "Bring Emily," and taking me by the hand led me quickly down the dark passage to Lady D's. sitting room, the others following. He placed chairs for us all, drew over a little table, and sat down. It was pitch dark. Immediately a hand was laid on the back of my head. He said, "They will touch you with flowers." Both Mrs. Wynne and I felt them. He said to Mrs. Wynne, "It was John who touched you." We heard at a little distance the sound of flowers being stirred and broken, and immediately some were placed in our hands. Mr. Home said, "Take Daniel's hands, dear Emily, we want you to be able to tell others that you held his hands, and felt his feet." While Mr. Home's hands and feet were thus in contact with Mrs. Wynne's, we all simultaneously felt flowers waved across our faces, heads, and hands. Mrs. Wynne put up her hand to try and grasp them, but failed. Mr. Home laughed, and said, " No, Emily, you cannot catch it—we do not wish you to yet." Flowers were then given to us all; Adare received a white azalea with this message, through Mr. Home, " For Florence." Then another flower was given us, with the message, " This for Augusta, and leaves or a flower for all the dear ones—for all the children. We wish to say one word if you will call the alphabet, Adare." He did so, and " *Love* " was given, by a flower placed in my hand, the stalk being pulled for each letter. I tried to feel the hand, but the flower was drawn back by the stem, till my arm was stretched out. We all then observed a light, resembling a little star, near the chimney piece, moving to and fro; it then disappeared. Mr. Home said, " Ask them in the name of the Father, the Son, and the Holy Ghost, if this is the work of God." I repeated the words very earnestly; the light shone out, making three little flashes, each one about a foot higher above the floor than the preceding. Mr. Home said, " We are able to make it brighter and stronger, because you asked solemnly, and in the name of God." We then heard a sound of something moving, and a shower of flowers fell about us. Loud raps announced the presence, as we supposed, of Dr. Elliotson. Mr. Home (or Dr. Elliotson speaking through him), uttered a short and beautiful address, which, unfortunately we cannot recall; but he made use of a simile ending with the words,—" As the sand on the shore." I felt a little heap of sand laid upon the back of my hand. In his address he said, " You have been baptized in the name of the Father, the Son, and the Holy Ghost; be now baptized as a truth seeker." I then felt a drop of some liquid fall on my head. Mr. Home then said, " Emily, would you like to feel the sand?" Mrs. Wynne replied, " Yes;" and a small quantity was placed on the back of her hand. He then said, " Emily, you will feel a kiss on the brow, and also on the lips." She felt something, which she afterwards described as more resembling two moist fingers than an ordinary kiss. I asked, " What spirits are here?" Mr. Home answered, " Augusta, Emily's father, mother, and brother; also others." Mrs. Wynne seemed grieved at the absence of one very dear to her: Mr. Home in a subsequent *séance*, at Garinish, (p. 126) alluded to this. He then addressed us and those dearest to us in very affectionate terms, and seemed very happy; he ended by saying, " We have been so pleased at being able to make these manifestations. You did not witness much at the Abbey, nor did we promise that you would; what we wanted was to keep you up late enough for this, and it has happened as we wished. And now, darlings, you will return to the hall, and sit by Daniel at the piano; Daniel's power is becoming exhausted; there will probably be no manifestations to-morrow evening, but we will let him know; he is not very well, but he does not like saying so." We then got up, went back to the hall, and sat down as directed at the piano; Mr. Home awoke almost immediately. It was half-past three o'clock. I took a candle and returned to the room we had been in; I found the little table and the ground about it strewed with flowers. The table on which the flower pots stood was about eight feet distant from the other; there was a good deal of sand in the flower pots. Adare and I went up to Mr. Home's room, and smoked a cigarette; Mr. Home was in bed. We began talking about Spiritualism, and I said, "I am quite sure that L—— was concerned in what went on last winter here."* "*Yes*" was suddenly said by three distinct raps in a distant part of the room. I made other remarks, which were similarly joined in by raps; but I was very tired, and cannot sufficiently recall them to insert them here.   D.

No. 60.—*Garinish, March 9th.*

While my father, Home, and I were at dinner, we all felt a current of cold air, and the table vibrated. This occurred two or three times, and seemed to be interrupted by the servants coming in and out. At about ten o'clock, Home joined me in the dining room, where I was writing alone, he seemed uneasy and I asked him if he was not feeling well. "Oh, yes," he said, "I am quite well; but there is a strange influence about that I do not know." Shortly after, raps came upon the table, and the following messages were given. "*Owing to conditions, we fear we shall not be able before Thursday; but we will try to-morrow. Humphrey May.*" "*Use this table.*" "*Tell Uncle* (word confused) *not to be over anxious.*" I took the messages to my father, and he joined us in the dining room, observing how curious it was that Humphrey May should come, that he had never been with us before, that he had never been at Garinish, and that he could not understand why he came. "There is one," he said, "that I should have supposed would have come here before all others, and I should also have thought Dr. Elliotson would have made some communication, because he told us the other night at Adare that he would do

---

* I subsequently found that the occurrences to which I alluded, chiefly took place before L—— arrived at Adare.

so." We began talking about some *séances* that were held at Adare, without Home, alluding particularly to one, the written account of which Home happened to be holding in his hand. The alphabet was called for, and this message given: "*The writing that you hold in your hand is all nonsense.*" Soon after, Home went into a trance; he got up and said, "The light is too strong for Dan." I blew the candles out, leaving a good fire-light in the room, and began searching for a pencil to take notes. He said, "The light will do nicely now, never mind about taking notes, you will be able to record what Dan says better without doing so; we will endeavour to impress you with it to-morrow, and you will remember the substance, if not the exact words; by trusting entirely to us, we shall be able to assist you more than if you took notes, and trusted to them; what I am going to say now is important you must try and remember it. Certain conditions are necessary for us to be able to make any manifestations; by conditions, I mean not only the state of the external atmosphere, but also the state of your minds and bodies; certain electrical conditions are necessary. Now, it often happens that some spirit—though possibly a perfect stranger to all of you—is possessed of the particular quality that is necessary to supply a deficiency and make the conditions favourable, he would then be called in. Sometimes three or four of them club together, and by that means supply something that is wanting, or take away some quality that is in excess, and equalize the atmosphere so as to be able to make manifestations. Those spirits that love you best, that are most anxious to communicate, that would naturally be nearest and dearest to you, may not have the peculiar quality that is necessary to harmonize with the condition of yourselves, and of the external atmosphere on any particular day, and they cannot then make communications, it is impossible, for it is all a matter of physical conditions; they are then obliged to communicate through other spirits who harmonize with the existing conditions. That is one reason why Humphrey May came to-night. You often wonder why those you love best do not come to you, it is simply because the conditions are such that they cannot make themselves known. Now the other night the spirit that Emily was anxious about was standing outside the circle, Emily thought it most strange that she did not say anything to her, but if she had entered the circle it would have entirely destroyed the arrangements, and there could have been no more manifestations; it is surely better to have any communications than none at all. This explains also why it is generally a bad plan to ask questions; after things have been arranged, some spirit steps into the circle to answer a question, and not being in harmony, the whole thing is thrown out of gear. It is like making delicate experiments in electricity; or like photography—to go no further than that, if, when you are mixing your chemicals in a dark room, one single ray of light enters, all is destroyed; so it is where a spirit enters the circle whose physical condition does not harmonize with the state of the atmosphere, and of your minds and bodies. The conditions are very bad to-night; you saw what difficulty we had in giving those messages, the raps were feeble and uncertain (we had observed this), the word '*Uncle*' ought to have been '*Dunraven;*' we spelled out '*dun,*' and then the letters became all confused, we could not indicate the right ones. You heard those raps that came afterwards— you would scarcely believe that they were made by Dr. Elliotson, so different were they from those he usually makes; yet so it was. Oh! there has been a curious influence here all the afternoon—an old man, his name is Thomas—Thomas Trench; he has a bald head—a large bald head." My father asked if he had come with Towny Trench.—"Yes, he came with him; he belongs to him. Dr. Elliotson says, that if the conditions are favorable, he wants to make some experiments on Thursday; he is so anxious about it, he wants to invent some more perfect means of keeping up a constant communication; it is very doubtful if he will ever succeed. He knows your mind, Dunraven, and he would like to make his experiments with you; he is very much interested in the matter, and so will you be also when you join us; you will take a great pleasure in experimentalizing." Home then went to the door of the drawing room, made a gesture of disapproval, and said, pushing the door open as he spoke, " No, you must not do that, please." We heard a dull sound in the drawing room. Home laughed and said, " That is Thomas, he does not approve of your investigations, and he thought he would make a very terrible noise in there, that would frighten you and put a stop to it all and destroy the conditions; but he cannot do so." I said, " Why on earth does he disapprove; do you not mean Henry Thomas?"—" Oh dear no, he is a great experimentalizer in electricity; no, I mean the Thomas I told you of, Thomas Trench." I said, " Why does he object?"—" Oh, it is entirely against his principles, and he thought he would make a very weird horrible noise and frighten you, and stop it." My father said, " Will he then seek to influence Towny against Spiritualism?"— " Most decidedly he will; oh, most decidedly. There is another reason besides that which I have already mentioned, why Humphrey May came to us to-night. It is true that he was never here; but his brother Arthur has been, and will be here again. Arthur has, or rather had, no real religious opinions; he was not accustomed to pray; his heart was not softened and lifted to God in prayer. When he hears what occurred to-night, it will have an effect upon him. He knows that Dan, I mean Dan Home, could never have heard of Humphrey, that Humphrey was never here, and was probably the last person in the world that any of you were thinking of; and the fact of his coming will strike Arthur the more forcibly; it will be like a little test to him. Besides this, he was very fond of you, Dunraven, and also of Adare." After this, Home sat by the fire making passes, and magnetizing his wrist. He said, "Daniel's wrist is swelling, and hurts him." He then walked over towards the window, and stretching out his arm, we heard a sound as of some one's fingers snapping near it. He said, "That is Dr. Elliotson magnetizing Dan's hand." Home placed his hand upon my head, but immediately said, "No, was your father will do better," and placed it on his head. He said, "Listen;" and my father heard raps upon the hand. Home took the sheet on which the *séance* before mentioned was written, and asked us to hold it by the corners with him; we did so, and raps came upon it; then lifting up the sheet of paper, he said, "It is all black now; there is a good deal that is not right here, there is more in it than you see. Now, do you think that if a person were to participate and help in doing something wrong, and, when the others were suspected, were to keep silence, and let them bear all the blame, do you think that person would be right?" My father replied, "No, I think they would be very wrong." "And so do we," Home said, and throwing the paper down, added, "You see where we have thrown it?" "On the floor," I said. "Yes, just in front of the fire." I was going to put the paper in the fire, but my father thought we had better keep it. Home said, "Oh, certainly, keep it; it is interesting if only as a psychological study; you will, however, lose it some day." Soon after this, Home awoke. Although I had blown out the candles when Home went into the trance; the room was well lighted all the time by the fire.　　　　　　　　　　　　　　　　　　A.

No. 61.—*Séance, March* 11*th.*

This evening while Mrs. Blackburn, Home, and myself were sitting reading in the drawing room, raps came upon the table. Soon after, we, that is Major and Mrs. Blackburn, my father, Home, and myself, at Home's suggestion sat round the table that we had been told on Tuesday night to use. We had slight physical manifestations, the table was made light and

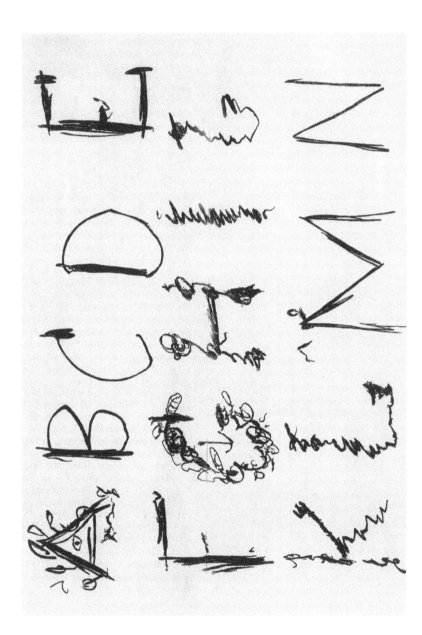

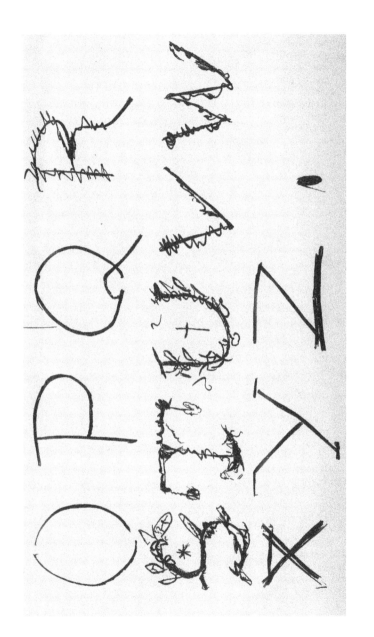

heavy at request, and was tilted three times towards each of us. The spirits occasionally answered our remarks as to what they were doing, whether they were endeavouring to concentrate the power, &c., &c., by affirmative or negative tilts. Mrs. Blackburn becoming slightly under influence, and a good deal agitated Home asked if the spirits would take it from her? The answer was by two raps meaning "*perhaps*" or "*presently.*" He afterwards placed his hands upon hers, and the shaking left her, and was communicated to him. Home now went into one of those strange trances in which he is unable to speak; he bandaged his eyes with a handkerchief, walked about the room a little, then brought the candle, two sheets of paper and a pencil, and placing them on our table, sat down; then spreading open one of the sheets he commenced writing the alphabet on it in large capital letters. He proceeded with a firm bold touch as far as the letter F, when his hand became violently tremulous, he went on to the letter L, the shaking of his fingers gradually increasing, when he made a gesture as if he could not proceed, and handed the paper and pencil to me. I finished the alphabet. He then, following the lines that I had made, traced over the letters R, S, T, U, V, W, with the same tremulous motion of his hand, and proceeded to decorate with leaves and flowers the letters A, G, S, T, U. He drew a cross in the letter U, a heart pendant on T, a star or double cross in S, an anchor in G, something resembling a bird in A, and marked the letters A and U with the figure 2.* He then got up and fetched a pen, handed me a fresh sheet of paper and the pencil, turned the alphabet towards my father, sat down and gave us the following messages, by indicating the letters with the pen. "*We hope to have great power, God being our helper.*" "*You see what ones they are.*" None of us could understand what the last sentence "*You see what ones they are*" referred to. Home spelled out "*The ones we have decorated.*" We then, on looking at the alphabet, found that the decorated letters spelled "*Augusta.*" the letters A and U, which occur twice in the word, being marked on the alphabet with the numeral 2. Home got up and went into the dining room, where we had been smoking after dinner, but returned immediately, much affected—as we supposed, by the tobacco smoke; he appeared to have difficulty in breathing, was much distressed, and groped about as if he could not see: † he caught hold of my hand and sat down. I observed that he was affected by something, and consequently the spirits had lost perfect control over him; Home nodded, as much as

---

* A fac simile of the alphabet is here appended.

† The effect of the tobacco smoke in partially obstructing the clairvoyant power was very curious to witness.—D.

I

to say, that is the case. He got up, went into the open air for a few minutes and returned quite right. He then made us leave our places, moved the table close to the window, placed the accordion on the window shelf, and spelt out by the written alphabet, "*Bring in the cloth.*" I accordingly brought the cloth from the dining room, covered our table with it, and sat down. On my father remarking that he had not spoken in the trance, Home made him and Mrs. Blackburn feel his jaws : they were locked and perfectly rigid ; he then sat down, and shortly after awoke. We had a series of curious but not very powerful manifestations ; the window curtains were drawn partially across the window, and in answer to the suggestion of one of us that perhaps the spirits did this to cover the accordion on which possibly they might be about to try and play, "*Yes*" was rapped out. Home saw on three or four occasions, and my father saw once, little flashes of light playing over the keys of the accordion. We heard that a small table behind Home was moving, and after the *séance*, we found it had been lifted on to the sofa. The table was now raised in that very peculiar manner which we had remarked at Adare, by successive lifts (five or six of them), to the height of about two feet, and then gently set down ; after which, "*Take the instrument*" was spelled. My father remarked that we might expect music, as this action of the table—imitating so curiously that of the bellows of the organ when being filled, usually preceded it.* Home took the accordion, and it played for a short time, chiefly harmonies. He then placed it on the ground, when a few chords and notes were played. We heard raps on the table, floor, walls, and outside the window ; and the spirits occasionally joined in our conversation by rapping, "*Yes*" or "*No.*" At one time we were speculating as to how Mr. Mahony would treat the subject of Spiritualism, and some one said that he would not judge of it fairly, for that he would condemn it at once without any investigation; the following message was immediately given : "*Judge not lest ye be judged.*" I observed that the manifestations were weak ; and that there appeared to be some obstruction, when this was given : "*Be prayerful.*" We recognized Dr. Elliotson's presence by his peculiar raps. Mrs. Blackburn remarked that they were not so loud as they had been in the gallery at Adare. He spelled out the word, "*servants,*" implying probably that if he were to rap as forcibly here as he had done at Adare, the servants might hear him, being in a room nearly under us. Home again became entranced; he got up, and put out the candle, so that the room was lighted only by a bright fire. My father said to me, "It is

---

* That this was the object aimed at by this peculiar motion of the table was afterwards told us, *vide* p.

curious that we have not had stronger manifestations, because the first message we received was to the effect that they would have great power." Home said, "You are mistaken, we said 'we *hope* to have great power;' we have to harmonize and arrange the room, we shall be able to do more another night. Dunraven, you were remarking that when Dan was in a trance no physical manifestations ever occurred; do you and Maria (Mrs. Blackburn) come here." He made them stand by a small heavy table in the centre of the room. My father said, "I thought Dr. Elliotson wished to try some experiments with me." Home answered, "Yes, this is one of the experiments; he is very anxious also to be able to communicate with you when you are quite alone, he does not know whether he can, but he will try and develope you sufficiently for that." They then had a series of the usual manifestations, raps, and vibrations, the table tilting in different directions, and being twice raised slightly off the ground. Home was very particular in making them observe closely the position of his hands and feet, in order, as he said, "That you may be able to assure others that Dan could not possibly have done all this." Suddenly the small table rose quickly into the air to such a height, that Mrs. Blackburn and my father could no longer keep their hands' upon it; it rose so suddenly that Mrs. Blackburn gave a start. The table beginning to fall, Home said, "Take it, or it will fall." When they had placed it on the ground, Home observed, "That was badly managed, it is a great pity but it is our fault; Dr. Elliotson says he ought to have told you what he was going to do, Maria was startled and you both let go, and therefore the table fell; if he had warned you, and you had allowed your hands to slip down the legs as it rose, so as not to break the continuity suddenly, it would probably have left your hands, and risen without contact with you until it touched the ceiling.* We will try and do it again; Adare and John, come here." We joined them, and Home told us all to place our fingers lightly under the edge of the table in order that we might let them slide down the legs without ever quite taking them off it. The table rose to a height of about three feet, but came to the ground again directly, and fell over on its side; Home told us not to move it, but presently he said "Yes, put it on its legs we have not power now; the influence has returned to the large table, go back to your places." We did so, and the Major not finding a chair near him, and the light being by this time faint. Home put one into his hand. The Major was going to sit down upon nothing, as he had by mistake placed the chair with the seat

* The room is about ten or eleven feet high.

turned away from him; Home stopped him saying, "No, no, Major, you are going to sit on the wrong side of the chair." We all laughed and Home joined in saying, "That was very funny was it not? very funny to see John trying to sit down at the back of the chair." Home then took his seat, and said, "Dr. Elliotson was anxious to try the experiment, and to see whether he could make manifestations when Dan was in a trance, and he succeeded; you had all the usual phenomena, the levitation of the table, raps, tiltings, and vibrations, but it required a great effort to do it; it is much more difficult, because the greater part of the influence is centred upon Dan while he is mesmerised. We are just as anxious as you are, Dunraven, to pass through the present phase of manifestations, but we must do our appointed work, and you will find that ultimately it is all for the best. It would be much pleasanter to converse with you and answer your questions; but then, however well we might answer them, people would account for that, by all sorts of theories, such as mind-reading, &c., &c. Now, no amount of clairvoyance or mind-reading would suffice to raise a table in the air higher than your heads. We must fulfil our appointed duties and you will know some day that it is all for the best." Home began to laugh and said, "It was very funny John's turning the chair the wrong way; your godmother (speaking to Mrs. Blackburn) is laughing so about it, it recalls another incident. You know John's mother has answered his letter, but she has not answered his question about Isabella; she and John's sister purposely would not do so, because they said, "it will never do to have John turning everything upside down in this sort of way." It amused Dr. Elliotson very much, that did; he was there when they said so. Dr. Elliotson is fond of you, Major (taking the Major's hand and shaking it cordially); he likes you very much; he says you are so steadfast, and an honest, brave, man. Dan is going to awake now." After Home awoke, we had some slight manifestations, which gradually died away. Home said he felt that the influence had entirely gone, and that he was fatigued. In speaking about the answer to the letter, Home referred to his having at Adare, when in a trance, told Major Blackburn to ask his mother about Isabella, and about Margaret Henderson *(vide p.* 109*).* No one had told Home that an answer had been received, or even that the Major had written.   A.

No. 62.—*Séance, March 12th.*

About half-past nine o'clock, Home proposed a *séance*. We placed the table by the window, in the position to which it had been moved the previous night, and covered it with a cloth. The party consisted of Major and Mrs. Blackburn, my father, Home, and myself. We had no manifestations whatever; and after sitting for half-an-hour my father said he thought there was no use in waiting any longer, having for a certain reason a strong feeling that nothing would occur. Home said that although he had often known *séances* to fail as regards manifestations, yet in all his experience he never remembered a room to feel so entirely devoid of any spiritual presence. At his suggestion, we all, with the exception of Mrs. Blackburn, took a walk out of doors for about a quarter of an hour. On our return we again sat round the table, but Mrs. Blackburn, not feeling very well, did not join us. We had no manifestations whatever; and after waiting a short time gave it up in despair. My father and Mrs. Blackburn went into the dining room; the Major, Home, and I remained and sat at a small table, to see if we could get any message. Almost immediately faint raps came upon the table, and the word "*Impossible*" was spelled out. We joined the others, and told them what had occurred. Mrs. Blackburn went to bed, and we were sitting round the supper table talking, when I suddenly felt a current of cold air. Home also perceived it, and said, "There is a strong influence about me." We heard raps on the table and furniture. Presently, at Home's suggestion, we returned to the next room, and again sat round the small table. We had faint physical manifestations; Home became under influence, and his hands were much agitated. He had been complaining during the evening of a feeling of great depression; he now said that he felt all right. He got up, and acting under an uncontrollable impulse, walked about the room, his hands and arms being strangely waved about and agitated; he made mesmeric passes over us all, and said (referring more especially to my father), "Your brains are overworked, you have had your thoughts too much concentrated on one subject, and have been writing too much. (We had been engaged in recording the *séances* at Adare). The atmosphere that spirits utilize in making manifestations emanates from the head, and in consequence of your brains being overworked, there is absolutely none flowing from you." He made passes for some time over my father's forehead, the back of his head, and behind his ears, occasionally going to the table at which we had previously been seated, and extending his fingers over it as though withdrawing some influence from it. While walking about he suddenly stopped in the middle of a sentence with a violent gasp, and sinking on his knees went into a trance. He got up, walked about, apparently conversing with some one, and then, taking each of us in turn by the hand, led us to the other table, placed chairs for us, and signed to us to sit down. My father requested me to bring paper and a pencil; but Home shook his head, and afterwards brought them himself. He then commenced arranging the furniture in the most minute detail, consulting apparently all the time with some one. He placed the small round table near us and behind my father, and moved a chair up to it; he altered the position of several of the chairs in different parts of the room, placed the miniature portrait of his wife on the small round table, and the case containing little Dannie Cox's photograph on the large table behind me, then going to the bookcase he took out several books, looked into them and replaced them; at length he appeared to find what he wanted, for he took out a volume, folded his hands across it on his breast, and after standing for a few seconds in a most reverential attitude, sunk down upon his knees and appeared to pray earnestly; then rising to his full height he held the book as high as he could above his head and placed it upon our table. On looking at the volume afterwards we found it to be, "Jesus Christ; His Times, Life, and Work," by E. de Pressensé. He again commenced making mesmeric passes about the room. Coming to me he passsed his hand sharply across my shoulders from left to right, did the same to Major Blackburn, then to my father, and finally to himself; then reversing the action, he commenced with himself making the pass from right to left, and went over us all in the same way; this curious movement he repeated three times. He now put out the candle leaving us with no other light but that of the fire, rubbed his hands, smiled, and nodded when I remarked that I thought we should have some manifestations as he seemed to be contented. Having taken his seat he altered the position of two vases of flowers on the table in such a way, as to make with the book, which he placed back upwards transversely between them, the form of a cross. The accompanying diagram shews the arrangement of the various articles. They are marked by capital letters in their original positions, while the altered places of those that were moved, are indicated by small letters.

Home awoke, and we had all the usual physical phenomena; very strong currents of cold air, vibrations of the table, &c., &c. On two occasions during the *séance*, the table was raised about a foot in the air and remained there poised for some time, oscillating

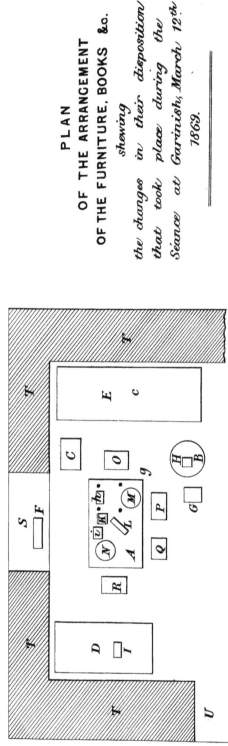

PLAN
OF THE ARRANGEMENT
OF THE FURNITURE, BOOKS, &c.

shewing

*the changes in their disposition
that took place during the
Séance at Garinish, March 12th.
1869.*

A. Table at which the Séance was held.
B. Small Table placed on A, as shewn
    by the four dots.
C. Small Table placed on E at c.
D. Table on which Daniel Cox's Photograph
    was placed by Mr Home.
E. Sofa.
F. Accordion on the Window-Shelf.
G. Chair moved to g.
H. Mrs Home's Miniature moved to h.
I. Daniel Cox's Photograph moved to i.

K. Primeval Man by the Duke of Argyll.
L. Pressense's Life of Christ.
M.N. Small Vases holding Flowers.
O. Mr Home's Chair.
P. Lord Ds Chair.
Q. Major Blackburn's Chair.
R. Lord A's Chair.
S. Window-shelf.
T. Wall of the Room.
U. South Window.
    Scale. ¼ Inch to a Foot.

gently from side to side. We now all heard a movement about vase N, and Home and I, both saw a hand upon it; I said that the vase was moving; Home insisted that it was not, and requested me to place my hand upon it; I did so, and found that it was moving slowly round, but the sound we heard was caused by the hand rubbing against the side of the vase; I saw the hand all the time. We now heard a rustling among the flowers, and Home said, " The fingers have closed over a flower and taken it away." I did not see the flower taken, but the hand at that moment disappeared. Home and I both observed a hand rise above the edge of the table near the window, and place a flower upon it; I then lost sight of the hand, but Home said he saw it carry the flower across the table, and place it near my father; my father saw the flower all the time moving as it were of itself, for he could not distinguish the hand that conveyed it. He took the flower, and asked if it was for him. The following was spelled out: " *Yes and we will give you another soon.*" My father remarking that he was very anxious to see a hand, the following messages were given: " *Place your hand over the flowers.*" He did so over vase N, and we all heard—and my father, Home, and I, saw, a hand moving among the flowers. " *Now on them.*" He did so, and the hand became much more distinctly visible to him. I said to my father, " I suppose you were told to place your hand there in order that they might draw some power from you to enable them to make the hand sufficiently material for you to see it distinctly. " *Yes,*" was answered by three loud raps. Sacha's (Home's wife's) miniature was now carried from table B, and placed upon our table; none of us saw anything supporting it, but we observed it placed quietly upon Home's hands, and then gliding off them it moved across the table until it remained stationary on the corner near the window. The case was closed when Home put it upon table B, at the commencement of the *séance;* it was open when laid upon our table. Home and I now distinctly saw a hand place little Dannie Cox's photograph (I) on the edge of our table next the window, and then push it a little further on to the table. It will be remembered that this photograph was placed by Home at the commencement of the *séance* on table D. Home and I perceived a whole arm and hand between our table and the window, it was slightly luminous, and appeared whiter than the white tablecloth. The hand pushed the accordion, F, along the shelf S, and then grasping it, took it off; the accordion fell, but not heavily, to the ground. All saw and heard the accordion moved. Home said, " I am sure that was little Dannie, because I saw a small figure; his shoulders were plainly visible; apparently he had not power sufficient to enable him to carry the instrument gently to the ground." This was spelled out, " *Yes, it was Dannie.*" Previous to the accordion moving, the muslin curtains were drawn out so as partially to hide it; this required some force to effect, as the curtain rings did not run easily on the line. A very pretty manifestation now occurred; Home called my father's attention to the fact, that the reflection of a hand was visible on the glass, covering his wife's miniature. My father also saw it, but was not sure whether it was the reflection or the actual hand; he placed his own hand just above the glass, and still saw in it the reflection of a small hand, moving backwards and forwards. He said, " I see it distinctly, the fingers are small and delicate." He asked whose hand it was, and the following was spelled out, " *The fingers are those of Caroline.*" The accordion was carried under the table to Home; he took it, and a short, but very beautiful harmony was played. Home replaced it on the floor, and chords were heard, when no one was touching it. In some of the messages also the letters were indicated, by notes played on the accordion. The following was now given. *Seek rather to know the present condition of the immortal soul* (the word soul being emphasised) *than,*"——here the message broke off abruptly. Home repeated the alphabet twice, and nothing occurred; but while saying it over the third time, a hand placed a book on the table; the message then continued, "*In good time, and with God's permission, the one will elucidate the other.*" On looking at the book, we found it to be " Primeval Man," by the Duke of Argyle. The message would therefore appear to mean, " *Seek rather to know the present condition of the immortal soul, than* to speculate about that of primeval man; *in good time, and with God's permission, the one will elucidate the other.* The book " Primeval Man " was at the commencement of the *séance* lying on a table in the centre of the room, at a distance of six or eight feet from us. The second flower that was promised to my father was now placed on the table near his hand; none of us saw anything supporting it, but Home perceived the flower moving in the air. A flower came from the direction of where Home was sitting towards me; it dropped on the edge of the table close to me, and fell on the floor: I saw it in the air. Home and I perceived a hand place something on the shelf under the window, and we saw a hand with a flower raised above the side of the table next the window; Home stretched out his hand towards it, and the flower dropped on the floor. Both my father and Home were repeatedly touched; I also, on four occasions, was most palpably touched by a hand patting my knee. Some one remarked that Major Blackburn had not been touched, soon after he declared that he felt a hand touch his knee; he asked who it was, and the name "*John*" was spelled. I said, "Do you know who John is?" he replied, "My father's name was John, but I do not know whether it was he that touched me." The words, "*Yes, your father*," were spelled; and then, "*We wish John also to see the hand; place your hand above, and then on, the flowers.*" Major Blackburn did so; we all heard the flowers rustling, and Home and I saw the hand doing it. The Major saw nothing while his hand was over the flowers; but when he touched them, he also saw the hand, though indistinctly. We now heard loud raps upon the small table C, and looking round, found that it had been lifted up and placed upon the sofa E at *c*; so quietly was it done that we should not have noticed it, had the spirits not called our attention by rapping upon it. My father asked if they had moved it in the same way last night; the answer was, "*Yes.*" The chair G was moved up to *g*, and the table B was moved close to it. The table B was then raised in the air (no one touching it), and placed gently, but without hesitation, upon our table A. The table B has four legs, like a camp stool; they rested where the four dots are marked, close to the vases, books and portraits, without touching any of them. We now felt very strong vibrations in our table; it was tilted from side to side, and so strongly towards my father's side, that he put out his hand expecting the small table B to fall over upon him; but nothing moved. About this time we heard curious sounds in the air; Home said, "Do you hear their voices? I will talk, never mind what I say the more I talk the plainer you will hear them." He went on speaking for two or three minutes, during which time we heard strange noises like high-pitched voices at a little distance, the louder he spoke the louder the sounds became, they were most peculiar; we could not hear any articulate words. Mrs. Blackburn, who had retired to bed in the room under that in which we were sitting, told us next day that she had heard strange sounds; and she imitated them so well, that we at once recognised that she really had heard the voices. Home then went into a trance, and said, "We are so very glad to have been able to effect what has been done for you; but the state of the external atmosphere, and the fact of Dan being ill, are very much against us; we have not been able to do by any means all that we intended. Dr. Elliotson was most anxious that you should have some manifestations to-night, he hopes circumstances may be more favourable to-morrow; he would like to come to you Dunraven, and talk to you, and enter upon serious subjects. Dan will awake now; when he does you will stay where you are, and Adare will get a candle, that you may note down accurately the position of everything. We must now go. May God

Almighty, in His infinite goodness, for ever lead and guide you nearer and nearer to Him." Home having awoke, I brought in a candle, and we noted down the position in which we found the different articles that had been moved. Some doubt was expressed as to whether a chair in the middle of the room had been stirred; a spirit rapped three times to say " *Yes*," that it had.　　　　　　　　　　　　　　　　　　　　　　　　　　　　　　　　　A.

No. 63.—*Séance, March* 13*th*.

Present:—My father, Home, and myself. Home and I had been a good deal affected and depressed to-day by the weather— a strong, drying east wind had been blowing for two or three days. After dinner when seated in the drawing room we heard raps upon the furniture, and Home soon suggested that we should sit round the table. I went to my bed room to put on a dressing gown, placing my snuff box (the same heavy silver one mentioned at page 26 in the account of some wonderful manifestations at Mr. Jones's house, at Norwood) in my waistcoat pocket. On returning to the drawing room, I laid the snuff box (why, I do not know) on a bookcase standing against the wall at the side of the room opposite to the window where stood the table at which my father and Home were already seated. We had slight physical manifestations, and then Home went into a trance. As usual, he began by arranging the furniture; he placed the small round table between his chair and my father's, and about a foot from our table, laid his wife's miniature upon it, and arranged the two vases of flowers in the same positions they had occupied the previous evening. He went over to the bookcase, sat down on the ground, and opened several books, as if looking for one in particular. He brought over a small prayer book with a cross on it, which he placed on the flowers in the vase near me. He then sat down on the sofa, (*vide* diagram of the room, in last night's *séance*), and almost immediately put his hand on the window shelf, touching a book which was lying there. He gave a slight start, grasped the book, felt it all over, and then with great reverence kneeled down, placed the book against his forehead and on the top of his head, apparently praying earnestly; he then slowly rose up, and holding the book he extended his arm at full length, and appeared to be raised in the air several inches. The table hid his legs and feet, but I think it was a case of elevation not elongation, for he appeared to be moved a little forwards, and in becoming shorter, he seemed to alight on the floor. He then placed the book on the table in exactly the same position as on the previous evening. I guessed, by the effect the book produced—so similar to what happened last night, that it was the same, *viz.*, Pressensé's "Life of Christ" which turned out to be the case. He now took a large railway plaid of mine, and placing it over his head and gathering it in at the waist so as to resemble a monk's cowl or habit, he commenced walking about the room. He stood between us and the bookcase with his back to us, and was apparently elongated, but only slightly. He then bowed himself repeatedly to the ground; and was occupied for a little while about his dress, and doing something with his hands which we could not well see as he had his back turned to us; it appeared as if he were going through some religious ceremony. The plaid began slipping gradually off him, but was replaced upon his shoulders. (Home said afterwards before he awoke that the plaid had been replaced by spirits, I did not notice at the time whether he touched it himself or not, and cannot therefore vouch for the fact.) A second time it began to slip, and fell to the ground; Home appeared to be very unhappy, and taking the plaid, he placed it on the floor, and seating himself at the end of the sofa, he retreated along the edge by starts, his countenance showing indications of great pain, his look being fixed all the time upon the plaid; then leaning his head upon his hand, he rocked himself from side to side. His distress was most painful to witness; he groaned and sobbed as if in despair. After a while he took the "Life of Christ," and kneeling down appeared to pray fervently, pressing the book to his forehead. He then sat down and began to speak somewhat as follows, "The same spirit is here that visited Adare in his room, and that was in the Abbey; he was very anxious to come to you once more, and took this opportunity because you are alone. What Dan has been doing is intended as an allegory, he (the spirit) wished to shew you that when he first took the monkish habit, it raised and elevated him, and the grace of God was in him; then, if you remember, Dan was elevated in the air; afterwards he became less worthy of it, and the habit nearly fell off Dan, but was replaced by the spirits; Dan did not do it himself. But he committed a great crime—a grievous sin against God and man—and he became altogether unworthy of the habit, and it fell from him; then you saw the misery and remorse he felt in thinking of what he had done, and how he had fallen from his former position, and had lost all the blessings he ought to have gained; you saw also the comfort that prayer and the contemplation of the "Life of Christ" were to him. He was so anxious to come to you again, for he wishes to thank you; he is not happy, but he is very different to what he was; then all was dark, now he sees a little glimmer of the light of hope like a star leading him on. You have prayed for him, you have prayed for all unhappy spirits in the like condition as himself, and it is a comfort to him; he is very thankful and declares he will do all he can to be of service to you. He says, 'I pray you, thanks;' he does not talk like the others, he does not speak English as they do. He is going now and says again, 'I pray you, thanks.' Home repeated the words, 'I pray you, thanks,' two or three times, his voice becoming gradually fainter and fainter, as if to signify that the spirit was slowly leaving us." He then spoke about our last visit to the Abbey at Adare, and our going to Desmond Castle. He said something of this sort: "You made a mistake in taking the females to the ruins; we told you not to take them (*vide* p. 99) ; and you would have had more manifestations had you not done so. It did not so much signify at the Castle, where the influence is quite different from that at the Abbey. The influence of religion does not exist there, it was a place of warfare, blood was shed upon the ground, but the blood has long since passed by chemical operations into various forms, and has disappeared; all the associations are gone, there was no abiding influence about that place; even the chapel was not the same as the Abbey, for it was only in times of danger that religious services were conducted there. The Abbey is very different, there the ground is hallowed and consecrated by religion and prayer, and it will for ever bear their impress; that influence can never be lost, it appeals to your souls and deeply affects you; you all felt the difference because in the Abbey, in the consecrated ground, there is an indestructible influence whereas in the Castle all is passed, changed, and gone." Soon after this, Home awoke. We had slight physical manifestations, which gave me the impression that owing to adverse circumstances, the spirits were unable to do what they intended. Home suddenly said, "I saw something bright move across the floor this minute." My father said he also saw it. Directly after, we all heard sounds, as if some metallic substance was being lifted up and thrown down again on the floor under the table and the following message was given: "*This is the last time that we will reprove you about a habit that can do you no possible good.*" Neither my father or Mr. Home could at all understand this; but the meaning struck me at once, and I said, "The message is for me, and it refers to my taking snuff." "*Yes*," was the reply. I said, "Do you wish me to give it up entirely." "*Don't take too much*," was rapped out. I said, "I think they have brought my snuff-box across the room from where I left it, and that is what we heard under the table." "*Yes*," was again rapped. I asked if they wished to give me the box, the answer was, "*Yes*." I said, "Shall I put my hand down for it?" "*No*," was answered. Shortly after I saw quite distinctly an arm and hand holding the snuff-box open, rise from under the table, and moving to the shelf under the

window, tilt the box over slightly, and then shake out a quantity
of snuff upon some papers that happened to be there; the arm
and hand then withdrew, still retaining the box. The hand was
more distinct than the arm, and appeared very white, and slightly
luminous. I could see the fingers quite plainly, and also the
manner in which they grasped the box; Home also saw the
hand, arm, and box, my father could not, owing to the position
in which he was sitting, but on standing up he saw a dark
heap lying on the paper. I felt the box touch my knee, and
asked if I should put my hand down for it. "*Yes*," was
answered, by tapping my knee three times with it. I put
my hand under the table, and the box was placed in it by
a hand; I felt the tips of the fingers, and the inside part of
the thumb quite distinctly; the skin felt quite natural, but
somewhat wrinkled, conveying the idea of an aged hand. I said
" Are the snuff-box and the message given me by my grandfather?" The following message was given : " *Your father saw*
it passing, so did Dan. It is from your grandfather." I asked,
" Grandfather Goold?" " *Yes, Goold.*" My father then expressed a desire to know what spirit had written out the
ornamental alphabet last night. The following was given:
" *It was directed by the same one that directed the music; the*
name was indicated by the decorated letters." After a pause, the
words " *Take instrument*" were spelled out. Home took the
accordion, and it was beautifully played with tremolo effects.
My father said something about wishing that it could be played
in his hand. Home said he thought they would do so, and shortly
after his chair was pushed back from the table, which I supposed
was done in order to pass the accordion to my father; it was
not however given to him. We now saw a hand approach the
vase nearest me, and take a flower from it, and presently the
flower was placed upon the edge of the table, and moved across
it in little jerks, as though it were flipped by a finger; we
could see no hand or anything supporting it. The flower was
taken off the table, and the following message was given : " *We*
will give you the leaf you saw leave the table." Directly
after my father was touched on the knee, and putting his hand
down, he felt first the flower and then fingers touch him; he
then expressed a wish to feel the whole hand. Home said, " I
am sure they will try, they generally are able at first to
make only the fingers apparent to you." A spirit assented.
He kept his hand down for some little time, but at length
took the leaf, not succeeding in feeling more than the fingers;
this however occurred two or three times. The small table
then moved of itself, close up between my father and Home,
and Sacha's portrait was taken from it, and placed upon our
table. On two or three different occasions during the evening,

we heard curious sounds; once my father and Home heard, as it were, some one whistling; I could not perceive it at all. At another time, we all heard a sound as of some one trying to articulate near the door; this also ended in a whistling. On another occasion, we heard some one trying to make their voice audible to us, apparently outside the window. Home now went into a trance; while waiting for him to commence speaking, my father and I were talking about the absence of tests; he appeared rather annoyed, saying, that there had been in fact no real tests of identity given, and that everybody was remarking the same thing. I mentioned the great difficulty of giving really satisfactory tests, and reminded him that one striking effect had been given; (referring to the imitation of the organ bellows and tremolo) and asked why he did not try and question them in some way that would serve as a test, it being as easy for him to recollect some past event or conversation, as it was for them to recall one, that he also remembered. Home began speaking about the extreme difficulty they had experienced in making any manifestations. "The state of the external atmosphere is such," he said, " as to render it all but impossible. We act by using certain emanations from you, flowing through your brains; now, the state of the weather, this east wind, has dried all that up, we have next to nothing to work with. It affects you all, more especially Dan, but you can all feel it, and complained to-day of being depressed and irritated; under better circumstances you would have seen the hand that carried Sacha's portrait, and the hand that held the flower. You observed also that we could not carry the flower over the table steadily, but were obliged to push it along the surface." He then changed the subject to that of tests; speaking to my father, he said, " Do not be impatient, all will come right in time, you shall have tests given you, you have already had some; remember that what you might think an excellent test to-day, on reflection, you might consider to be worth nothing. Would you have us recall a past conversation? That might be done by mind-reading, and would not be at all a good test. We are the best judges of what we do; we work for others as well as for you who are here. We have a certain appointed work, and it must be done; we have not really been able to do half enough yet in the way of physical manifestations; circumstances have been so much against us, that we have failed in nearly all we wished to effect. We know all the difficulties and trials that surround you; but you do not see the difficulties that we have to contend against. Physical manifestations are very necessary; be patient and some day you may arrive at other things. We do not ask you to have faith in us; we only ask that you will be patient and prayerful in investigating." Home had apparently great difficulty in speaking; he now called me over to him, and bidding me sit down, said, " You understand all about this, we cannot impress Dan properly with what we want him to say; circumstances are so adverse that we have scarcely any control over him. Ah, I see the entrance at Adare; your mother is standing there, she appears to be giving directions about planning the garden and walks." My father said, " Do you mean the lodge gate?" " No, no; I mean the little gate where the notice is put up, ' These grounds are strictly private;' she is standing there between the two clumps of shrubs; ah, it is all confused, I cannot make it out. Your father intends going to the Abbey some night by himself, he wants to find out about those birds; he will see a sort of bright luminous cloud; your mother will be there." My father said, " But I never had any intention of going to the Abbey." Home appeared much astonished; " Are you sure?" he said. " Yes," said my father, " quite sure." " Well," said Home, " that is very strange, the idea must have been in your mind, and you have forgotten it, for some of us had arranged what to do the night that you went; one spirit was going to make the same whistling sound like a bird, and you were to see the luminous cloud." I asked, " Were they then not real birds that we heard whistling?" " No, they were not birds." Home then threw himself back, and taking my hand, said, " We cannot influence Dan properly, your father had better ask questions." My father said, " I thought Elliotson was going to have made some experiments." " Yes, he was anxious to, and tried, but he could not succeed; he attempted to make his voice heard by the door, and instead of being like a voice, it sounded to you like a whistle; the conditions are very bad, we have been able to do scarcely anything to-night, besides your minds are not favourable—they are disturbed, and out of harmony." My father declined to put any questions, so I asked about a certain disputed answer of Dr. Elliotson's that had been given us in the gallery at Adare. Home said, " Your father was right: he did say ' Yes;' afterwards he said he would come by the sea; you were mistaken." After a pause, he said " Your grandfather is really anxious about your taking so much snuff; he did not like to put it any stronger than he did in saying that it could do you no possible good; but he is anxious about it, because he thinks it will harm your nervous system. He says, if you like to take an occasional pinch, that will not hurt you; but he does not like to see you take as much as you do at present. (turning to my father) Dr. Elliotson is here and has brought a girl with him: her name is Dawson, she is short and appears so stooping as to be almost deformed; I cannot make out her Christian name. Harriet,—Harriet; no, that is not it: she will not tell me—how very odd!" My father said: "I have a very vague recollection of a mesmeric patient of the name of Dawson; but I don't think her name was Harriet."* Home now said, "Dan must awake, Adare, go back to your place." Home being exhausted, we went at once into the dining room to supper. During the whole time that I was sitting by Home, I could see the shadowy form of a figure appearing white and slightly luminous, standing close to my father. He perceived nothing. In moving to my place, I could not avoid passing right through the figure, but as I approached it, it disappeared. Soon after we had gone into the dining room, my father being at the table, and Home sitting on the floor, near the fireplace, with his hand resting against the wall, he suddenly said: "Adare, I hear raps for the alphabet;" and the following was given: "*Ellen Daw*——" "Oh, Dawson," my father said. "*Yes*," was rapped out. Home said, "Ellen Dawson, Ellen Dawson; Who on earth is she? I never heard of such a person." "Oh," my father replied, "It is the Christian name of a mesmeric patient which you could not make out in your trance." Now this is a curious fact. The name Ellen having been in my father's mind for a moment, had Home mentioned it in his trance, it might have been attributed to ordinary clairvoyance or mind-reading on his part; but coming as it did through raps, it could not be accounted for in that way. My father had said to me in the course of the evening, "I have not the same confidence in what is said in a trance; it may be accounted for by mind-reading or clairvoyance; but if a name or a message be given through raps, even if it be read from my mind, it must be attributed to some intelligence other than that of the medium, or any one in the room. † Directly after the *séance*, I poured the snuff back into my box, from the paper on the ledge under the window where we had seen it deposited. After supper, my father said, "Let us go and see if the snuff is there." I said that I had already removed it; but we went and found remnants of snuff still on and among the papers, quite sufficient to prove that it had been there.—A.

---

* My father says that he had a notion Ellen was the name; however, he did not mention this aloud.

† On reference to the *Zoist*, Ellen Dawson appears as a patient of Mr. Hind's, and a clairvoyant. My father recollects her at Dr. Elliotson's. She is mentioned in *séance* No. 14, p. 34 in connection with Mrs. Hennings and Dr. Elliotson.

[The following occurrences were witnessed and recorded by me after Mr. Home's return to London]:—

No. 64.—Séance, Ashley House, March 29th, 1869.

Present:—Mr. Rudall, Mr. McKenzie, Mr. Jencken, Home, and myself. After a short time we experienced slight physical manifestations, raps, vibrations, &c., &c. The table was raised about one foot off the ground; it was raised a second time about two feet, and after remaining stationary in the air for some seconds, it rose to the height of at least five feet, rolling and swaying with a movement like that of a ship at sea; it descended slowly with a strong vibratory motion, accompanied by a sound resembling that of a railway train. I asked if these peculiar movements had any definite meaning; the answer was " *Yes.*" By asking several questions which were answered " *Yes*" or " *No*," it appeared that the movements had reference to me, and that I ought to understand the meaning. Flowers and fern leaves were brought from the chimney piece and given to us. We now, at Mr. Rudall's suggestion, shut the folding doors, thereby excluding all light save that entering by the window. Home went into a trance. He clapped his hands (the sign adopted by Adah Menken to signify her presence), and going to the window, folded the curtains round him, leaving only his head clear. We all saw a very curious appearance form itself above his head; it looked at first like a lace handkerchief, held out by a stick or support of some sort; soon however it became more distinct and appeared to be a shadowy human form enveloped in drapery; it was about two feet in length. Some one present remarked that it exceedingly resembled a " vignette " heading one of Adah Menken's poems. Home said (speaking as Menken) " Yes, that is it, that is what I wish to imitate; I will try and make my form visible to you." The surface of the wall to Home's right became illuminated three or four times; the light apparently radiating from a bright spot in the centre. Across the portion of wall thus illuminated we repeatedly saw a dark shadow pass; it appeared to me to be rather the shadow cast by a solid substance than the actual form itself. Home's collar stud dropped on the floor, and a spirit brought it and placed it on my head, touching my brow while doing so; Home remarked that it was shining like a little star upon my forehead, he told me to take care of it until Dan should awake. After Home awoke we had some more physical

K

manifestations, flowers were again brought to us, we were all touched, Mr. Rudall received several messages, apparently from his father, the clock was made to strike in answer to some question, we heard a heavy step in the passage and the folding doors were opened and shut, a sofa was moved from the wall to our table, and a chair was carried across the room.

No. 65.—*Séance, Ashley House, April 3rd.*

Present:—Mrs. Gregory, Miss Douglas, Mr. Charles Blackburn, Mr. Fuller, the Master of Lindsay, Home, and myself. We had tolerably strong physical manifestations, lasting for a short time, after which Home went into a trance. He walked about and was elongated in the usual manner. He then stood still before us, and stretching out his arms to their full length, a palpable elongation took place in them. I said, "Can you manage that we may test that in some way; may I stand just in front of you, or will you place yourself against the wall?" Home replied, "Yes, certainly, we will do both." I accordingly placed myself just in front of him, with my arms extended along and touching his; his arms were elongated four or five inches, the others could judge of the extent pretty well by comparison with mine. While his arms appeared to be increasing in length, his chest became greatly expanded, and he said to me, "You see how it is, the extension is from the chest." He then placed himself against the wall, and extended his arms to their full natural length; I made a pencil mark at the tips of his fingers. His left arm was then elongated, I held the pencil against the wall, suffering it to be pushed along by his fingers, until he told me to make another mark. His right arm was then elongated, and I marked the movement in the same manner. The total elongation as ascertained by this means, amounted to 9½ inches. Home now stood by Miss Douglas, and talked to her for a considerable time, mentioning the spirits who were about her, recalling past circumstances of her life, and impressing upon her, that it was in her power to be of very great service to the cause of Spiritualism; he spoke also a good deal to Mrs. Gregory. Walking over to the fire-place, he took from thence, with his hand, a red-hot glowing ember, about the size of a small orange. Mrs. Gregory became nervous, fearing that he would request her to take it, he however went to Miss Douglas and said, "Now if you have sufficient faith, let me place this coal in your hand;" she replied, "I have faith, but I cannot overcome the physical dread, pray do not ask me to take it." Upon this, Home

said, " If you would only allow me to place it in your hand
it would not burn you; it does not burn Dan; it would not
harm him" (pointing to Lindsay). He then placed the coal
which had by this time become black, on Lindsay's head, but
almost immediately took it off, and saying, " That is not of
much use as an experiment, for the natural heat has almost
left the coal," he crumbled it in his hand and then threw it in
the fireplace. Presently he took another red-hot ember from the
fire, and holding it in his hand, spoke a few words to Miss
Douglas on the subject of faith. She held out her hand, and
he placed the coal in it. Miss Douglas was not in the least
burned, and said that it felt rather cold, like marble. After
allowing it to remain there a few seconds, Home took the coal
and requested Miss Douglas to touch it; she placed her fingers
near it, but withdrew them immediately, saying that it burned
her.* He then placed it in Mr. Blackburn's hand, previously
asking if he had any faith, who replied that he had. After he
had held it a short time he said it became hotter. Home then
took the ember, threw it away, smiled, and seemed pleased at the
success of the experiment. He now sat down and turning to
Lindsay, said, " Ah, what a pity it was that those little *séances*
that you held here in the winter were broken up (referring to
two or three occasions on which Lindsay, Captain Smith,
Home, and I had sat together). We told you that we wished
to speak on some very interesting subjects, and we would
have done so ; we were anxious also to have entered upon the
subject of the origin of certain of the ceremonies of your
Church. We have such difficulties to contend with ; we had
got the conditions so very favorable at that time, the party was
harmonious and we could have done so much ; but then, you
see, when we have arranged everything on the spiritual side, it
is all broken up on the material,—on your side." Turning to
one of those present, he said, " That arrangement of seven with
which we impressed Fred (Fuller). Oh ! if that could have been
managed it would have been of such use. We could and would
have conducted a series of experiments so wonderful, so clearly
proved, and so easy to record, that it would have been impossible
to doubt them." (This had reference to an impression that
seven were to form themselves into a society for the study of
occult science). In reply to Fuller, he said, " We still have
hopes about that arrangement; we think there may possibly
be a future for it." Home now spoke in a totally different

---

* I am informed by Miss Douglas and the Master of Lindsay that Lord
Adare has omitted to state that Mr Home put this coal between his coat and
shirt under the arm, and that no mark of singeing or burning was visible on
the shirt.—D.

tone of voice, addressing us in the same style and delivery as in the portions of *séances* recorded in pages 84, 85, and 91. He said something to this effect: "You think that baptism is a thing of to-day—a ceremony instituted but 1,800 years ago! Come with me away to the banks of the distant Ganges, travel with me far back in the annals of time, and I will shew you races of men dwelling there who worshipped senseless gods of wood and stone—and yet not much more senseless than the god that some among you worship now—and who had the same ceremony of baptism, which was obligatory for them before an infant could be admitted to the benefits of their church and religion. Will you travel still further back with me into ages long anterior to this, and see the altars dripping with blood—aye, with human blood—and the priest decked with flowers standing in his place, and the people bowing down, and the sacrifices offered. Blood I see on every page—blood! blood! blood! True it is, that in later ages it was that of bulls and of goats, of doves and pigeons. And what is your religion now to many of you but blood; still the same—blood to appease a God! Ah, it is fearful—it is too horrible, blood! and sacrifice! to propitiate your God, your Maker, your Father, the infinitely perfect and loving Creator of all things." Home spoke at great length on these subjects; but I cannot recal to mind the exact language he made use of. After he awoke we had some curious manifestations. A small camp chair was raised off the floor and carried round the table, touching each of us in turn, and finally was placed on the centre of the table, where it remained. The sofa was moved up to us. We received no messages during the *séance*.

No. 66.—*Ashley House.*

On the 4th or 5th of the month, in the evening, I was seated at the table in Home's room at Ashley House writing; he was seated at the opposite side, reading; we heard raps upon the door; Home said "Your grandfather has come in, do you not see him sitting in that chair yonder?" "I see no one," I answered; "Which grandfather do you mean?" "Your father's father; you will at any rate hear him." I heard a sound as if some one sitting on the chair he had mentioned had put his foot on the ground. Home, while speaking, went into a trance. The chair moved very slowly up to the table (no one touching it) a distance of eight feet eleven inches. "He is moving the chair," Home said, "He is pleased to be able to do that, he says you never saw a much prettier manifestation than that; Ah! he has gone over there now." Another chair moved close up to me, a distance of about a foot. Home said "He is sitting in that chair near you; he has come because he wishes to speak to you; you are rather in difficulties he thinks." He then spoke to me about certain private matters. Presently Home said " Your mother does not wish you to think that she forgot you because she said so little about your marriage; she could not say more then, and after all what could she do more than pray God's blessing upon you in this as she would in everything that you undertake, honestly, and with a desire to do that which was right. She has much more to say on the subject, but not now."

No. 67.—Ashley House.

On the night of the 6th I got home about eleven o'clock. I found Home already in bed. He told me that he was very unwell; that he had left the house; on his way to Gower Street that he had suddenly lost consciousness on turning out of Ashley Place, and that he remembered nothing more until he found himself in bed. Home soon went to sleep and began to talk and mutter; after what he had said I attributed it to bodily illness, and did not pay much attention, however I soon found that he was in a trance. The first distinct words he uttered were "But I am not an Hindoo." The room shook for some minutes very violently as if people were dancing on the floor below. Home said, " Oh, do stop that dancing, they must not do it, it is not kind." The shaking of the floor almost immediately ceased; I asked if people had been dancing below, but received no answer. Home turned to me and speaking in a firm loud voice, said, " Ah, dear me, the poor little dog has gone !" " What dog ?" I asked. " Why, little white sister*—she has gone just now. Are you not sorry, Adare ? They will be so grieved about it. She has passed from earth; but she is not destroyed, she is like a little spark of electricity, now a small globe of light, it is moving on, in time it will come in contact with some other substance and be absorbed." " Absorbed into what ?" I asked. " Oh, into some higher form of animal life. Some spirits could catch it, for although I said it was like a little globe of light, still you know on leaving the body it had the appearance of the little dog, and some spirits might capture it and keep it for a

---

* A little dog belonging to Mrs. S. C. Hall. Home, I believe, knew that the dog was ill; but could not have heard of its death, which took place between 10 and 11 o'clock. I had no idea that the dog was even ill.

time, but eventually it would be absorbed, for that is the law of nature, and they could not overrule it. It has no sensation or consciousness now; its condition of being, its organization, was not sufficiently high to permit of its retaining its individuality." " But," I said, " are there not animals in the other world ?" " Oh dear yes, God in his goodness has made variety in the spirit world, as he has in your world; there would be no beauty without variety; there are dogs and horses and many animals. The Red Indians were not wrong in their ideas of the ' happy hunting ground,' their Seers saw these things in visions, and they really exist." " But," I observed, " although they might hunt they could never kill the animals." " Oh no, of course they could not shed their blood, but they could conquer them ; it is difficult for you to understand, but you know yourself that the real charm of all hunting consists rather in showing your superiority over the animal, in overcoming it, than in the mere shedding of blood and killing." " But," I asked, " if some animals retain their individuality, and continue to exist in the next world under the same form that they had here, and others are as you say absorbed, where is the line drawn ? what is it that causes one to be absorbed, while another retains its individuality ?" " Oh, I do not say that the animals in the next world ever existed on earth, it does not seem to me that they did, I only know that they are there, and I see that the life of animals upon earth is eventually absorbed into other forms. I do not know that your animals ever continue to exist in the spirit-world."

" You heard those Hindoos dancing just now ?" " Yes," I answered, " I heard what I thought were people dancing on the floor below us." " Oh, it was not caused by mortals, there is no one living on that floor now ; they were spirits—Hindoos." " What on earth do they want here," I asked. " Well, they are very anxious about their Trinity." " But why should that bring them here ?" " They do not seem to have any special object in being here, but they are occupied with that subject, and that is why they are on earth ; they are very advanced Hindoos, and they want to prove that their Trinity is not different from your Trinity as you suppose; there is a good deal going on now in the world in the way of investigating these subjects. These Hindoos are anxious about this; they say there is not so much difference as you think ; for instance, they assert that their second person Christna was incarnated as your second person Christ was." Question : " Had they a personal devil ?" " Yes ; and they say that Christna was tempted of the devil in the same way as Christ." The substance of Home's conversation after this I forget ; it led somehow to his saying, " When this zone shall have become torrid, of course the forms of animal and vegetable life, will be much changed." Question : " Do you mean that the temperature is changing?" " Oh, yes, these will be the torrid zones, and the torrid zones will become cooler; there is a very marked change taking place now." Question : " I suppose the change will be so gradual, that life will not be affected?" " Life will not be affected, the change is gradual, but it is quite apparent to us." Question : " Has the heat of the two last seasons anything to do with this, or was it quite abnormal?" " No, it was not entirely abnormal, it had to do with the great change that is taking place." Question : " Then will the frigid zones round the poles become warmer?" " Oh yes, certainly; do you know it is true that there is land to the North beyond where explorers have yet penetrated, and there are tribes of men living there, and they yet retain the traces of a by-gone civilization. They are of the old Semitic or original Hebrew race." Question : " But how could they ever get there; it could not have been in historic times?" In answer to this question, I distinctly heard a voice quite different to Home's say, " Oh dear, no." Home said, " Did you hear him?" " Yes," I answered, " I heard him quite plain." " I am glad you did;" he said " Oh dear, no." He is rather difficult to understand, this spirit; he seems a little confused, but he declares he has seen these people, and that he could bring the spirit of one of them with him. He says there are distinct traces of Hebrew to be found in their language. You know there are traces of the old original Hebrew in the language of the Brahmins. The ancient Hebraic tribes were a most migratory people, always wandering and fighting ; their idea even of God was a warlike, bloodthirsty being, and they were always fighting and quarrelling among themselves and their neighbours, and doing so in the name of the Lord. They have wandered all over the earth, and have left their marks in many places. There are signs of a civilization that you know nothing of, in North America; it was derived from the same source. Historians have conjectured that they crossed the narrow channel of a few miles in breadth; and they are correct. As to those people I spoke of in the North, they penetrated there long before history ; oh, there were lions and tigers in these latitudes at that time. The Hebrews were very bad historians; they kept no records; tradition served as history for them, even in very much later times; they were very careless, and kept their records very badly." I remarked, " What an interesting thing it would be to reach these people if they exist." " This spirit declares that it will be done ; he says there is an expedition fitting out now, and he thinks it will be successful." " Fitting out in England ? " I asked. " No in America; it seems that this spirit is interested in it, and that is the reason why he is on earth." " Have I ever known him ?" I enquired, " Oh dear no, he has left the earth long ago." " How interesting it would be," I remarked, " to go on such an expedition." Home laughed at me and said, " Yes, you look very like going on that sort of an expedition just now; look and feel very strong don't you, just at present; quite fit to go through that awful bitter cold ?" Home reverted to the Hindoos, and then began speaking about Spiritualism in general, " Oh ! " he said, " what a blessing it is to know that the world will one day be spiritualised, that mortal man in the flesh will walk and talk face to face with his brother, who has left the body." " Well," I observed, " I do not see much likelihood of that time coming soon; if it were so, death would no longer have any terrors, it would not be even a separation." " You cannot see it, but I can; what I say will inevitably come true. Death ought not to be considered a separation, death is a development, and should have no terrors; was it not part of Christ's mission to take away the sting and terror of death ?"

I began speculating as to the probability of the population ever becoming excessive over the whole earth. Home said, " No, that will not be the case; when countries become much over populated, the people are carried off by epidemics, by emigration and other causes." But emigration," I said, " only relieves one country at the expense of another. If population increases as it does at present, the time must come when there will be no outlet for emigrants; and surely it cannot be natural or right that people should be carried off by plagues and famines." " Epidemics and famines are quite in the natural order of things; and the misery resulting from them may seem much greater to you than it in reality is." " But still," I insisted, " such things do cause great distress." " Yes, to a certain extent you are of course right; and there are other causes that will eventually act to check the increase of the human race. Cannot you understand that men, by cultivating the intellectual qualities, the higher organs contained in the upper portion of the brain will arrive at such a condition, that their sole gratification and pleasure will be in the pursuit of all that is beautiful, harmonious, and good ?—the upper portions of the brain will become more fully developed, the lower parts being neglected will become less and less, the animal nature weaker, and man will no longer find the same pleasure in the gratification of his lusts and passions; man will become spiritualised, and will be very different to what he is now." Soon after this, Home awoke. He spoke for such a length of time, that a great deal of what he said has entirely escaped my memory.

Allan Kardec died on Sunday the 4th. On the Wednesday or Thursday following, as Home and I were in the dressing room, at about 11 o'clock in the morning, we heard loud raps on the floor between us. The alphabet was asked for and the following message given: " *Bon jour, mon ami Daniel, je crois que je me suis trompé un peu la bas en fait d'identité, Allan Kardec.* " Home asked a few questions which were answered by raps.

No. 68.—*Ashley House, April 10th.*

Last night Mr. J—— and I walked to Ashley House with Home from Fitzroy Square. Home complained of feeling nervous, as is usually the case after an unsuccessful *séance*. He sat down at the piano, and commenced playing ; while so engaged he went into a trance. I extinguished one of the candles, and placed the other on the floor. We heard sounds as of some one walking up and down the passage, and raps upon the door and walls. Mr. J—— felt, during the whole evening, a strong current of very cold air blowing about him. Home walked about the room apparently in great distress ; he moaned and sat down on the floor and seemed to mourn over something. Suddenly the character of the influence changed. Home came over to where I was sitting on the sofa, and made me lie at full length upon it ; by the attitude he assumed I recognized the spirit he calls " the nameless doctor." He stood beside me apparently lost in thought for a minute or two, then kneeling down, made me unbutton my waistcoat, began sounding my chest as doctors do ; he then rubbed and patted over the chest, loins, and legs, occasionally turning round as if to ask advice from some one ; his efforts were principally directed to my right side, he frequently pointed to it and turned his head as if to call some one's attention to that particular spot. He placed his mouth to my right side and exhaled a deep breath ; the heat I felt was something extraordinary. When he had finished, Home seemed pleased with what he had done, smiled and rubbed his hands as if delighted. The first influence now seemed to return ; he sat down on the floor evidently in great distress ; then lay flat on his back and extended his arms in the form of a cross. His body became rigid and he was palpably elongated, and was almost raised off the ground ; he may have been completely off, but I think not; it was evident, however, by the swaying vibratory motion of his body that it was not resting naturally on the ground. While this was taking place two chairs moved slightly of themselves. Home got up, knelt upon one knee, and simulated a man endeavouring to raise a heavy body. He appeared to fail once or twice; at last he raised it, and supporting it on his knee, carried it with great difficulty to a chair near at hand, where he placed it and sat down on the floor, apparently much exhausted. He beckoned to me, and when I approached told me in French to bring a chair, and sit near him; I did so, and he spoke in French somewhat to the following effect. " What we have been trying to represent to you by acting, is the condition of Allan Kardec. The body that was extended on the ground in the form of a cross, and that was elongated, was his; he suffered a good deal for truth; and in symbolism as you know, the cross signifies truth; but then he was not enlightened; he refused the light, he was obstinate, and would not enlighten himself upon it, and that makes him unhappy now; it seems to weigh upon him, he cannot raise himself above his former ideas and prejudices. We tried to represent that by the difficulty of raising the heavy body. He is sitting here in this chair; he does not move; he would not come into the room at first, you heard him walking in the passage. There are many spirits here of his ' entourage.' Of his followers, and he had many of them, some of the spirits will not come into the room, I know not why; you hear them in the passage; there are two just behind here that I do not like at all." Presently Home gave a cry almost amounting to a scream, and shuddering pointed to the opposite side of the room and said in English, " Who are those fearful looking men? Oh, what are they doing? They are eastern, their feet are bare, as also their legs up to the knees, they will not show their faces, they cover them with a sort of cloak; oh this is horrible, they are hiding and lying in wait for something They are so totally undeveloped, so earthy and material, they could shed blood, they could take man's life." " Do you mean," I said, " to tell me that these spirits could kill a man?" " Oh yes," he answered, " they could, but they can do no harm here at all; it was in a city where the sun cast broad alternate bands of light and shadow; I can see them among the olive trees gliding in and out; they are so fearfully undeveloped, so material; they could harm a man if he had not power over them; *that* must come by prayer." I asked Mr. J—— if he had any idea what all this meant. He replied, " Yes, I think I know." Home got up, took a striped rug off the sofa, and covering his shoulders, head, and face with it, began walking about the room in a stealthy manner, hiding behind the furniture, and crawling about flat upon the ground, apparently lying in wait for some one. Suddenly he put his hand upon the candle, and left us in almost total darkness. I could just distinguish him gliding about the room, and crawling on the floor. At one time he stood up and was elongated; he came close to me and said, " What did they do to his brother?" " Whose brother?" said Mr. J——. " Why, yours." " Oh, good gracious," cried Mr. J——; " How strange;" and so saying he sank back in his chair. Home added, " He is not dead; he is quite safe." I spoke two or three times to Mr. J—— after this, but received no answer. Home said, " He is under influence." Presently, Home sat down on the floor beside me and said, " He is under influence; the tall strong man who is influencing him will move something." A chair behind me moved of itself. Home leaned his head against my knee; it appeared most extraordinarily heavy. I placed my hand upon it, and the weight was removed. " Did you feel," he said, " the weight on Dan's head? That was the influence of only one of those men; they are so strong, so very material." Mr. J—— became much affected; he sobbed violently, seemed in great distress, spoke in Arabic with great rapidity, and said, " Oh, S——! S——!" (his brother's name), and then " Chalini! chalini!" which means " Leave me! leave me!" I began asking Home about what had puzzled me very much, namely, his having asserted that spirits could do bodily harm to man. He said, " Yes, they can; I will tell you later. Dan must awake to take the influence off J——." Home suddenly awoke, and asked what was going on. I told him that Mr. J—— was under influence, upon which he took his hands, and he immediately awoke, and was much astonished at finding that he had been crying violently.

I slept in Home's room; after we had gone to bed he went into a trance and said " Of course not; why of course they could not, Adare." " Could not do what?" I asked. " Why could not do harm here." " You are referring to those spirits," I said. " I never thought they could do harm here; but could they hurt as man under any circumstances?" " Yes, they could; you see his brother had been mixed up in some magical incantations, where sacrifices where offered. Now, if a man sold himself to such spirits as those, if he gave himself to them for any purpose, they could do as they liked with him." " But," I asked " could they take his life? Could they for instance strike him with a knife?" " Certainly, why not? you have seen table, chairs and heavy objects moved by a spirit, why not a knife also." " But that would not be fair play, he could not strike them back," I said. " No, he could not; but they could not touch him unless he was willing. You see it would be necessary that he should have allowed them to gain power over him, if for any purpose he did that, they could then so use their influence as to make him do whatever they chose. They did not hurt his brother, they carried him off, it was as if he had fallen among bandits.[*] There is more truth than you suppose in the stories of the old magicians, and the precautions they adopted to protect themselves from the undeveloped and material influences with which they surrounded themselves. Your mother stood just behind you when Dan's head became so heavy against your knee; she influenced you to put your hand on his head, she was anxious a little about Dan, a little fearful that he might be hurt. Of course you know no harm could come to him." Home now awoke, he had a distinct impression of the sort of influence that had been about him, and said "I feel very strange, so dreadfully crafty and sly, if I were to give way to my feelings I should do all sorts of curious things, I should hide behind the curtains, and go to Mr. J——'s room and try to frighten him." I told Home a little of what had occurred so as to account for these strange feelings.

No. 69.

[The following account of what occurred to Mr. J—— during the night, was related to me by him two or three days afterwards. He said] :—

"I went to bed in the spare room, but did not immediately put out the candle. I was lying with my face turned towards the wall, when suddenly the bed-clothes were pulled so violently as nearly to uncover me. I jumped up in bed, and the movement ceased. After watching a few minutes I lay down and the clothes were again sharply pulled. This was repeated three times; I could not detect anything touching the clothes, in fact the moment I sat up to watch all movement ceased. While this was going on I heard distinct raps all about the room. I now turned round and saw a number of figures near the window, moving about, apparently conversing; they were of a grey or whitish colour, the features in profile were very distinct, and the hands especially so; but I could not see how they rested on the floor, as the lower extremities finished in vapour or cloud. I used every means in my power to induce them to look at me

---

[*] I am not certain whether this sentence conveys Home's meaning quite correctly.

and answer my questions, by raps or otherwise, but in vain. I begged them to speak, and exercised my will as forcibly as I could to make them do so, but they would not take the slightest notice of me; I accordingly got out of bed and slowly approached them. When I was within about three paces of them they divided in two rows on each side of the window, as if to allow me to pass, and turning round, bent their heads and looked down towards me; at the next step they all separated, and I experienced a feeling of intense cold; when close upon them they disappeared. I walked slowly backwards, and when I had retreated three or four yards, the forms became visible. I went to bed but never closed my eyes; the figures remained near the window moving about as if in conversation, until a quarter to seven when they disappeared. After going towards them the first time, in order to make sure that I was thoroughly awake, I went to a cupboard, opened it, and found a box of brown biscuits of which I ate two; I also found a Highland sporran, and read the monogram on the hilts of the knives. After dressing in the morning, I examined the cupboard, found the box of biscuits, and ascertained that I had read the monograms correctly; I also walked all over the house during the night in search of Home's room, but could not find it. I spoke to the figures repeatedly in English not in Arabic."

No. 70.

[The following strange story was also related to me on the same occasion by Mr. J——. As it evidently bears upon the occurrences related in p. 154, I have determined to break through the rule hitherto adhered to of relating only what took place in my own presence. I had the story direct from Mr. J——, who received it from his brother. Mr. J—— at my request wrote to his brother in the East, to enquire if anything had happened to him on the Friday when the strange occurrences mentioned in pp. 154, 155, took place, but no answer has as yet been received.]

"About three years ago, my brother S. was residing in my father's house, in the town of ——, in the East, studying 'Nahawi,' that is the grammatical Arabic, the language of the 'Koran'—quite a different tongue from the vernacular. One day he was much astonished at receiving an answer in 'Nahawi' from a poor labouring man, to whom he had addressed some question; he entered into conversation, and found that this man was well educated, and he also noticed that in the evening he was dressed in a style quite incompatible with his rank of life; in fact he appeared much superior to the class to which he belonged. One day, soon after their first meeting, this labourer, whom I will call 'the native' as I cannot mention his name, told my brother that he had something of importance to communicate if he would promise secrecy. He then informed him that in a field outside the town, belonging to his father, there was something buried that he was determined to obtain by means of what in the East is called 'magic;' he said that he had already tried but had failed, that he was determined to succeed even at the risk of his life, but that it was necessary for him to obtain the co-operation of some member of the family; if my brother would assist him, he promised to give up anything of value that might be found, bargaining only to be allowed to keep a certain scroll or parchment. My brother agreed, and on the following Friday they commenced operations. I may mention here that in Mahomedan countries it is supposed that Friday is the only day on which magic can be successfully practised. S. and the native left the town just before the gates were shut, at sunset, and proceeded to the field in question; arrived there they sat down cross-legged on the ground, at right angles to each other, and about four or five yards apart, the native warning S. not to mind him, and on no account to scream, as that would involve considerable danger to both. The native commenced burning incense and repeating invocations or prayers, bowing his head to the ground; very soon loud thrusts or blows were heard on the ground and several forms became visible, issuing apparently out of the earth. These figures commenced walking round the two men. On passing S. each figure stooped down and threw a handful of dust into his face; his clothes were covered with dust afterwards. On passing the native, each figure struck him on the head; he, however, took no notice whatever of them, merely bowing his head down, adding fresh incense, and mumbling something to himself. After a time the figures disappeared into the ground, and the native said that all was over for that night.

" On the second Friday the same ceremonies were gone through, except that the incense was of a different kind, with like results; the forms appeared, but suddenly a tremendous shower of dry bones fell over them. S. could not tell where they came from, but they appeared to come from behind him so as to be directed against the native. The native jumped up and said that something had occurred to interrupt the arrangements, and that they must immediately go.

"On the third Friday the usual invocations and incense burning were gone through, and the figures appeared and commenced walking round, and throwing dust as on the first occasion. Suddenly the figure of a gigantic black man appeared out of the ground, armed with a great stick or club, with which he belaboured the native in the most fearful manner; while a great commotion took place among the other figures—instead of moving slowly round, they were all rushing about as if in a state of great agitation. The native took no notice at first of the black man, merely crouching himself closer to the ground, increasing the ardour of his incantations, and adding fresh incense. At length, however, he said in Arabic, 'Well, well, be it so; if you must have it, you shall.' After this, all was quiet.

"On the following Friday they again went out; but this time the native carried with him a live lamb concealed under his burnous, which, after they were seated on the ground, he proceeded to kill and skin. They went through the usual incense burning, &c., &c.; and first the figures appeared, and then the black man rose from out of the ground, and advanced in a menacing attitude towards the native, preparing to strike him with his club. The native held up the lamb to him, and the figure took it and disappeared again into the earth. S. declares that the earth literally opened, and that the black figure descended, bearing the lamb through the aperture. In a few minutes the black figure reappeared, and a conversation ensued between him and the native; the latter seemed very angry, declared that he had complied with all their requests, that the black man was not the spirit that he wanted at all, and that he had been duped. The altercation was suddenly interrupted by a shower of dry bones, upon which the figure disappeared; and the native jumping up, seized S.'s arm and hurried him away, saying that they were watched.

"It appears that my father noticed that S. absented himself from home every Friday, and becoming uneasy he set some one to watch him. He was seen to leave the city at sunset in company with this native; but none would follow them, as they did not like the idea of spending the night outside. On the last Friday, however, one bolder than the rest followed them, and concealing himself behind a rock, witnessed their proceedings. On the Saturday following a formal complaint was laid before the Governor of the town, the native was banished for life, and S. came over to England. After an absence of two years, my brother returned to the town, and a few weeks afterwards I received a letter from him, saying: Imagine my intense surprise, the same native is here, but no one recognizes him, he says he is determined to go on with his project if I will assist him; I can see no difference whatever in his appearance, he is not disguised in any way, and yet not a soul in the town has the slightest notion that he is the man who was banished three years ago."

No. 71.—Ashley House.

On the 10th, Home went into a trance, and said, " Allan Kardec,—apoplexy." " Did he die suddenly ? " I asked. " Of apoplexy—fell down stairs. You must not sleep in the same room with Dan at present, it is not good for either of you, your magnetism is mutually injurious, you take strength from each other; your nerves are in an excited state, I can see them emitting a phosphorescent light, they are stretched to the extreme verge of tension." " They are then in an unhealthy state," I said. " Yes, in a condition that must be checked, it is exactly as if you had taken too much stimulant. In the daytime it does not matter how much you are together, it is at night when you are asleep that the injury is done; you are not well; if you slept in the same room with a healthy man it would do you good." " I have been thinking," I said, " that mesmerism might be of service to me, what is your opinion ?" " The magnetism of a strong healthy man would do you much good, the mesmeriser should be a fair man, a few passes every day not sufficient to induce sleep would be of use to you, it would be good for Dan also." " I think change would do me good," I remarked. " Travelling is very good for you." I asked, after a long pause, " Do you think it would also suit Florence's constitution ? " Home said, " Oh yes it would not hurt her, but she has a talent that must not be neglected." " What is that—music ?" I enquired. " Composition, the composition of music." I said, " You would not like that to be neglected ?" " It must not be neglected." " That is rather awkward," I added. " No, it need not be; she would have great facility in learning stringed instruments; for instance the violin; of course they would all laugh at first, but you need not mind that. Dear me, how curious! Oh no, certainly not, L—— ought not to pass away." "L—— M—— do you mean ?" I asked, " No, L—— N——, she had more influence almost than any of them over O——; her magnetism kept him in check, she has lost it in a great measure now; he is all hoity toity fly-away. What a curious habit he has got into of tossing his head back in that way; dear me, he is very excited, there is something all wrong about it, when I go there it all seems confused, I cannot make it out well !

" Allan Kardec says that spirits very soon forget events that happened on earth, they have no way of computing time; they even forget their birthdays; if they want to get a date they often have to go and look for it." "But why," I said, " should they take the trouble to look for dates? what can it matter to them." " Oh, they are obliged to do so sometimes for tests and things of that sort." Home then awoke.

No. 72, *Ashley House.*

On, I think, the 15th, Mr. Ward Cheeney and Mr. Arnold, two Americans, friends of Home came to see him. Soon after they had gone, I heard raps upon the table at which I was seated. Home was walking about the room at the time. I called his attention to the raps, and he came and sat down near me. The alphabet was called for, and the name " *Carry*" was spelled out. Home said to me "That is Mrs. Cheeney;" then addressing her:—

"I am so glad, dear, that you have come to me again, is Julia with you often?"

" *Yes,*" was answered.

"Why does she not speak to me? Does she not like me?"

" *Oh yes, she is the same as ever, but your mission does not always consist of love messages being given you. When we would do so, we are sometimes unable by reason of your exhaustion; but you know, so long as you are true to God, your mission, and yourself, that we love you.*"

Home, pointing to me, said, " He is going to America." Two raps were made signifying uncertainty; Home added, " I hope you will like him."

" *Yes,*" was said, and then, " *I hope that you may be at my earthly habitation when you are there, in order that I may welcome you.*"

Home continued, " He is going to be married; I hope you will like his wife."

" *I dont know her. What is her name?*"

"Miss Florence Kerr. Will you go and see her?"

Two raps were given, signifying *perhaps.* " Adare will be dining there to-night; will you go with him?

" *Yes; I shall call her Florence. Do you not find this to be a subject fraught with very vast importance?*"

" Is that message to me?" I asked.

" *Yes.*"

" Certainly, I consider it a subject of great importance."

" *Standing on the threshold, peering through the chinks.*"

L

" Of the other world ? " I asked.

" *Yes.*"

Home observed " That is just like her, there was a good deal of poetry in her nature ; I have some very pretty lines of hers." He was interrupted by the words "*Such doggrel*," being spelled out; after this the sounds became gradually fainter, and we had no more messages.

No. 73.—*Ashley House.*

On Friday, the 16th, I was present at a meeting of one of the sub-committees of the Dialectical Society. The *séance* was not satisfactory. The Master of Lindsay, Mr. Bergheim, Home, and myself, afterwards adjourned to Lindsay's room, in Grosvenor Square. We sat round a small table, and had some physical manifestations. Home was in an excessively nervous state. Presently he went into a trance, and began to laugh; he spoke to me for some time as A—— B——. Home then said " That same spirit is here about W—— B——. It is too late now to do all he wanted; he wished to have prevented all this business about X——." " Oh," said Lindsay, " He could have done nothing, for W—— could have no influence over X——." " He says he could have succeeded." " I am sure he could not," continued Lindsay, " for they are not even on speaking terms." " Well, he says that W—— being susceptible, he would have got such influence over him, that X——, would have noticed it, and it would have had a good effect upon him; however, it is too late now, still he wants W—— to meet Dan. He will pass away before his natural time." " Who?" said Lindsay, W——?" " Yes." " Is he then ill?" I asked. " Oh, no; not in that way; it will probably be in some wild frolic or row, or something of that sort. This spirit used to howl at W—— when he was at school." Lindsay remarked, " That is very curious, I had not thought of it before, but now I remember that W—— told me of that. Did it frighten him?" " Oh, yes; he used to howl at him and frighten him a good deal, so much so that one night he got up and slept with one of the other fellows; he was afraid to be alone." Home turned to me and said, " You must look out, boy, there seems to be a storm brewing for you." " If you would tell me what it is," I said, " perhaps I might avoid it." " It is of no great consequence; it will be but a storm in a coffee pot. Oh, Dan is very weak, very weak indeed." Home sank back in his chair, he was seized with a violent spasm in the chest, and was in great pain. Presently he said, " They are magnetizing me." He fell into a natural sleep, and awoke in a short time much better. Home went home, I remained some time longer. Lindsay asked Mr. Bergheim to mesmerise him; he did so, and soon put him to sleep. After he had awoke him, Mr. Bergheim asked Lindsay to try upon him, no one having as yet succeeded in mesmerising him. After a few passes, he went off; he became very uneasy, placed his hand on his forehead and said, "It is all wrong." Lindsay asked him whether there was too much weight on his head; whether he should take some off, or put more on. He replied, "No, it is not that, but it is all wrong, I am being cross-mesmerised." (This is curious, as no one else was attempting to influence him). As he seemed so uneasy, Lindsay awoke him. He told us he did not remember saying anything about cross-mesmerising, but that the last thing he recollected was seeing a figure or form of some sort standing beside Lindsay. He also saw the figure. After some time, Lindsay mesmerised him again; as on the first occasion, he became very restless and excited; he extended his right arm, and kept it in that position for fully half an hour; Lindsay could not induce him to alter it. He spoke Arabic with great rapidity in long sentences, and occasionally repeated single words which I wrote down as well as I could. He appeared to be, or to think himself to be, under some influence more powerful than Lindsay. He said among other things, "Mabidah ('she won't'). Oh, dear, she won't come. Ta-âli, ta-âli ('come, come!'—word feminine and applicable to a woman only). Rahat! ('she is gone'). Allah! (God) Bedosh, or Behash (he won't, or she won't) Hakil Inglêse or Hekil Inglêse, or Yihkil Inglêse, or Hakal, Inglêse, (English talk, or speak English, or he speaks English, or he spoke English)." Lindsay repeatedly tried to make him speak English, but he said, "he won't let me." Lindsay endeavoured to influence him to move, but he always replied, "he won't let me, I would if I could, but he won't let me, he is so strong." Presently he said, "Chalini! chalini! (leave me, leave me,) don't let him come near me." Lindsay walked round in a circle, making passes, and said, "there, he cannot come inside that." Mr. Bergheim said, "Ah, she has come," and appeared to stroke and caress some one's head and hair. "He cannot speak English and won't let me." "Ah, Ta-âli (oh, come) Chalini! chalini! (leave me, leave me) Rah, (he is gone). Oh, he has gone, and she has gone with him." He appeared so distressed that Lindsay said, "I will awake him." He sat up and said, "You cannot, he has gone, and you cannot awake me." Lindsay began making upward passes, saying, "nonsense, of course I can awake you." Mr. Bergheim shouted at him, "You cannot, you cannot, he must come back or I shall die, you cannot awake me; oh, bring him back." Lindsay said, "All right, he shall

L 2

come". I opened the door and Lindsay added, "There, he has come." Mr. Bergheim heaved a deep sigh, and said, "Oh, yes, he has come back," he became quite quiet and soon awoke, but was in a nervous state for some time.*

No. 74.—*Ashley House, April.*

Last night soon after we had gone to bed, we both heard raps upon the wall. The alphabet was called for and the following messages given, "*Come come, Dan, cheer up! You have been overdoing it lately, we intend giving you a rest from the day after to-morrow till the 29th; your power will be taken from you.*" Home said, "I am sorry for it." "*We think it best,*" was answered. Home went into a trance; he said, "Your grandfather is here, he is not pleased." He spoke to me for a long time, representing my grandfather, saying at the close of the conversation, "You must be prepared, boy, for some change; it seems that something will soon occur to alter your prospects." "Can you not tell what it is," I asked. "No we cannot tell you, Oh! it is nothing to do with your marriage; no, it just seems that something will occur to alter your plans, that is all." "I wish to ask a question," I said. "Do so," he replied. "Dan suddenly asked me yesterday, shuddering, to take my hand off the table where we were both writing; when I asked him some time after what his motive had been for doing so, he told me that my thumb was all covered with blood. Now, there was really no blood upon my thumb; was that merely a defect in Dan's vision, or the result of his imagination, or was there anything more in it?" After a pause Home answered, "We do not know what that could have meant, it might have been a foreshadowing of something, or merely the reflection of the red table cloth, or some purely physical effect of Dan's brain, or vision; we do not remember the occurrence—Stop! wait a minute" (after a pause), "Ah! Sacha says it was not imagination or deception on Dan's part, he was in one of those very curious conditions into which he sometimes falls, and it was a foreshadowing of something that will occur, blood will flow, you may perhaps cut your finger or something of that sort, it does not follow that it will be your thumb. Sacha sends all manner of love to Dan, and wishes you to tell him that he must not be low-spirited, more than he can help; it is not right, he has never wanted as yet, she says it is extremely unlikely that he will be permitted to want now." I said, "I want to ask your opinion about what occurred in

---

* I mention the occurrences of this evening, as although outside the present limits of "Spiritualism," they seem to bear a strong resemblance to what took place at Ashley House, mentioned in pp. 154, 155.

Lindsay's room." "We do not know exactly to what you refer; but we will tell you about it some time or other. Dan is very weak and ill, we have been having a regular council about him." "I hope you will be able to do him good," I said. "Oh yes, we hope so, he is overworked; and he worries himself about leaving the house, and is distressed about a lot of jewels and precious stones. It is not right of him to give way so, he should have more faith. Poor little L—— will we fear have a relapse, but she must not be cast down; she will get better again; she ought to be very careful not to do too much this summer." " You mean in the way of society," I observed, " seeing too many people?" "Yes, certainly. Your mother seems anxious about you, she says your position is not a very easy one; you have a difficult path to follow, and must be careful." I said, "It seems hard that if I am in difficult circumstances I should have lost the advantage of her advice; there are so few people with whom I can take counsel." "Ah, but that is just what she does not want you to feel. She says you have not lost the benefit of her advice; she can influence you. If you will, when in doubt as to what course to pursue, pray earnestly to God for guidance, and sit down quietly to think the matter over, she says you may be sure she will be there, and will be enabled to help you to form a right judgment. She smiles, and says, 'You may even smoke your cigar you know, my boy, if you like; just sit down quietly by yourself, desiring earnestly and prayerfully to do what is right, and I am certain to be with you, and will endeavour to influence your mind so that you may come to a right con- clusion about Bergheim.' You need never be nervous at any- thing of that sort; no harm could have come of it; no spiritual influence could or would hurt him. You might have known that; you know how sensitive Dan is, and that he is continually subjected to all sorts of influences, at all times, even when walking in the streets; and yet you know they cannot harm him." "But," I said, "you spoke the other night of spirits having power even to kill a man : how do you mean then that no danger could ensue from a man becoming under a strong influence as Bergheim was, or as Dan often is." "Insomuch as the man is willing, harm might come. As I told you the other night, if anyone were voluntarily to agree to certain conditions, were to submit themselves to a spiritual influence, to obtain a certain end, harm might ensue from that, but in no other way; Bergheim could not have been hurt, he would have awoke all right, he is of a very nervous excitable temperament, that was the cause of it. Danger might arise in another way, a person might throw himself into a deep trance. If Dan in his present very weak condition were to will himself to go into a trance, he might do so, and the result might be disastrous, we are obliged to watch over him very closely. Dan will not awake, he will fall into a natural sleep now."

No. 75.—Séance, Grafton Hotel, Albermarle Street, May 26th.

At about 10 o'clock I went to the Comtesse de Pomar, and found already assembled and seated round the table the Comtesse de Pomar, Mrs. Crawford, Madame de Galiano, Mrs. H. Senior, Mr. Bergheim, and Home; they had had slight physical manifestations. One of the ladies was not very well, and another was expecting to be obliged to leave every minute —two circumstances which no doubt acted unfavourably upon the harmony of the party. Soon after my arrival Home went into a trance; he was apparently much distressed by the black crape on Madame de Pomar's dress. Getting up, he took a black shawl that she had laid on a chair, and expressing by his countenance the greatest disgust, he opened the door of an inner room and threw the shawl down. On coming back he whispered as he passed me, "We do not like it at all—there is too much black. You see there are four what *you* call widows here; we cannot bear mourning." He stroked and patted my forehead; and going round to Mrs. ——'s son, he bent over him, looked into his face and caressed his hair. He took a small round table that was standing in the corner of the room, and said, still in a whisper, "Paula and Marie must not have too much confidence in this, it is an undeveloped influence that communicates with them, and they are not fully developed as mediums, they must not place implicit reliance on what is told them, but use their own sense about it." On returning to his chair—as he passed me— he clapped his hands (Adah Menken's sign), and whispered, "I hope you are very happy. It was not far from here that I met you." Mr. Bergheim and I were talking, in a very low tone, about crystals, mirrors, and eastern magic in general, and the strange things that had occurred at Ashley House in connection with Mr. J——'s brother. Home became much agitated, gasped occasionally for breath, had difficulty in speaking, and made passes before him as if waiving something off. "Oh," he said, "you must not talk of that, you bring such a fearful influence about you; the moment your minds are turned in that direction, the influence comes as it were pouring in, I wish you could understand this, you would see how necessary is prayer to bring a good influence about you; and if you wish for that which is bad, it will inevitably come. Oh, it is very dangerous, we cannot bear you to have anything to do with magic, that incense of blood is fearful." I interrupted him saying, "I have not used any incense." Home continued, " Oh, yes ; I know, I know. You must not have anything to do with it ; you do not know how dangerous it is. Pray leave that magic alone ; what is the use of it? it is but curiosity and can do you no good. Would you place yourself in the power of the lowest men on earth? Would you bring the worst and most degraded of mortal influence about you? You would not; then why do so among spirits? I tell you you do not know the danger; they are so fearfully low, the very lowest and most material of all ; you might almost call them ' accursed.' They will get a power over you that you cannot break through. Have nothing to do with it. Try and get a good influence about you, one that will raise and elevate you, not one to drag you down lower and lower. You would be afraid of the worst and most brutal of your fellow-men. You have more cause to fear those spirits who correspond to them if you encourage and let them gain power over you. No, *he* has not found it yet." Bergheim said to me, " Have you told him the story? how does he know anything about this?" Home laughed, and speaking to Madame de Pomar said, " They are wondering at Dan speaking about subjects with which he is not acquainted, as if we did not know all about it." Turning to us he continued, " No, *he* has not found it, he has got your letter; yes I think he will answer it in a little time, he does not quite know what to do. I say again, have nothing to do with magic. Mind! there is a storm coming, if that box arrives, if the house is not burned or smashed to pieces it will be a wonder. Seek by prayer to repel evil influences, do not encourage them." Soon after, Home awoke. We had tolerably strong physical manifestations, but nothing remarkable occurred, and afterwards the three following messages were given through the alphabet, with short intervals between them : " *We find material hindrances impeding our manifestations.*" " *The influences are too various.*" " *We must, though reluctantly, say ' good night.'* "

[The three following *Séances* are recorded by Lord Dunraven] :

No. 76.—Séance, No. 7, Buckingham Gate, June, 25.

Present :—Sir Robert Gore Booth, Augusta Gore Booth, Mrs. Honywood, Arthur Smith Barry, Miss A—— P——, Miss C—— R——, Mr. Home, and myself. In a very short time vibrations and slight movements of the table occurred. These were followed by raps on and about the table. Augusta was lying on a low couch close to the ground. The five raps for the alphabet being given, we received the following message: "*The position of Augusta absorbs our atmosphere; raise her.*" We placed her couch on a sofa, and brought it up to the table. The sofa presently moved a few inches from the table, which was shortly moved up to it. She mentioned that the couch was shaken, and also that she was touched several times. Being just then strongly touched on the knee, I asked, "Has any one else been touched?" "*You,*" was immediately rapped out. Mr. Home remarking that the influence seemed chiefly on one side, we received the following message: "*We are obliged to keep to this side of the table.*" This was on Augusta's side, opposite to that at which the two young ladies sat. Mr. Home remarking, that, if the white table cloth was put on the table, hands might visibly move under the cloth, we accordingly put one on. He asked if there was an accordion in the room. Arthur Barry fetched one from the sideboard, and placed it on the table. Some movements under the cloth were seen about the edge of the table near Augusta, and in other places. As no intimation was given about the instrument, Mr. Home took it, holding it with one hand as usual, at the under edge of the table. A sort of prelude was played with slight tremolo effect. We then had the following message, the letters being chiefly indicated by notes on the instrument: "*There is spiritual discord—we pray for harmony.*" The word discord was given by a horrid discord being played; while harmony was expressed by beautiful soft chords. While the playing was going on, Arthur Barry and the two young ladies were requested to look under the table to see how the instrument was held and moved. Just after the last message, we received the following: "*An undeveloped influence prevents our*" . . . . . here some slight break occurred, and then it went on, "*but with prayer— earnest prayer—we will dispel it.*" This was shortly followed by: "*We must dispel the discord; Arthur, sit opposite.*" He removed to the chair opposite Mr. Home, changing places with Sir Robert. Mrs. Honywood was next to Mr. Home, and Sir Robert was next to her. Mr. Home's chair was partly turned round, and slight movements of the table and of Augusta's sofa took place. The alphabet being called for, the following message, addressed to Mr. Home, was given: "*You were surprised, Dan, that you were turned round; we wish to convince an undeveloped spirit that you could not trick, even if you wished to do so.*" Mr. Home expressed the greatest wonder what this could mean. "Convince a spirit," he said, "how very odd; an undeveloped spirit; I cannot understand it at all." He then reminded me of the *séance* in which he employed the fire test to satisfy spirits (*No.* 30). I said, "Ask if any one else understands what this message signifies." He pointed to each of us; and when his hand was directed to me and to Mrs. Honywood, three raps were given. Some rather undecided indications were heard when opposite one of the young ladies. Soon after, this message was sent: "*Robert, change with Barbara*" (Mrs. Honywood). Slight movements were now seen under the cloth near Augusta, and near Sir Robert. Augusta was touched several times; Mr. Home remarking that this might be for some good purpose. We received the following: " *It is with intent to heal, and with God's aid we will.*" This was nearly all spelled out by notes on the accordion; each of the letters of the word "God" being indicated by very soft chords, and the last two words by very loud notes. This was followed by, "*Patience, darling.*" The accordion was now played with great power, like a sort of jubilant hymn. It was pulled with such force that Mr. Home was obliged to hold it with both hands. At one time it was drawn away till Mr. Home's arm was stretched out; the instrument being quite horizontal; the arm and accordion bending round the head of Augusta's couch. It also rested on the edge of the couch, and was played there. Then it was brought round across the table back to Mr. Home's body, and carried under the table. This was a curious manifestation. He placed it on the ground, and it moved about under the table, touching me and others. Soon after this, as Mr. Home was talking, he was arrested in the middle of a sentence—his words died away—his half outstretched arm seemed to become rigid, and he passed into the trance. He got up and walked about the room, apparently in a very uncomfortable state. Going over to the piano he played a few chords, but quickly left off, seeming cold and distressed. He again walked about for a little while, when, coming over to Augusta's sofa, he knelt down as if in prayer; then taking her hands he patted them, and made passes down her arm. After this he went behind Arthur Barry, and putting his hands on his head he exclaimed, "It is much too cold here!" He next came and stood behind me for a few seconds, and then nearly behind Miss C. R's. chair, when he delivered a short address, beautifully expressed; but of which unfortunately I retain but a slight recollection. Every word was admirably chosen, referring chiefly to this undeveloped spirit. He began something to this effect: That a home was once opened for the souls of men; but through sin it was closed and sealed. From the moment a man is born, the door of heaven is closed against him; but he is given a golden key which unlocks the golden gate by which he may enter in, and let out the golden waters of the lake.

That key is prayer, through which our spirits, force their way before the seat of God. That Spiritualism is not a subject for idle curiosity, but for stedfast pursuit. Then speaking of occupations, he said, that even such amusements as music, drawing, &c., if carried on too much, would lead you away from higher pursuits, and ought to be resisted. He ended by saying, " There is much we would see altered ; you must pray ; do not doubt ; it will be done ; only pray, all will come right." This was obviously addressed to the lady behind whose chair he stood. Turning to Arthur Barry he said, " You don't under-stand this now, but you will by-and-bye ;" alluding no doubt to what will be explained further on. Approaching Mrs. Honywood, he said, " Barbara, your father is here ; you have been uneasy in your mind lately, but never mind, all shall be made smooth." Then putting his hand on Sir Robert's shoulder, he said, " You were touched by two hands, belonging to two very dear to you, one large, the other smaller and more delicate. Augusta, you felt a hand touching you, and a small pointed finger put into your hand (which she did); this was your grandmother ; she is very much pleased ; they would like to have done more, but they could not." Rapidly approaching me, he said with emphasis, " You knew well who was playing." After this he sat down and awoke, remarking how very silent we all were. No more manifestations occurred of any interest ; one of the ladies left the room, and Mr. Home soon after said he felt tired, and we broke up the *séance.*

At supper some one remarked that a chair was being moved to the table ; while our attention was called to this, another chair moved rather quickly five or six feet to within a foot of the table, near Mr. Home. This was seen by all present. His chair was turned half round, and he took his feet off the ground while being moved. There were no further manifestations.

The occurrences which form the remarkable feature of this *séance* require explanation. Some days ago I had the oppor-tunity of seeing Miss C—— R—— write, under supposed spirit-influence, in my presence. I obtained permission to put a few questions. Among them I asked, " What do you think of Mr. Home ?" Miss R—— wrote instantly, " He has a certain degree of power, but a vast amount of trickery." In answer to another question was written, " He (Home) deceives people by pretending that he can call up the spirits of their friends, &c." These and other answers made me think that this was probably a deceitful spirit. The young lady being very anxious to be present at a *séance,* I invited her to this one, expecting that something curious would probably occur. I mentioned the circumstances to Mrs. Hony-wood, but neither she nor I had any communication with Mr. Home on the subject. At the *séance* he had no idea who she was. The reader will now perceive the remarkable drift of what took place. The first message bearing on the case was, " We are obliged to keep to this side of the table," that is, the side opposite Miss C—— R——. The next was, " There is spiritual discord, &c." Then followed that about the undeveloped influence; and afterwards in addition, the remarkable one addressed to " Dan" (Mr. Home) where the very word "*trick*" is employed which was written by Miss C—— R—— with reference to Mr. Home. These messages were, so to say, supplemented by the beautiful and pointed address uttered by Mr. Home, when in a trance, standing behind Miss R's. chair. Some days previous, I had mentioned to two friends, very conversant with spiritualistic manifestations, the character of several of the answers written through Miss C—— R——, and they both pronounced them to proceed from an undeveloped or low spirit; one of a class which appears to be by no means uncommon, particularly with young or incipient mediums. These friends were ignorant of Miss R.'s name, or that she was to be at a *séance* with Mr. Home. They, it will be observed, used the word "*undeveloped*," the same as was employed in the messages this evening; and they both recommended the same remedy, as was urged by Mr. Home in the trance, namely earnest prayer. The table was lifted off the ground, but only a few inches. The drawer of the table on Augusta's side was suddenly opened.

No. 77.—Séance, No. 7, Buckingham Gate, July 1.

Present:—The Dowager Duchess of St. Albans, Lady ——, Mrs. Honywood, Mrs. Stopford, the Honorable Mrs. ——, Arthur Smith Barry, Sir R. Gore Booth, Augusta Gore Booth, Mr. Home, and myself. We sat round the same table which we used on the last occasion, the room being lighted as before by one lamp, with the shade over it. We quickly had strong vibrations, and raps of various kinds, some of them very loud. I said " I wonder if it is Dr. Elliotson?" " *Yes*," was answered by three loud raps. The table was slightly moved in different directions, and strongly tilted; but I observed that when inclined, objects slipped down it. The Duchess of St. Albans was touched, both audibly and visibly to others. The Duchess's scarf was pulled so strongly that she said had it not been for the brooch it would have been pulled off. Mrs. ——, Mr. Home, and I were also touched. The accordion was taken by Mr. Home, and it commenced playing in the usual manner. Mr. Home said, " If you will ask for some air they will perhaps play it." The Duchess asked for " Home, sweet Home," which was given at first by single notes and afterwards by chords. The Duchess and Mrs. Stopford looked under the table while the instrument was being played. It was drawn about outside the table and back again. It was placed in the Duchess's hands, and played when she alone held it. It was then put down under the table, where it moved about, touching different persons' feet. It came up on my legs, and I took hold of it. I asked was it the same spirit that played the other night, and was answered by the alphabet, " *A rude imitation only.*" After a little while we got the following : " *All present are loving friends and messengers from God.* Part of this message was given by the accordion ; the word God being indicated by soft chords. I asked if they would play the same air as they did at Adare. No reply was given. Mrs. Honywood's handkerchief was taken from her. Mrs. —— felt a hand placed in hers.

Some time after this, a little pencil with which I had been writing dropped out of my hand, much to my surprise, and fell at my feet. I tried to find it, but could not. Shortly after, Mr. Home said, " I see a hand moving about the Duchess's shoulder. She felt something coming down over her shoulder, and we then perceived a slight object on the edge of the table cloth in front of her. I saw it come, or placed there. Some one said, " It is a little pencil." "Oh," I said, " I dare say it is mine," which on examination it proved to be. We then got this message : " *We took it from Dunraven for you ; take it.*" I gave the pencil to the Duchess. A drawer that was exactly opposite Lady D——, shot out quite suddenly, so as to startle her ; this happened several times. It was also shut. Once it was opened so far, that although they tried they could not shut it. The cloth was moved as if by hands under it. Mr. Home saw hands, as did Mrs. ——. She also saw dark forms behind the screen and near the door. Presently we received the following message, partly on the accordion : " *God bless you, One who watches over you ;*" and then "Oft in the stilly night" was softly played. This was the air I alluded to when I asked if they would play the air they had played at Adare ; but I was not the least thinking of it at this time. Soon after, Mr. Home went gradually into a trance. He got up, bandaged his eyes and walked about. He knelt down beside Augusta, and patted her arms sharply, and made passes down them. He came round, and stood behind several of us. When between Arthur Barry and me, he spoke in a loud whisper, saying that Lady D—— might become a medium if she wished it ; that she had decided mediumistic powers. I said, " Will she succeed ?" " That depends," he replied, " entirely on herself, not upon us." He said

that a beautiful spirit was standing near her, and that her power
would be good, and the manifestations delicate in accordance with her nature, which is pure; he added more to
the same effect. He also said to Smith Barry, "Arthur, the
spirit that touched you was from D——'s influence." Then in a
sort of side whisper, he said to me, "You will explain to them
that Dan always calls people by their christian names. A
spirit, Arthur, pressed on your knee with one hand, while
picking up the pencil with the other." He also said to Mrs.
——, "I see the spirit of Arthur (her husband?), standing
behind you." And he said something about George, which
was, I believe, addressed to Mrs. Honywood. He then returned to his chair, and soon awoke. Scarcely the slightest
manifestation occurred after this, and we left the table. At
supper nothing took place. I omitted to state that the table was
raised on one occasion at least 18 inches from the floor; also
that a very curious manifestation occurred—an extraordinary
rattling inside the drawer, very strong and loud. Our chairs
also vibrated, and so did, once or twice, the floor. The variety
of raps, and the strength and frequency of the vibrations at this
séance were remarkable. The principal object aimed at appeared
to be to convince the Duchess and Lady D——, by the physical
manifestations, of the reality of some invisible power.

No. 78 —Séance, 7, Buckingham Gate, July 7th.

Present (in the order in which we sat):—The Dowager
Duchess of St. Albans, Mr. Home, Mrs. Stopford, Sir R. Gore
Booth, Lady ——, Capt. G. Smith, myself, Miss Gore Booth,
and Mrs. Honywood. We sat at the same table, and with the
same light as before, but without the table cloth. For some time
we had but slight manifestations: they were merely vibrations
and faint cold currents. I was touched twice, and hearing some
one making a remark about being touched, I said, "Who
was touched?" The alphabet was called for, and the word
"*Dunraven*" was spelled out. Mr. Home then went into a
trance; he bandaged his eyes; then walked about a little.
Afterwards he appeared as if talking to a spirit, making a good
deal of pantomime, occasionally placing his hands round the
glass of the lamp, apparently to diminish the light; he then put
it on the table. He sat down and began forming an alphabet,
as he did at Garinish; after making a few letters he pushed the
paper over to Captain Smith who completed it. He then gave
us the following message by pointing at the letters: "*We will do
the best we can, but the conditions are not favorable.*" Then,
"*Elizabeth*" was spelled, which no one seemed to understand.

Mr. Home then put the Duchess's scarf over his head and face, but soon removed it. He took her hand and placed it to his jaws to shew that they were locked, so that he could not speak. He then spelled out, "*You are too positive ;*" and soon afterwards, "*There is a strange mixture of unbelief, not existing the last time we met.*" I remarked, "I think I know what may account for this difference;" alluding to my having in my pocket a relic which a friend had particularly requested me to wear. He pointed out this message: "*It matters but little to us ; believe in God and love each other.*" Then underlining some of the letters, he put numbers, 1, 2, 3, &c., to several of them. He showed this to the Duchess, not wishing, apparently, that we should see what he was about; however, she did not seem to understand the meaning of what he did. It occurred to me to try the effect of putting away the relic, so I got up, and walking across the room, quietly placed it among some books on the sideboard. Mr. Home then pointed out the word "*Talk.*"

Soon after he got up; walked over to the sideboard, and returned and sat down. Then taking a piece of paper, he wrote in large letters, "Where did you put it?" I replied, "Can't you find it?" He went over again to the sideboard and came back, and, sitting down, showed me a cross which he wore, and which he partly drew out from his shirt collar. After this he took the lamp and placed it on the sideboard, and while there two of the party saw something in, or rather on one of his hands, when the hand was open. This must have been the relic. He afterwards returned to the chair and sat down. Captain Smith saw the relic on the table before Mr. Home sat down. We saw it become visible just before he placed his hands on each side of it. He then pushed it across the table to me. The relic is contained in a little circular box, about 1½ inches diameter. Soon after this Mr. Home awoke.

We had vibrations of the table and raps. Mr. Home's chair was turned round; he took his feet off the ground, and was either lifted up bodily several inches, or elongated; but subsided almost immediately. Mr. Home asked for the accordion. He took it; and some chords were played, with a discord among them. We then received the following: "*Slight want of harmony.*" Mr. Home asked if any of us should change places; "*Yes,*" was replied. Mr. Home, by pointing to us consecutively, made out that the Duchess was to change with him. The accordion was moved all round Mr. Home, and played some notes, when his arm was stretched out; it was placed at the Duchess's back, resting on her, and was played in that position. It was then drawn under the table, Mr. Home holding it, and given to Lady ——, who took it, and held it for a short time. Very faint sounds

were heard; after which we got the message, " *Dan, take it.*"
It played for a little time, and he then placed it under the table.
Presently I felt a very sharp blow on the shin, and found the accordion had struck me. Mrs. Stopford being obliged to go, left
the room. Mr. Home remarked that he was sure we should have
better manifestations now. We almost directly received the
following message by raps : " *We told you that the influences were
contending ; there is a change for the better.*" Mrs. Stopford's
chair now moved up to the table. Captain Smith said he saw
a form move it, and then sit in it. Three notes, for " *Yes,*"
were sounded by the accordion. The table was then
slowly tilted to one side, and then the other, as if they
were trying to lift it; it then ascended more than a foot,
and with two or more lifts, something like what was done at
Adare. After this the accordion was beautifully played with
tremolo effect at the end. It was then put under the table. Sir
Robert was touched by a hand that came from under the table
cloth. Captain Smith saw a spirit form and hand coming from
under the table. Mr. Home also saw hands. Captain Smith
asked who was sitting at the other end of the room. The word
" *Father*" was spelled out; also " *William.*" This word was given
by Lady——'s dress being pulled. Captain Smith said, "There is
a reason why the chair moved up to the table; will you tell us?"
No answer. " Do I know it?" " *Yes*" was rapped out. Then,
" *Sit at a small table four.*" Mr. Home then pointed to us all to
know who should go, and the Duchess, Lady——, Sir Robert, and
he were chosen, by raps. The small table was tilted into Mr.
Home's lap. They then were told by raps, " *Put a bit of paper
on the table.*" This they did. They took the cloth off, and the
table was raised above 45° on one side, when the paper slipped. It was replaced. The table was again inclined and
the paper was slowly moved, rather up, then in different
directions. After this the paper became luminous; it was
probably the hand holding it. The table was then inclined
almost vertically, but the paper did not move. The table was
also made to feel light or heavy according to the wish of the persons present. This was done very strongly. They now sent the
following message by raps :—" *They do this to let you see* (a
pause), *now return to the large table.*" Very soon we had
the following :—" *We are called away nearer God, good night.*"
We then left the table, at which we had been sitting for two
hours and a half. At supper we were talking about Lady——'s
glove being lost last evening, and upon some one asking
whether it had been found, some one else said, "I wish the
spirits would tell us what became of it." Then we began
talking about Mr. Home looking for the relic, and how it was

brought to the table, whether by him or by a spirit. The subject continuing we were sent the following:—"*He had it in his hand at the side-board, but we placed it on the table.*" These messages corroborated Captain Smith's opinion that Home did not place it there. Raps were heard all about, on the table, near the ceiling, and in different places. We received the following:—"*The reason he could not find it was that another spirit had taken it and brought it to the table.*" Then immediately followed, "*And we are very good, are we not, Dan?*" Upon which Mr. Home laughed immoderately, as did also Mrs. Honywood. It was all a mystery to us, but afterwards he told us the meaning of the message. It was about the prettiest manifestation of the evening, but unfortunately I am precluded from giving any explanation. Mrs. Honywood knew the circumstances of the case, and what the spirits meant by their forbearance in Dan's favour.

The cross which Mr. Home wore round his neck, and which he exhibited to me when he gave me the relic, was a Russian one, bearing this inscription, " In Thee O Lord have I placed my trust, hell and the powers thereof may strive, but Thou art mighty and shalt prevail." The relic is said to contain a portion of the true cross.

The following interesting details were furnished to me by Captain G. Smith. " It was quite at the beginning of the *séance* that I saw an object without apparent form move near you under the table, and approach Miss Gore Booth." Home said, " I think they are trying to form hands." The answer, " *Yes,*" was faintly rapped out. Previous to Mrs. Stopford leaving the room, indeed almost from the commencement, I had seen a tall spirit sometimes standing against the window nearest the door, sometimes sitting in an arm chair between the window and door. When Mrs. Stopford arose to go, he arose from his arm chair, and swept forward to the door. I fancied he was going out with her, but he returned to the chair. The impression made on my mind was that, for some good reason, he was prevented from entering the circle. When Mrs. Stopford left the room, the large table in the centre covered with flowers and books moved twice, each time nearer Mr. Home and the Duchess, and on each occasion he moved his arm chair too ; I think no one saw this latter movement but myself. It was then as if to frustrate any further attempts on his part to enter the circle, that Mrs. Stopford's chair was taken by a spirit, (in appearance like a pillar of cloud) and moved up to the table. When the door was opened for supper, the spirit in the arm chair passed out in front of me."

ADDENDA.

No. 1.

Captain Gerard Smith has kindly furnished me with the following notes relative to the *séances* at which he was present :—

In *No.* 46, the hand which brought the sprig of box was distinctly visible as it pushed the curtains aside, which partially overhung the window, and at our request it was again subsequently shown on the table, close to where Home was sitting.

P. 41, with regard to the foot note, I am able distinctly to state, that the only occasions upon which Home left the room were to fetch the lemon, and at the conclusion of this particular manifestation, to replace it in the spot he had taken it from.

No. 49, P. 94, when I entered the room Home was walking about with the accordion held in his left hand only, and it was playing; not a distinct air, but a plaintive kind of dirge, now loud, and then dying away till it became inaudible. When the spirit moved from Lord Adare's side it seemed to pass over the table with a sound like the rustling of silver paper ; Home then rose and stood at the window with his right arm extended, and the spirit seemed to sweep down until it rested with both hands on his outstretched arm, looking up into his face. From the position in which I sat, the profile of the face was perfectly visible to me, and when the two faces approached each other to kiss, there was no apparent difference in the degree of density of the two figures.

I have nothing further to add. The remainder of the manifestations which occurred when I was present, have been most accurately and truthfully described.

GERARD SMITH,
Captain, Scots Fusilier Guards.

No. 2.

I have collected a few cases, illustrating some of the most extraordinary of the phenomena, mentioned in the preceding *séances.*

The following remarkable case of the fire test has been kindly furnished me by Mrs. S. C. Hall :—

M

" 15, Ashley Place,
" July the 5th, 1869.

" Dear Lord Dunraven,—You have requested me to recall
the circumstances of a *séance* that took place here several weeks
ago. I have much pleasure in doing so, but I never take notes.
I am, however, certain of the facts; though I shall not be able
to place them in the order in which they occurred.

" We were nine (a greater number than Mr. Home likes);
we were seated round the table as usual, in the small drawing
room, which communicates with a much larger room; the
folding doors were pushed back into the wall, and the portiers
unclosed. I think there was one lamp burning over the table,
but a very large fire was blazing away in the large room—I know
there was a great deal of light. The Master of Lindsay, the
Rev. Mr. Y——, and his wife, Mr. Hall and myself, Mr. Home,
and the Misses Bertolacci were present. We sat for some little
time before the tremulous motion that so frequently indicates
stronger manifestations commenced, but it was quickly followed
by raps, not only on the table, but in different parts of the
room; the table was moved up and down,—lifted perfectly off
the ground—made 'light' and 'heavy' at the request of one
or two of the gentlemen present; and after the lapse of, I
suppose, nearly an hour, Mr. Home went into a trance. Presently
he pushed his chair, or his chair was pushed away—quite away
from the table. He got up; walked about the room in his usual
manner; went to the fire-place; half knelt on the fender stool;
took up the poker and poked the fire, which was like a red-hot
furnace, so as to increase the heat; held his hands over the fire
for some time, and finally drew out of the fire, with his hand,
a huge lump of live burning coal, so large that he held it in *both*
hands, as he came from the fire-place in the large room into the
small room; where, seated round the table, we were all watching
his movements. Mr. Hall was seated nearly opposite to where
I sat; and I saw Mr. Home, after standing for about half a
minute at the back of Mr. Hall's chair, deliberately place the
lump of burning coal on his head! I have often since wondered
that I was not frightened; but I was not; I had perfect
faith that he would not be injured. Some one said—' Is it
not hot?' Mr. Hall answered—' Warm, but not hot!'
Mr. Home had moved a little away, but returned, still in a
trance; he smiled and seemed quite pleased; and then proceeded
to draw up Mr. Hall's white hair over the red coal. The
white hair had the appearance of silver threads, over the
red coal. Mr. Home drew the hair into a sort of pyramid, the
coal still red, showing beneath the hair; then, after, I think,
four or five minutes Mr. Home pushed the hair back, and, taking

the coal off Mr. Hall's head, he said (in the peculiar low voice in which, when in a trance, he always speaks), addressing Mrs. Y——, 'Will you have it?' She drew back; and I heard him murmur, 'Little faith—little faith.' Two or three attempted to touch it, but it burnt their fingers. I said, 'Daniel, bring it to me; I do not fear to take it.' It was not red all over, as when Mr. Home put it on Mr. Hall's head, but it was still red in parts. Mr. Home came and knelt by my side; I put out my right hand, but he murmured, 'No, not that; the other hand.' He then placed it in my left hand, where it remained more than a minute. I felt it, as my husband had said, 'warm;' yet when I stooped down to examine the coal, my face felt the heat so much that I was obliged to withdraw it. After that Mrs. Y—— took it, and said she felt no inconvenience. When Mr. Hall brushed his hair at night he found a quantity of cinder dust. Mr. Home was elongated, and all the manifestations that evening were very remarkable; but I believe your Lordship requested me to relate only what I remember of the coal test.

"Dear Lord Dunraven, sincerely yours,
"ANNA MARIA HALL."
(Mrs. S. C. Hall).

_____

No. 3.

The following is an additional case of the fire test witnessed at a *séance* held at Lady Louisa ——'s, at Brighton, furnished me by the Countess M. de Pomar. Lady Gomm has permitted me to make use of her name in corroboration of the statement about the red-hot coal being placed in her hand.

"Mr. Home went into a trance; he walked about the room; played the piano; stood behind Mr. Douglas's chair, who also went into a sleep or trance; and Mr. Home appeared to be speaking with some one about him, and to magnetize him; he said it was for his good, and would remove his head-ache finally. Mr. Home went to the fire and took out a large red-hot mass of coal, which he held in his extended hands, and blew upon to keep it alight. He walked up and down the room with it, then went to Lady Louisa and wanted to put it in her hands, but she drew back. He then said, 'No, you must not have it, for if you have no faith, it will burn you.' Lady Gomm extended her hands, saying, 'I will take it without fear, for I have faith.' Mr. Home then placed the burning mass in her hands, and she did not feel it at all, although she held it for at least one minute. It was afterwards put on a sheet of paper which directly began to blaze and had a great hole burned in it."

For EU product safety concerns, contact us at Calle de José Abascal, 56–1°, 28003 Madrid, Spain or eugpsr@cambridge.org.

www.ingramcontent.com/pod-product-compliance
Ingram Content Group UK Ltd.
Pitfield, Milton Keynes, MK11 3LW, UK
UKHW010335140625
459647UK00010B/614